SUPER HOROSCOPE

Your Most Comprehensive and Revealing Individual Forecast

CANCER

June 21 - July 20

2001

BERKLEY BOOKS, NEW YORK

The publishers regret that they cannot answer
individual letters requesting personal horoscope information.

2001 SUPER HOROSCOPE CANCER

PRINTING HISTORY
Berkley Trade Edition / July 2000

All rights reserved.
Copyright © 1974, 1978, 1979, 1980, 1981, 1982
by Grosset & Dunlap, Inc.
Copyright © 1983, 1984 by Charter Communications, Inc.
Copyright © 1985, 1986, 1987, 1988, 1989, 1990, 1991, 1992, 1993, 1994, 1995,
1996, 1997, 1998, 1999, 2000
by The Berkley Publishing Group.
This book may not be reproduced in whole or in part, by
mimeograph or any other means, without permission.
For information address: The Berkley Publishing Group,
a division of Penguin Putnam Inc.,
375 Hudson Street, New York, New York 10014.

The Penguin Putnam Inc. World Wide Web site address is
http://www.penguinputnam.com

ISBN: 0-425-17454-9

BERKLEY®
Berkley Books are published by The Berkley Publishing Group,
a division of Penguin Putnam Inc.,
375 Hudson Street, New York, New York 10014.
"BERKLEY" and the "B" logo
are trademarks belonging to Penguin Putnam Inc.

PRINTED IN THE UNITED STATES OF AMERICA

10 9 8 7 6 5 4 3 2 1

CONTENTS

THE CUSP-BORN CANCER	4
The Cusps of Cancer	5
THE ASCENDANT: CANCER RISING	6
Rising Signs for Cancer	8
THE PLACE OF ASTROLOGY IN TODAY'S WORLD	10
Astrology and Relationships	10
The Challenge of Love	11
Astrology and Science	12
Know Thyself—Why?	14
WHAT IS A HOROSCOPE?	16
The Zodiac	16
The Sun Sign and the Cusp	17
The Rising Sign and the Zodiacal Houses	17
The Planets in the Houses	20
How To Use These Predictions	21
HISTORY OF ASTROLOGY	22
ASTROLOGICAL BRIDGE TO THE 21st CENTURY	28
THE SIGNS OF THE ZODIAC	31
Dominant Characteristics	31
Sun Sign Personalities	56
Key Words	58
The Elements and Qualities of the Signs	59
THE PLANETS OF THE SOLAR SYSTEM	67
The Planets and the Signs They Rule	67
Characteristics of the Planets	68
THE MOON IN EACH SIGN	78
MOON TABLES	85
Time Conversions	85
Moon Sign Dates for 2001	86
Moon Phases for 2001	90
Fishing Guide for 2001	90
Planting Guide for 2001	91
Moon's Influence Over Plants	91
Moon's Influence Over Health and Daily Affairs	92
CANCER	93
Character Analysis	94
Love and Marriage	101
CANCER LUCKY NUMBERS FOR 2001	128
CANCER YEARLY FORECAST FOR 2001	129
CANCER DAILY FORECAST FOR 2001	133
November and December Daily Forecasts for 2000	231

THE CUSP-BORN CANCER

Are you *really* a Cancer? If your birthday falls during the fourth week of June, at the beginning of Cancer, will you still retain the traits of Gemini, the sign of the Zodiac before Cancer? And what if you were born late in July—are you more Leo than Cancer? Many people born at the edge, or cusp, of a sign have difficulty determining exactly what sign they are. If you are one of these people, here's how you can figure it out, once and for all.

Consult the cusp table on the facing page, then locate the year of your birth. The table will tell you the precise days on which the Sun entered and left your sign for the year of your birth. In that way you can determine if you are a true Cancer—or whether you are a Gemini or Leo—according to the variations in cusp dates from year to year (see also page 17).

If you were born at the beginning or end of Cancer, yours is a lifetime reflecting a process of subtle transformation. Your life on Earth will symbolize a significant change in consciousness, for you are either about to enter a whole new way of living or are leaving one behind.

If you were born during the fourth week of June, you may want to read the Gemini book as well as Cancer. Because Gemini holds the keys to the more hidden sides of your personality, many of your dilemmas and uncertainties about the world and people around you can be revealed. You can tune in to your secret wishes, and your potential for cosmic unfoldment.

Although you feel you have a lot to say, you will often withdraw and remain silent. Sometimes, the more you say the more confused a situation can get. Talking can drain you, and you are vulnerable to gossip. You feel secure surrounded by intimates you can trust, but sometimes the neighbors—even your own relatives—seem to be talking behind your back and you sense a vague plot in the air.

You symbolize the birth of feeling, the silent but rich condition of a fertilized seed growing full with life. The family is always an issue. At best you are a "feeling" type whose power of sensing things remains a force behind everything you think and do.

If you were born the fourth week of July, you may want to read the horoscope book for Leo as well as Cancer, for Leo could be your greatest asset. You need a warm embrace, the comfort and safety of being cared for, protected, fed. You need strong ties to the past, to the family. Attachments are natural for you. You want to be your own person, yet you often find ties and attachments prohibiting you from the rebirth you are anticipating. You may find it hard to separate yourself from dependencies without being drawn backward again and again.

You symbolize the fullness of growth, the condition of being nearly ripe, the new life about to emerge from the shadows into the sunshine.

THE CUSPS OF CANCER

DATES SUN ENTERS CANCER (LEAVES GEMINI)

June 21 every year from 1900 to 2010, except for the following:

June 20	June 22		
1988	1902	1915	1931
1992	03	18	35
1996	06	19	39
2000	07	22	43
2004	10	23	47
2008	11	26	51
	14	27	55

DATES SUN LEAVES CANCER (ENTERS LEO)

July 23 every year from 1900 to 2010, except for the following:

			July 22			
1928	1953	1968	1981	1992	2001	2010
32	56	69	84	93	2002	
36	57	72	85	94	2004	
40	60	73	86	96	2005	
44	61	76	88	97	2006	
48	64	77	89	98	2008	
52	65	80	90	2000	2009	

THE ASCENDANT: CANCER RISING

Could you be a "double" Cancer? That is, could you have Cancer as your Rising sign as well as your Sun sign? The tables on pages 8–9 will tell you Cancer people what your Rising sign happens to be. Just find the hour of your birth, then find the day of your birth, and you will see which sign of the Zodiac is your Ascendant, as the Rising sign is called. The Ascendant is called that because it is the sign rising on the eastern horizon at the time of your birth. For a more detailed discussion of the Rising sign and the twelve houses of the Zodiac, see pages 17–20.

The Ascendant, or Rising sign, is placed on the 1st house in a horoscope, of which there are twelve houses. The 1st house represents your response to the environment—your unique response. Call it identity, personality, ego, self-image, facade, come-on, body-mind-spirit—whatever term best conveys to you the meaning of the you that acts and reacts in the world. It is a you that is always changing, discovering a new you. Your identity started with birth and early environment, over which you had little conscious control, and continues to experience, to adjust, to express itself. The 1st house also represents how others see you. Has anyone ever guessed your sign to be your Rising sign? People may respond to that personality, that facade, that body type governed by your Rising sign.

Your Ascendant, or Rising sign, modifies your basic Sun sign personality, and it affects the way you act out the daily predictions for your Sun sign. If your Rising sign indeed is Cancer, what follows is a description of its effect on your horoscope. If your Rising sign is not Cancer, but some other sign of the Zodiac, you may wish to read the horoscope book for that sign as well.

With Cancer on the Ascendant, that is, in the 1st house, the ruling planet of the 1st house is the Moon. The Moon here gives you an especially keen ability to sense patterns and changes in the environment. The Moon in this position makes you more than just receptive; it makes you reactive and adaptive. You can integrate the most fleeting, irrational impressions received from the environment. There is, however, the danger that such sensory overload, so to speak, could inhibit your ability to act appropriately in a given situation.

Cancer in the 1st house accentuates your ambitiousness. Tenacity, a strong Cancer trait, is translated here into a highly developed power of focus. You can focus your energy on several levels at once—social, emotional, even psychic—in order to realize your aims. But always the scene of struggle and realization is personal rather than public, concrete rather than abstract. Your three basic loves—food, home, money—are all personal ones. Power is not a burning issue for you, but on the other hand, concepts of right and wrong are. You may also hide behind your concepts, posing as a more intellectual person than you really feel, whenever you become too timid to express your strongly emotional nature.

Sympathy and sensitivity are basic personality traits for Cancer Rising. That combination may lead to a subjective view of the world, one which has little in common with the views of other people. For that reason, you may appear to be shy, when in fact you are merely retiring from a possible occasion of misunderstanding or conflict. You prefer to protect yourself and those you love from any pain or suffering. You want to provide a comfortable haven for all the hurt creatures of the world. You can, therefore, be labeled a homebody or a mothering type.

Although the concept of home is central in your life, you are not a stick-in-the-mud; indeed, you do not necessarily like to be rooted in one place. You would like a family, to nurture and protect it, to develop and instill pervasive attitudes of right conduct. If you don't have a natural family, you will be happy serving a community cause, even if that service takes you far and wide and results in reversals of fortune along the way. There may be many travels and voyages in the lifetimes of those of you with Cancer Rising. Home is where your heart is. Possessions, too, have little meaning for you unless they are connected with a special person or intimate situation.

Supportiveness to others continually wars with inner insecurity, making you doubt the value and extent of your attachment. You need to feel appreciated by everyone in your immediate environment. Emotional satisfaction may be more compelling than honor and success. You could enter secret love affairs or alliances just for the personal gratification they provide, and despite the dangers they pose. There may be an aura of mystery surrounding you, inspired partly by your fondness for secrets, partly by your hidden, inaccessible, unsteady emotionality, partly by your success in isolation; some of you may engender enemies and long-standing rivals as a result.

Intuition and imagination are the key words for Cancer Rising. You can put them to use in the service of a fruitful lifestyle, or you can squander them in complaints. You are at your best when you are building something.

RISING SIGNS FOR CANCER

Hour of Birth*	Day of Birth		
	June 20–25	June 26–30	July 1–5
Midnight	Pisces; Aries 6/22	Aries	Aries
1 AM	Aries	Taurus	Taurus
2 AM	Taurus	Taurus	Taurus
3 AM	Gemini	Gemini	Gemini
4 AM	Gemini	Gemini	Gemini; Cancer 7/3
5 AM	Cancer	Cancer	Cancer
6 AM	Cancer	Cancer	Cancer
7 AM	Cancer; Leo 6/23	Leo	Leo
8 AM	Leo	Leo	Leo
9 AM	Leo	Leo; Virgo 6/30	Virgo
10 AM	Virgo	Virgo	Virgo
11 AM	Virgo	Virgo	Virgo
Noon	Virgo; Libra 6/24	Libra	Libra
1 PM	Libra	Libra	Libra
2 PM	Libra	Libra; Scorpio 6/29	Scorpio
3 PM	Scorpio	Scorpio	Scorpio
4 PM	Scorpio	Scorpio	Scorpio
5 PM	Scorpio; Sagittarius 6/23	Sagittarius	Sagittarius
6 PM	Sagittarius	Sagittarius	Sagittarius
7 PM	Sagittarius	Sagittarius; Capricorn 6/27	Capricorn
8 PM	Capricorn	Capricorn	Capricorn
9 PM	Capricorn	Aquarius	Aquarius
10 PM	Aquarius	Aquarius	Aquarius
11 PM	Pisces	Pisces	Pisces

*Hour of birth given here is for Standard Time in any time zone. If your hour of birth was recorded in Daylight Saving Time, subtract one hour from it and consult that hour in the table above. For example, if you were born at 9 AM D.S.T., see 8 AM above.

Hour of Birth*	Day of Birth		
	July 6–10	July 11–17	July 18–23
Midnight	Aries	Taurus	Taurus
1 AM	Taurus	Taurus	Taurus; Gemini 7/19
2 AM	Gemini	Gemini	Gemini
3 AM	Gemini	Gemini	Gemini
4 AM	Cancer	Cancer	Cancer
5 AM	Cancer	Cancer	Cancer; Leo 7/23
6 AM	Leo	Leo	Leo
7 AM	Leo	Leo	Leo
8 AM	Leo	Leo; Virgo 7/15	Virgo
9 AM	Virgo	Virgo	Virgo
10 AM	Virgo	Virgo	Virgo; Libra 7/23
11 AM	Libra	Libra	Libra
Noon	Libra	Libra	Libra
1 PM	Libra	Libra; Scorpio 7/15	Scorpio
2 PM	Scorpio	Scorpio	Scorpio
3 PM	Scorpio	Scorpio	Scorpio; Sagittarius 7/23
4 PM	Scorpio; Sagittarius 7/7	Sagittarius	Sagittarius
5 PM	Sagittarius	Sagittarius	Sagittarius
6 PM	Sagittarius	Capricorn	Capricorn
7 PM	Capricorn	Capricorn	Capricorn
8 PM	Capricorn	Aquarius	Aquarius
9 PM	Aquarius	Aquarius	Pisces
10 PM	Pisces	Pisces	Pisces; Aries 7/22
11 PM	Pisces; Aries 7/7	Aries	Aries

*See note on facing page.

THE PLACE OF ASTROLOGY IN TODAY'S WORLD

Does astrology have a place in the fast-moving, ultra-scientific world we live in today? Can it be justified in a sophisticated society whose outriders are already preparing to step off the moon into the deep space of the planets themselves? Or is it just a hangover of ancient superstition, a psychological dummy for neurotics and dreamers of every historical age?

These are the kind of questions that any inquiring person can be expected to ask when they approach a subject like astrology which goes beyond, but never excludes, the materialistic side of life.

The simple, single answer is that astrology works. It works for many millions of people in the western world alone. In the United States there are 10 million followers and in Europe, an estimated 25 million. America has more than 4000 practicing astrologers, Europe nearly three times as many. Even down-under Australia has its hundreds of thousands of adherents. In the eastern countries, astrology has enormous followings, again, because it has been proved to work. In India, for example, brides and grooms for centuries have been chosen on the basis of their astrological compatibility.

Astrology today is more vital than ever before, more practicable because all over the world the media devotes much space and time to it, more valid because science itself is confirming the precepts of astrological knowledge with every new exciting step. The ordinary person who daily applies astrology intelligently does not have to wonder whether it is true nor believe in it blindly. He can see it working for himself. And, if he can use it—and this book is designed to help the reader to do just that—he can make living a far richer experience, and become a more developed personality and a better person.

Astrology and Relationships

Astrology is the science of relationships. It is not just a study of planetary influences on man and his environment. It is the study of man himself.

We are at the center of our personal universe, of all our relationships. And our happiness or sadness depends on how we act, how we relate to the people and things that surround us. The emotions that we generate have a distinct effect—for better or worse—on the world around us. Our friends and our enemies will confirm this. Just look in the mirror the next time you are angry. In other words, each of us is a kind of sun or planet or star radiating our feelings on the environment around us. Our influence on our personal universe, whether loving, helpful, or destructive, varies with our changing moods, expressed through our individual character.

Our personal "radiations" are potent in the way they affect our moods and our ability to control them. But we usually are able to throw off our emotion in some sort of action—we have a good cry, walk it off, or tell someone our troubles—before it can build up too far and make us physically ill. Astrology helps us to understand the universal forces working on us, and through this understanding, we can become more properly adjusted to our surroundings so that we find ourselves coping where others may flounder.

The Challenge of Love

The challenge of love lies in recognizing the difference between infatuation, emotion, sex, and, sometimes, the intentional deceit of the other person. Mankind, with its record of broken marriages, despair, and disillusionment, is obviously not very good at making these distinctions.

Can astrology help?

Yes. In the same way that advance knowledge can usually help in any human situation. And there is probably no situation as human, as poignant, as pathetic and universal, as the failure of man's love.

Love, of course, is not just between man and woman. It involves love of children, parents, home, and friends. But the big problems usually involve the choice of partner.

Astrology has established degrees of compatibility that exist between people born under the various signs of the Zodiac. Because people are individuals, there are numerous variations and modifications. So the astrologer, when approached on mate and marriage matters, makes allowances for them. But the fact remains that some groups of people are suited for each other and some are not, and astrology has expressed this in terms of characteristics we all can study and use as a personal guide.

No matter how much enjoyment and pleasure we find in the different aspects of each other's character, if it is not an overall compatibility, the chances of our finding fulfillment or enduring happiness in each other are pretty hopeless. And astrology can help us to find someone compatible.

Astrology and Science

Closely related to our emotions is the "other side" of our personal universe, our physical welfare. Our body, of course, is largely influenced by things around us over which we have very little control. The phone rings, we hear it. The train runs late. We snag our stocking or cut our face shaving. Our body is under a constant bombardment of events that influence our daily lives to varying degrees.

The question that arises from all this is, what makes each of us act so that we have to involve other people and keep the ball of activity and evolution rolling? This is the question that both science and astrology are involved with. The scientists have attacked it from different angles: anthropology, the study of human evolution as body, mind and response to environment; anatomy, the study of bodily structure; psychology, the science of the human mind; and so on. These studies have produced very impressive classifications and valuable information, but because the approach to the problem is fragmented, so is the result. They remain "branches" of science. Science generally studies effects. It keeps turning up wonderful answers but no lasting solutions. Astrology, on the other hand, approaches the question from the broader viewpoint. Astrology began its inquiry with the totality of human experience and saw it as an effect. It then looked to find the cause, or at least the prime movers, and during thousands of years of observation of man and his *universal* environment came up with the extraordinary principle of planetary influence—or astrology, which, from the Greek, means the science of the stars.

Modern science, as we shall see, has confirmed much of astrology's foundations—most of it unintentionally, some of it reluctantly, but still, indisputably.

It is not difficult to imagine that there must be a connection between outer space and Earth. Even today, scientists are not too sure how our Earth was created, but it is generally agreed that it is only a tiny part of the universe. And as a part of the universe, people on Earth see and feel the influence of heavenly bodies in almost every aspect of our existence. There is no doubt that the Sun has the greatest influence on life on this planet. Without it there would be no life, for without it there would be no warmth, no division into day and night, no cycles of time or season at all. This is clear and easy to see. The influence of the Moon, on the other hand, is more subtle, though no less definite.

There are many ways in which the influence of the Moon manifests itself here on Earth, both on human and animal life. It is a well-known fact, for instance, that the large movements of water on our planet—that is the ebb and flow of the tides—are caused by the Moon's gravitational pull. Since this is so, it follows that these water movements do not occur only in the oceans, but that all bodies of water are affected, even down to the tiniest puddle.

The human body, too, which consists of about 70 percent water, falls within the scope of this lunar influence. For example the menstrual cycle of most women corresponds to the 28-day lunar month; the period of pregnancy in humans is 273 days, or equal to nine lunar months. Similarly, many illnesses reach a crisis at the change of the Moon, and statistics in many countries have shown that the crime rate is highest at the time of the Full Moon. Even human sexual desire has been associated with the phases of the Moon. But it is in the movement of the tides that we get the clearest demonstration of planetary influence, which leads to the irresistible correspondence between the so-called metaphysical and the physical.

Tide tables are prepared years in advance by calculating the future positions of the Moon. Science has known for a long time that the Moon is the main cause of tidal action. But only in the last few years has it begun to realize the possible extent of this influence on mankind. To begin with, the ocean tides do not rise and fall as we might imagine from our personal observations of them. The Moon as it orbits around Earth sets up a circular wave of attraction which pulls the oceans of the world after it, broadly in an east to west direction. This influence is like a phantom wave crest, a loop of power stretching from pole to pole which passes over and around the Earth like an invisible shadow. It travels with equal effect across the land masses and, as scientists were recently amazed to observe, caused oysters placed in the dark in the middle of the United States where there is no sea to open their shells to receive the nonexistent tide. If the land-locked oysters react to this invisible signal, what effect does it have on us who not so long ago in evolutionary time came out of the sea and still have its salt in our blood and sweat?

Less well known is the fact that the Moon is also the primary force behind the circulation of blood in human beings and animals, and the movement of sap in trees and plants. Agriculturists have established that the Moon has a distinct influence on crops, which explains why for centuries people have planted according to Moon cycles. The habits of many animals, too, are directed by the movement of the Moon. Migratory birds, for instance, depart only at or near the time of the Full Moon. And certain sea creatures, eels in particular, move only in accordance with certain phases of the Moon.

Know Thyself—Why?

In today's fast-changing world, everyone still longs to know what the future holds. It is the one thing that everyone has in common: rich and poor, famous and infamous, all are deeply concerned about tomorrow.

But the key to the future, as every historian knows, lies in the past. This is as true of individual people as it is of nations. You cannot understand your future without first understanding your past, which is simply another way of saying that you must first of all know yourself.

The motto "know thyself" seems obvious enough nowadays, but it was originally put forward as the foundation of wisdom by the ancient Greek philosophers. It was then adopted by the "mystery religions" of the ancient Middle East, Greece, Rome, and is still used in all genuine schools of mind training or mystical discipline, both in those of the East, based on yoga, and those of the West. So it is universally accepted now, and has been through the ages.

But how do you go about discovering what sort of person you are? The first step is usually classification into some sort of system of types. Astrology did this long before the birth of Christ. Psychology has also done it. So has modern medicine, in its way.

One system classifies people according to the source of the impulses they respond to most readily: the muscles, leading to direct bodily action; the digestive organs, resulting in emotion; or the brain and nerves, giving rise to thinking. Another such system says that character is determined by the endocrine glands, and gives us such labels as "pituitary," "thyroid," and "hyperthyroid" types. These different systems are neither contradictory nor mutually exclusive. In fact, they are very often different ways of saying the same thing.

Very popular, useful classifications were devised by Carl Jung, the eminent disciple of Freud. Jung observed among the different faculties of the mind, four which have a predominant influence on character. These four faculties exist in all of us without exception, but not in perfect balance. So when we say, for instance, that someone is a "thinking type," it means that in any situation he or she tries to be rational. Emotion, which may be the opposite of thinking, will be his or her weakest function. This thinking type can be sensible and reasonable, or calculating and unsympathetic. The emotional type, on the other hand, can often be recognized by exaggerated language—everything is either marvelous or terrible—and in extreme cases they even invent dramas and quarrels out of nothing just to make life more interesting.

The other two faculties are intuition and physical sensation. The sensation type does not only care for food and drink, nice clothes and furniture; he or she is also interested in all forms of physical experience. Many scientists are sensation types as are athletes and nature-lovers. Like sensation, intuition is a form of perception and we all possess it. But it works through that part of the mind which is not under conscious control—consequently it sees meanings and connections which are not obvious to thought or emotion. Inventors and original thinkers are always intuitive, but so, too, are superstitious people who see meanings where none exist.

Thus, sensation tells us what is going on in the world, feeling (that is, emotion) tells us how important it is to ourselves, thinking enables us to interpret it and work out what we should do about it, and intuition tells us what it means to ourselves and others. All four faculties are essential, and all are present in every one of us. But some people are guided chiefly by one, others by another. In addition, Jung also observed a division of the human personality into the extrovert and the introvert, which cuts across these four types.

A disadvantage of all these systems of classification is that one cannot tell very easily where to place oneself. Some people are reluctant to admit that they act to please their emotions. So they deceive themselves for years by trying to belong to whichever type they think is the "best." Of course, there is no best; each has its faults and each has its good points.

The advantage of the signs of the Zodiac is that they simplify classification. Not only that, but your date of birth is personal—it is unarguably yours. What better way to know yourself than by going back as far as possible to the very moment of your birth? And this is precisely what your horoscope is all about, as we shall see in the next section.

WHAT IS A HOROSCOPE?

If you had been able to take a picture of the skies at the moment of your birth, that photograph would be your horoscope. Lacking such a snapshot, it is still possible to recreate the picture—and this is at the basis of the astrologer's art. In other words, your horoscope is a representation of the skies with the planets in the exact positions they occupied at the time you were born.

The year of birth tells an astrologer the positions of the distant, slow-moving planets Jupiter, Saturn, Uranus, Neptune, and Pluto. The month of birth indicates the Sun sign, or birth sign as it is commonly called, as well as indicating the positions of the rapidly moving planets Venus, Mercury, and Mars. The day and time of birth will locate the position of our Moon. And the moment—the exact hour and minute—of birth determines the houses through what is called the Ascendant, or Rising sign.

With this information the astrologer consults various tables to calculate the specific positions of the Sun, Moon, and other planets relative to your birthplace at the moment you were born. Then he or she locates them by means of the Zodiac.

The Zodiac

The Zodiac is a band of stars (constellations) in the skies, centered on the Sun's apparent path around the Earth, and is divided into twelve equal segments, or signs. What we are actually dividing up is the Earth's path around the Sun. But from our point of view here on Earth, it seems as if the Sun is making a great circle around our planet in the sky, so we say it is the Sun's apparent path. This twelvefold division, the Zodiac, is a reference system for the astrologer. At any given moment the planets—and in astrology both the Sun and Moon are considered to be planets—can all be located at a specific point along this path.

Now where in all this are you, the subject of the horoscope? Your character is largely determined by the sign the Sun is in. So that is where the astrologer looks first in your horoscope, at your Sun sign.

The Sun Sign and the Cusp

There are twelve signs in the Zodiac, and the Sun spends approximately one month in each sign. But because of the motion of the Earth around the Sun—the Sun's apparent motion—the dates when the Sun enters and leaves each sign may change from year to year. Some people born near the cusp, or edge, of a sign have difficulty determining which is their Sun sign. But in this book a Table of Cusps is provided for the years 1900 to 2010 (page 5) so you can find out what your true Sun sign is.

Here are the twelve signs of the Zodiac, their ancient zodiacal symbol, and the dates when the Sun enters and leaves each sign for the year 2001. Remember, these dates may change from year to year.

ARIES	Ram	March 20–April 19
TAURUS	Bull	April 19–May 20
GEMINI	Twins	May 20–June 21
CANCER	Crab	June 21–July 22
LEO	Lion	July 22–August 22
VIRGO	Virgin	August 22–September 22
LIBRA	Scales	September 22–October 23
SCORPIO	Scorpion	October 23–November 22
SAGITTARIUS	Archer	November 22–December 21
CAPRICORN	Sea Goat	December 21–January 19
AQUARIUS	Water Bearer	January 19–February 18
PISCES	Fish	February 18–March 20

It is possible to draw significant conclusions and make meaningful predictions based simply on the Sun sign of a person. There are many people who have been amazed at the accuracy of the description of their own character based only on the Sun sign. But an astrologer needs more information than just your Sun sign to interpret the photograph that is your horoscope.

The Rising Sign and the Zodiacal Houses

An astrologer needs the exact time and place of your birth in order to construct and interpret your horoscope. The illustration on the next page shows the flat chart, or natural wheel, an astrologer uses. Note the inner circle of the wheel labeled 1 through 12. These 12 divisions are known as the houses of the Zodiac.

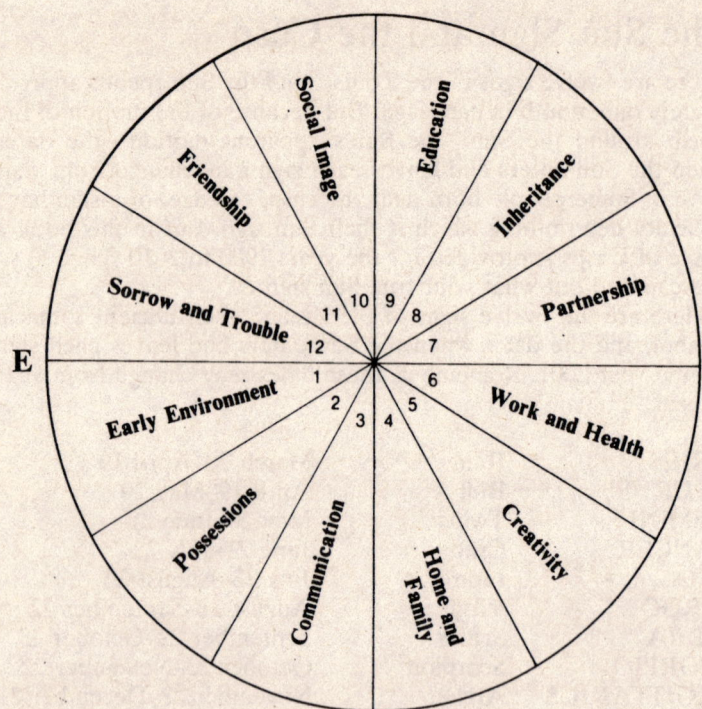

The 1st house always starts from the position marked E, which corresponds to the eastern horizon. The rest of the houses 2 through 12 follow around in a "counterclockwise" direction. The point where each house starts is known as a cusp, or edge.

The cusp, or edge, of the 1st house (point E) is where an astrologer would place your Rising sign, the Ascendant. And, as already noted, the exact time of your birth determines your Rising sign. Let's see how this works.

As the Earth rotates on its axis once every 24 hours, each one of the twelve signs of the Zodiac appears to be "rising" on the horizon, with a new one appearing about every 2 hours. Actually it is the turning of the Earth that exposes each sign to view, but in our astrological work we are discussing apparent motion. This Rising sign marks the Ascendant, and it colors the whole orientation of a horoscope. It indicates the sign governing the 1st house of the chart, and will thus determine which signs will govern all the other houses.

To visualize this idea, imagine two color wheels with twelve divisions superimposed upon each other. For just as the Zodiac is divided into twelve constellations that we identify as the signs, another twelvefold division is used to denote the houses. Now imagine one wheel (the signs) moving slowly while the other wheel (the houses) remains still. This analogy may help you see how the signs keep shifting the "color" of the houses as the Rising sign continues to change every two hours. To simplify things, a Table of Rising Signs has been provided (pages 8–9) for your specific Sun sign.

Once your Rising sign has been placed on the cusp of the 1st house, the signs that govern the rest of the 11 houses can be placed on the chart. In any individual's horoscope the signs do not necessarily correspond with the houses. For example, it could be that a sign covers part of two adjacent houses. It is the interpretation of such variations in an individual's horoscope that marks the professional astrologer.

But to gain a workable understanding of astrology, it is not necessary to go into great detail. In fact, we just need a description of the houses and their meanings, as is shown in the illustration above and in the table below.

THE 12 HOUSES OF THE ZODIAC

1st	Individuality, body appearance, general outlook on life	Personality house
2nd	Finance, possessions, ethical principles, gain or loss	Money house
3rd	Relatives, communication, short journeys, writing, education	Relatives house
4th	Family and home, parental ties, land and property, security	Home house
5th	Pleasure, children, creativity, entertainment, risk	Pleasure house
6th	Health, harvest, hygiene, work and service, employees	Health house
7th	Marriage and divorce, the law, partnerships and alliances	Marriage house
8th	Inheritance, secret deals, sex, death, regeneration	Inheritance house
9th	Travel, sports, study, philosophy and religion	Travel house
10th	Career, social standing, success and honor	Business house
11th	Friendship, social life, hopes and wishes	Friends house
12th	Troubles, illness, secret enemies, hidden agendas	Trouble house

The Planets in the Houses

An astrologer, knowing the exact time and place of your birth, will use tables of planetary motion in order to locate the planets in your horoscope chart. He or she will determine which planet or planets are in which sign and in which house. It is not uncommon, in an individual's horoscope, for there to be two or more planets in the same sign and in the same house.

The characteristics of the planets modify the influence of the Sun according to their natures and strengths.

Sun: Source of life. Basic temperament according to the Sun sign. The conscious will. Human potential.
Moon: Emotions. Moods. Customs. Habits. Changeable. Adaptive. Nurturing.
Mercury: Communication. Intellect. Reasoning power. Curiosity. Short travels.
Venus: Love. Delight. Charm. Harmony. Balance. Art. Beautiful possessions.
Mars: Energy. Initiative. War. Anger. Adventure. Courage. Daring. Impulse.
Jupiter: Luck. Optimism. Generous. Expansive. Opportunities. Protection.
Saturn: Pessimism. Privation. Obstacles. Delay. Hard work. Research. Lasting rewards after long struggle.
Uranus: Fashion. Electricity. Revolution. Independence. Freedom. Sudden changes. Modern science.
Neptune: Sensationalism. Theater. Dreams. Inspiration. Illusion. Deception.
Pluto: Creation and destruction. Total transformation. Lust for power. Strong obsessions.

Superimpose the characteristics of the planets on the functions of the house in which they appear. Express the result through the character of the Sun sign, and you will get the basic idea.

Of course, many other considerations have been taken into account in producing the carefully worked out predictions in this book: the aspects of the planets to each other; their strength according to position and sign; whether they are in a house of exaltation or decline; whether they are natural enemies or not; whether a planet occupies its own sign; the position of a planet in relation to its own house or sign; whether the sign is male or female; whether the sign is a fire, earth, water, or air sign. These are only a few of the colors on the astrologer's pallet which he or she must mix with the inspiration of the artist and the accuracy of the mathematician.

How To Use These Predictions

A person reading the predictions in this book should understand that they are produced from the daily position of the planets for a group of people and are not, of course, individually specialized. To get the full benefit of them our readers should relate the predictions to their own character and circumstances, coordinate them, and draw their own conclusions from them.

If you are a serious observer of your own life, you should find a definite pattern emerging that will be a helpful and reliable guide.

The point is that we always retain our free will. The stars indicate certain directional tendencies but we are not compelled to follow. We can do or not do, and wisdom must make the choice.

We all have our good and bad days. Sometimes they extend into cycles of weeks. It is therefore advisable to study daily predictions in a span ranging from the day before to several days ahead.

Daily predictions should be taken very generally. The word "difficult" does not necessarily indicate a whole day of obstruction or inconvenience. It is a warning to you to be cautious. Your caution will often see you around the difficulty before you are involved. This is the correct use of astrology.

In another section (pages 78–84), detailed information is given about the influence of the Moon as it passes through each of the twelve signs of the Zodiac. There are instructions on how to use the Moon Tables (pages 85–92), which provide Moon Sign Dates throughout the year as well as the Moon's role in health and daily affairs. This information should be used in conjunction with the daily forecasts to give a fuller picture of the astrological trends.

HISTORY OF ASTROLOGY

The origins of astrology have been lost far back in history, but we do know that reference is made to it as far back as the first written records of the human race. It is not hard to see why. Even in primitive times, people must have looked for an explanation for the various happenings in their lives. They must have wanted to know why people were different from one another. And in their search they turned to the regular movements of the Sun, Moon, and stars to see if they could provide an answer.

It is interesting to note that as soon as man learned to use his tools in any type of design, or his mind in any kind of calculation, he turned his attention to the heavens. Ancient cave dwellings reveal dim crescents and circles representative of the Sun and Moon, rulers of day and night. Mesopotamia and the civilization of Chaldea, in itself the foundation of those of Babylonia and Assyria, show a complete picture of astronomical observation and well-developed astrological interpretation.

Humanity has a natural instinct for order. The study of anthropology reveals that primitive people—even as far back as prehistoric times—were striving to achieve a certain order in their lives. They tried to organize the apparent chaos of the universe. They had the desire to attach meaning to things. This demand for order has persisted throughout the history of man. So that observing the regularity of the heavenly bodies made it logical that primitive peoples should turn heavenward in their search for an understanding of the world in which they found themselves so random and alone.

And they did find a significance in the movements of the stars. Shepherds tending their flocks, for instance, observed that when the cluster of stars now known as the constellation Aries was in sight, it was the time of fertility and they associated it with the Ram. And they noticed that the growth of plants and plant life corresponded with different phases of the Moon, so that certain times were favorable for the planting of crops, and other times were not. In this way, there grew up a tradition of seasons and causes connected with the passage of the Sun through the twelve signs of the Zodiac.

Astrology was valued so highly that the king was kept informed of the daily and monthly changes in the heavenly bodies, and the results of astrological studies regarding events of the future. Head astrologers were clearly men of great rank and position, and the office was said to be a hereditary one.

Omens were taken, not only from eclipses and conjunctions of the Moon or Sun with one of the planets, but also from storms and earthquakes. In the eastern civilizations, particularly, the reverence inspired by astrology appears to have remained unbroken since the very earliest days. In ancient China, astrology, astronomy, and religion went hand in hand. The astrologer, who was also an astronomer, was part of the official government service and had his own corner in the Imperial Palace. The duties of the Imperial astrologer, whose office was one of the most important in the land, were clearly defined, as this extract from early records shows:

> This exalted gentleman must concern himself with the stars in the heavens, keeping a record of the changes and movements of the Planets, the Sun and the Moon, in order to examine the movements of the terrestrial world with the object of prognosticating good and bad fortune. He divides the territories of the nine regions of the empire in accordance with their dependence on particular celestial bodies. All the fiefs and principalities are connected with the stars and from this their prosperity or misfortune should be ascertained. He makes prognostications according to the twelve years of the Jupiter cycle of good and evil of the terrestrial world. From the colors of the five kinds of clouds, he determines the coming of floods or droughts, abundance or famine. From the twelve winds, he draws conclusions about the state of harmony of heaven and earth, and takes note of good and bad signs that result from their accord or disaccord. In general, he concerns himself with five kinds of phenomena so as to warn the Emperor to come to the aid of the government and to allow for variations in the ceremonies according to their circumstances.

The Chinese were also keen observers of the fixed stars, giving them such unusual names as Ghost Vehicle, Sun of Imperial Concubine, Imperial Prince, Pivot of Heaven, Twinkling Brilliance, Weaving Girl. But, great astrologers though they may have been, the Chinese lacked one aspect of mathematics that the Greeks applied to astrology—deductive geometry. Deductive geometry was the basis of much classical astrology in and after the time of the Greeks, and this explains the different methods of prognostication used in the East and West.

Down through the ages the astrologer's art has depended, not so much on the uncovering of new facts, though this is important, as on the interpretation of the facts already known. This is the essence of the astrologer's skill.

But why should the signs of the Zodiac have any effect at all on the formation of human character? It is easy to see why people thought they did, and even now we constantly use astrological expressions in our everyday speech. The thoughts of "lucky star," "ill-fated," "star-crossed," "mooning around," are interwoven into the very structure of our language.

Wherever the concept of the Zodiac is understood and used, it could well appear to have an influence on the human character. Does this mean, then, that the human race, in whose civilization the idea of the twelve signs of the Zodiac has long been embedded, is divided into only twelve types? Can we honestly believe that it is really as simple as that? If so, there must be pretty wide ranges of variation within each type. And if, to explain the variation, we call in heredity and environment, experiences in early childhood, the thyroid and other glands, and also the four functions of the mind together with extroversion and introversion, then one begins to wonder if the original classification was worth making at all. No sensible person believes that his favorite system explains everything. But even so, he will not find the system much use at all if it does not even save him the trouble of bothering with the others.

In the same way, if we were to put every person under only one sign of the Zodiac, the system becomes too rigid and unlike life. Besides, it was never intended to be used like that. It may be convenient to have only twelve types, but we know that in practice there is every possible gradation between aggressiveness and timidity, or between conscientiousness and laziness. How, then, do we account for this?

A person born under any given Sun sign can be mainly influenced by one or two of the other signs that appear in their individual horoscope. For instance, famous persons born under the sign of Gemini include Henry VIII, whom nothing and no one could have induced to abdicate, and Edward VIII, who did just that. Obviously, then, the sign Gemini does not fully explain the complete character of either of them.

Again, under the opposite sign, Sagittarius, were both Stalin, who was totally consumed with the notion of power, and Charles V, who freely gave up an empire because he preferred to go into a monastery. And we find under Scorpio many uncompromising characters such as Luther, de Gaulle, Indira Gandhi, and Montgomery, but also Petain, a successful commander whose name later became synonymous with collaboration.

A single sign is therefore obviously inadequate to explain the differences between people; it can only explain resemblances, such as the combativeness of the Scorpio group, or the far-reaching devotion of Charles V and Stalin to their respective ideals—the Christian heaven and the Communist utopia.

But very few people have only one sign in their horoscope chart. In addition to the month of birth, the day and, even more, the hour to the nearest minute if possible, ought to be considered. Without this, it is impossible to have an actual horoscope, for the word horoscope literally means "a consideration of the hour."

The month of birth tells you only which sign of the Zodiac was occupied by the Sun. The day and hour tell you what sign was occupied by the Moon. And the minute tells you which sign was rising on the eastern horizon. This is called the Ascendant, and, as some astrologers believe, it is supposed to be the most important thing in the whole horoscope.

The Sun is said to signify one's heart, that is to say, one's deepest desires and inmost nature. This is quite different from the Moon, which signifies one's superficial way of behaving. When the ancient Romans referred to the Emperor Augustus as a Capricorn, they meant that he had the Moon in Capricorn. Or, to take another example, a modern astrologer would call Disraeli a Scorpion because he had Scorpio Rising, but most people would call him Sagittarius because he had the Sun there. The Romans would have called him Leo because his Moon was in Leo.

So if one does not seem to fit one's birth month, it is always worthwhile reading the other signs, for one may have been born at a time when any of them were rising or occupied by the Moon. It also seems to be the case that the influence of the Sun develops as life goes on, so that the month of birth is easier to guess in people over the age of forty. The young are supposed to be influenced mainly by their Ascendant, the Rising sign, which characterizes the body and physical personality as a whole.

It is nonsense to assume that all people born at a certain time will exhibit the same characteristics, or that they will even behave in the same manner. It is quite obvious that, from the very moment of its birth, a child is subject to the effects of its environment, and that this in turn will influence its character and heritage to a decisive extent. Also to be taken into account are education and economic conditions, which play a very important part in the formation of one's character as well.

People have, in general, certain character traits and qualities which, according to their environment, develop in either a positive or a negative manner. Therefore, selfishness (inherent selfishness, that is) might emerge as unselfishness; kindness and consideration as cruelty and lack of consideration toward others. In the same way, a naturally constructive person may, through frustration, become destructive, and so on. The latent characteristics with which people are born can, therefore, through environment and good or bad training, become something that would appear to be its opposite, and so give the lie to the astrologer's description of their character. But this is not the case. The true character is still there, but it is buried deep beneath these external superficialities.

Careful study of the character traits of various signs of the Zodiac are of immeasurable help, and can render beneficial service to the intelligent person. Undoubtedly, the reader will already have discovered that, while he is able to get on very well with some people, he just "cannot stand" others. The causes sometimes seem inexplicable. At times there is intense dislike, at other times immediate sympathy. And there is, too, the phenomenon of love at first sight, which is also apparently inexplicable. People appear to be either sympathetic or unsympathetic toward each other for no apparent reason.

Now if we look at this in the light of the Zodiac, we find that people born under different signs are either compatible or incompatible with each other. In other words, there are good and bad interrelating factors among the various signs. This does not, of course, mean that humanity can be divided into groups of hostile camps. It would be quite wrong to be hostile or indifferent toward people who happen to be born under an incompatible sign. There is no reason why everybody should not, or cannot, learn to control and adjust their feelings and actions, especially after they are aware of the positive qualities of other people by studying their character analyses, among other things.

Every person born under a certain sign has both positive and negative qualities, which are developed more or less according to our free will. Nobody is entirely good or entirely bad, and it is up to each of us to learn to control ourselves on the one hand and at the same time to endeavor to learn about ourselves and others.

It cannot be emphasized often enough that it is free will that determines whether we will make really good use of our talents and abilities. Using our free will, we can either overcome our failings or allow them to rule us. Our free will enables us to exert sufficient willpower to control our failings so that they do not harm ourselves or others.

Astrology can reveal our inclinations and tendencies. Astrology can tell us about ourselves so that we are able to use our free will to overcome our shortcomings. In this way astrology helps us do our best to become needed and valuable members of society as well as helpmates to our family and our friends. Astrology also can save us a great deal of unhappiness and remorse.

Yet it may seem absurd that an ancient philosophy could be a prop to modern men and women. But below the materialistic surface of modern life, there are hidden streams of feeling and thought. Symbology is reappearing as a study worthy of the scholar; the psychosomatic factor in illness has passed from the writings of the crank to those of the specialist; spiritual healing in all its forms is no longer a pious hope but an accepted phenomenon. And it is into this context that we consider astrology, in the sense that it is an analysis of human types.

Astrology and medicine had a long journey together, and only parted company a couple of centuries ago. There still remain in medical language such astrological terms as "saturnine," "choleric," and "mercurial," used in the diagnosis of physical tendencies. The herbalist, for long the handyman of the medical profession, has been dominated by astrology since the days of the Greeks. Certain herbs traditionally respond to certain planetary influences, and diseases must therefore be treated to ensure harmony between the medicine and the disease.

But the stars are expected to foretell and not only to diagnose.

Astrological forecasting has been remarkably accurate, but often it is wide of the mark. The brave person who cares to predict world events takes dangerous chances. Individual forecasting is less clear cut; it can be a help or a disillusionment. Then we come to the nagging question: if it is possible to foreknow, is it right to foretell? This is a point of ethics on which it is hard to pronounce judgment. The doctor faces the same dilemma if he finds that symptoms of a mortal disease are present in his patient and that he can only prognosticate a steady decline. How much to tell an individual in a crisis is a problem that has perplexed many distinguished scholars. Honest and conscientious astrologers in this modern world, where so many people are seeking guidance, face the same problem.

Five hundred years ago it was customary to call in a learned man who was an astrologer who was probably also a doctor and a philosopher. By his knowledge of astrology, his study of planetary influences, he felt himself qualified to guide those in distress. The world has moved forward at a fantastic rate since then, and yet people are still uncertain of themselves. At first sight it seems fantastic in the light of modern thinking that they turn to the most ancient of all studies, and get someone to calculate a horoscope for them. But is it *really* so fantastic if you take a second look? For astrology is concerned with tomorrow, with survival. And in a world such as ours, tomorrow and survival are the keywords for the twenty-first century.

ASTROLOGICAL BRIDGE TO THE 21st CENTURY

As the decade opens on a new century, indeed on a new millennium, the planets set the stage for change and challenge. Themes connecting past, present, and future are in play as new planetary cycles form the bridge to the twenty-first century and its broad horizons. The first few years of the new decade reveal hidden paths and personal hints for achieving your potential, for making the most of your message from the planets.

With the dawning of the twenty-first century look first to Jupiter, the planet of good fortune. Each new yearly Jupiter cycle follows the natural progression of the Zodiac. First is Jupiter in Aries and in Taurus through spring 2000, next Jupiter is in Gemini to summer 2001, then in Cancer to midsummer 2002, in Leo to late summer 2003, in Virgo to early autumn 2004, and so on through Jupiter in Pisces through June 2010. The beneficent planet Jupiter promotes your professional and educational goals while urging informed choice and deliberation. Jupiter sharpens your focus and hones your skills, providing a rich medium for creativity. Planet Jupiter's influence is protective, the generous helper that comes to the rescue just in the nick of time. And while safeguarding good luck, Jupiter can turn unusual risks into achievable aims.

In order to take advantage of luck and opportunity, to gain wisdom from experience, to persevere against adversity, look to beautiful planet Saturn. Saturn, planet of reason and responsibility, began a new cycle in earthy Taurus at the turn of the century. Saturn in Taurus until spring 2001 inspires industry and affection, blends practicality and imagination, all the while inviting caution and care. Persistence and planning can reverse setbacks and minimize risk. Saturn in Taurus lends beauty, order, and structure to your life. Then Saturn is in Gemini, the sign of mind and communication, until June 2003. Saturn in Gemini gives depth and inspiration to thought and feeling. Here, because of a lively intellectual capacity, the limits of creativity can be stretched and boundaries broken. Saturn in Gemini holds the promise of fruitful endeavor through sustained study, learning, and application.

Uranus, planet of innovation and surprise, started an important new cycle in January of 1996. At that time Uranus entered its natural home in airy Aquarius. Uranus in Aquarius into the year 2003 has a profound effect on your personality and the lens through which you see the world. A basic change in the way you project yourself is just one impact of Uranus in Aquarius. More significantly, a whole new consciousness is evolving. Winds of change blowing your way emphasize movement and freedom. Uranus in Aquarius poses involvement in the larger community beyond self, family, friends, lovers, associates. Radical ideas and progressive thought signal a journey of liberation. As the new century begins, follow Uranus on the path of humanitarianism. While you carve a prestigious niche in public life, while you preach social reform and justice, you will be striving to make the world a better place for all people.

Neptune, planet of vision and mystery, is enjoying a long cycle that excites creativity and imaginative thinking. Neptune is in airy Aquarius from November 1998 to February of 2012. Neptune in Aquarius, the sign of the Water Bearer, represents two sides of the coin of wisdom: inspiration and reason. Here Neptune stirs powerful currents bearing a rich and varied harvest, the fertile breeding ground for idealistic aims and practical considerations. Neptune's fine intuition tunes in to your dreams, your imagination, your spirituality. You can never turn your back on the mysteries of life. Uranus and Neptune, the planets of enlightenment and renewed idealism both in the sign of Aquarius, give you glimpses into the future, letting you peek through secret doorways opening into the twenty-first century.

Pluto, planet of beginnings and endings, began a new cycle of growth and learning late in 1995. Pluto entered fiery Sagittarius and remains there into the year 2008. Pluto in Sagittarius during its long stay over twelve years can create significant change. The great power of Pluto in Sagittarius is already starting its transformation of your character and lifestyle. Pluto in Sagittarius takes you on a new journey of exploration and learning. The awakening you experience on intellectual and artistic levels heralds a new cycle of growth. Uncompromising Pluto, seeker of truth, challenges your identity, persona, and self-expression. Uncovering the real you, Pluto holds the key to understanding and meaningful communication. Pluto in Sagittarius can be the guiding light illuminating the first decade of the twenty-first century. Good luck is riding on the waves of change.

THE SIGNS OF THE ZODIAC

Dominant Characteristics

Aries: March 21–April 20

The Positive Side of Aries

The Aries has many positive points to his character. People born under this first sign of the Zodiac are often quite strong and enthusiastic. On the whole, they are forward-looking people who are not easily discouraged by temporary setbacks. They know what they want out of life and they go out after it. Their personalities are strong. Others are usually quite impressed by the Ram's way of doing things. Quite often they are sources of inspiration for others traveling the same route. Aries men and women have a special zest for life that can be contagious; for others, they are a fine example of how life should be lived.

The Aries person usually has a quick and active mind. He is imaginative and inventive. He enjoys keeping busy and active. He generally gets along well with all kinds of people. He is interested in mankind, as a whole. He likes to be challenged. Some would say he thrives on opposition, for it is when he is set against that he often does his best. Getting over or around obstacles is a challenge he generally enjoys. All in all, Aries is quite positive and young-thinking. He likes to keep abreast of new things that are happening in the world. Aries are often fond of speed. They like things to be done quickly, and this sometimes aggravates their slower colleagues and associates.

The Aries man or woman always seems to remain young. Their whole approach to life is youthful and optimistic. They never say die, no matter what the odds. They may have an occasional setback, but it is not long before they are back on their feet again.

The Negative Side of Aries

Everybody has his less positive qualities—and Aries is no exception. Sometimes the Aries man or woman is not very tactful in communicating with others; in his hurry to get things done he is apt to be a little callous or inconsiderate. Sensitive people are likely to find him somewhat sharp-tongued in some situations. Often in his eagerness to get the show on the road, he misses the mark altogether and cannot achieve his aims.

At times Aries can be too impulsive. He can occasionally be stubborn and refuse to listen to reason. If things do not move quickly enough to suit the Aries man or woman, he or she is apt to become rather nervous or irritable. The uncultivated Aries is not unfamiliar with moments of doubt and fear. He is capable of being destructive if he does not get his way. He can overcome some of his emotional problems by steadily trying to express himself as he really is, but this requires effort.

Taurus: April 21–May 20

The Positive Side of Taurus

The Taurus person is known for his ability to concentrate and for his tenacity. These are perhaps his strongest qualities. The Taurus man or woman generally has very little trouble in getting along with others; it's his nature to be helpful toward people in need. He can always be depended on by his friends, especially those in trouble.

Taurus generally achieves what he wants through his ability to persevere. He never leaves anything unfinished but works on something until it has been completed. People can usually take him at his word; he is honest and forthright in most of his dealings. The Taurus person has a good chance to make a success of his life because of his many positive qualities. The Taurus who aims high seldom falls short of his mark. He learns well by experience. He is thorough and does not believe in shortcuts of any kind. The Bull's thoroughness pays off in the end, for through his deliberateness he learns how to rely on himself and what he has learned. The Taurus person tries to get along with others, as a rule. He is not overly critical and likes people to be themselves. He is a tolerant person and enjoys peace and harmony—especially in his home life.

Taurus is usually cautious in all that he does. He is not a person who believes in taking unnecessary risks. Before adopting any one line of action, he will weigh all of the pros and cons. The Taurus person is steadfast. Once his mind is made up it seldom changes. The person born under this sign usually is a good family person—reliable and loving.

The Negative Side of Taurus

Sometimes the Taurus man or woman is a bit too stubborn. He won't listen to other points of view if his mind is set on something. To others, this can be quite annoying. Taurus also does not like to be told what to do. He becomes rather angry if others think him not too bright. He does not like to be told he is wrong, even when he is. He dislikes being contradicted.

Some people who are born under this sign are very suspicious of others—even of those persons close to them. They find it difficult to trust people fully. They are often afraid of being deceived or taken advantage of. The Bull often finds it difficult to forget or forgive. His love of material things sometimes makes him rather avaricious and petty.

Gemini: May 21–June 20

The Positive Side of Gemini

The person born under this sign of the Heavenly Twins is usually quite bright and quick-witted. Some of them are capable of doing many different things. The Gemini person very often has many different interests. He keeps an open mind and is always anxious to learn new things.

Gemini is often an analytical person. He is a person who enjoys making use of his intellect. He is governed more by his mind than by his emotions. He is a person who is not confined to one view; he can often understand both sides to a problem or question. He knows how to reason, how to make rapid decisions if need be.

He is an adaptable person and can make himself at home almost anywhere. There are all kinds of situations he can adapt to. He is a person who seldom doubts himself; he is sure of his talents and his ability to think and reason. Gemini is generally most satisfied

when he is in a situation where he can make use of his intellect. Never short of imagination, he often has strong talents for invention. He is rather a modern person when it comes to life; Gemini almost always moves along with the times—perhaps that is why he remains so youthful throughout most of his life.

Literature and art appeal to the person born under this sign. Creativity in almost any form will interest and intrigue the Gemini man or woman.

The Gemini is often quite charming. A good talker, he often is the center of attraction at any gathering. People find it easy to like a person born under this sign because he can appear easygoing and usually has a good sense of humor.

The Negative Side of Gemini

Sometimes the Gemini person tries to do too many things at one time—and as a result, winds up finishing nothing. Some Twins are easily distracted and find it rather difficult to concentrate on one thing for too long a time. Sometimes they give in to trifling fancies and find it rather boring to become too serious about any one thing. Some of them are never dependable, no matter what they promise.

Although the Gemini man or woman often appears to be well-versed on many subjects, this is sometimes just a veneer. His knowledge may be only superficial, but because he speaks so well he gives people the impression of erudition. Some Geminis are sharp-tongued and inconsiderate; they think only of themselves and their own pleasure.

Cancer: June 21–July 20

The Positive Side of Cancer

The Moon Child's most positive point is his understanding nature. On the whole, he is a loving and sympathetic person. He would never go out of his way to hurt anyone. The Cancer man or woman is often very kind and tender; they give what they can to others. They hate to see others suffering and will do what they can to help someone in less fortunate circumstances than themselves. They are often very concerned about the world. Their interest in people generally goes beyond that of just their own families and close friends; they have a deep sense of community and respect humanitarian values. The Moon Child means what he says, as a rule; he is honest about his feelings.

The Cancer man or woman is a person who knows the art of patience. When something seems difficult, he is willing to wait until the situation becomes manageable again. He is a person who knows how to bide his time. Cancer knows how to concentrate on one thing at a time. When he has made his mind up he generally sticks with what he does, seeing it through to the end.

Cancer is a person who loves his home. He enjoys being surrounded by familiar things and the people he loves. Of all the signs, Cancer is the most maternal. Even the men born under this sign often have a motherly or protective quality about them. They like to take care of people in their family—to see that they are well loved and well provided for. They are usually loyal and faithful. Family ties mean a lot to the Cancer man or woman. Parents and in-laws are respected and loved. Young Cancer responds very well to adults who show faith in him. The Moon Child has a strong sense of tradition. He is very sensitive to the moods of others.

The Negative Side of Cancer

Sometimes Cancer finds it rather hard to face life. It becomes too much for him. He can be a little timid and retiring, when things don't go too well. When unfortunate things happen, he is apt to just shrug and say, "Whatever will be will be." He can be fatalistic to a fault. The uncultivated Cancer is a bit lazy. He doesn't have very much ambition. Anything that seems a bit difficult he'll gladly leave to others. He may be lacking in initiative. Too sensitive, when he feels he's been injured, he'll crawl back into his shell and nurse his imaginary wounds. The immature Moon Child often is given to crying when the smallest thing goes wrong.

Some Cancers find it difficult to enjoy themselves in environments outside their homes. They make heavy demands on others, and need to be constantly reassured that they are loved. Lacking such reassurance, they may resort to sulking in silence.

Leo: July 21–August 21

The Positive Side of Leo

Often Leos make good leaders. They seem to be good organizers and administrators. Usually they are quite popular with others. Whatever group it is that they belong to, the Leo man or woman is almost sure to be or become the leader. Loyalty, one of the Lion's noblest traits, enables him or her to maintain this leadership position.

Leo is generous most of the time. It is his best characteristic. He or she likes to give gifts and presents. In making others happy, the Leo person becomes happy himself. He likes to splurge when spending money on others. In some instances it may seem that the Lion's generosity knows no boundaries. A hospitable person, the Leo man or woman is very fond of welcoming people to his house and entertaining them. He is never short of company.

Leo has plenty of energy and drive. He enjoys working toward some specific goal. When he applies himself correctly, he gets what he wants most often. The Leo person is almost never unsure of himself. He has plenty of confidence and aplomb. He is a person who is direct in almost everything he does. He has a quick mind and can make a decision in a very short time.

He usually sets a good example for others because of his ambitious manner and positive ways. He knows how to stick to something once he's started. Although Leo may be good at making a joke, he is not superficial or glib. He is a loving person, kind and thoughtful.

There is generally nothing small or petty about the Leo man or woman. He does what he can for those who are deserving. He is a person others can rely upon at all times. He means what he says. An honest person, generally speaking, he is a friend who is valued and sought out.

The Negative Side of Leo

Leo, however, does have his faults. At times, he can be just a bit too arrogant. He thinks that no one deserves a leadership position except him. Only he is capable of doing things well. His opinion of himself is often much too high. Because of his conceit, he is

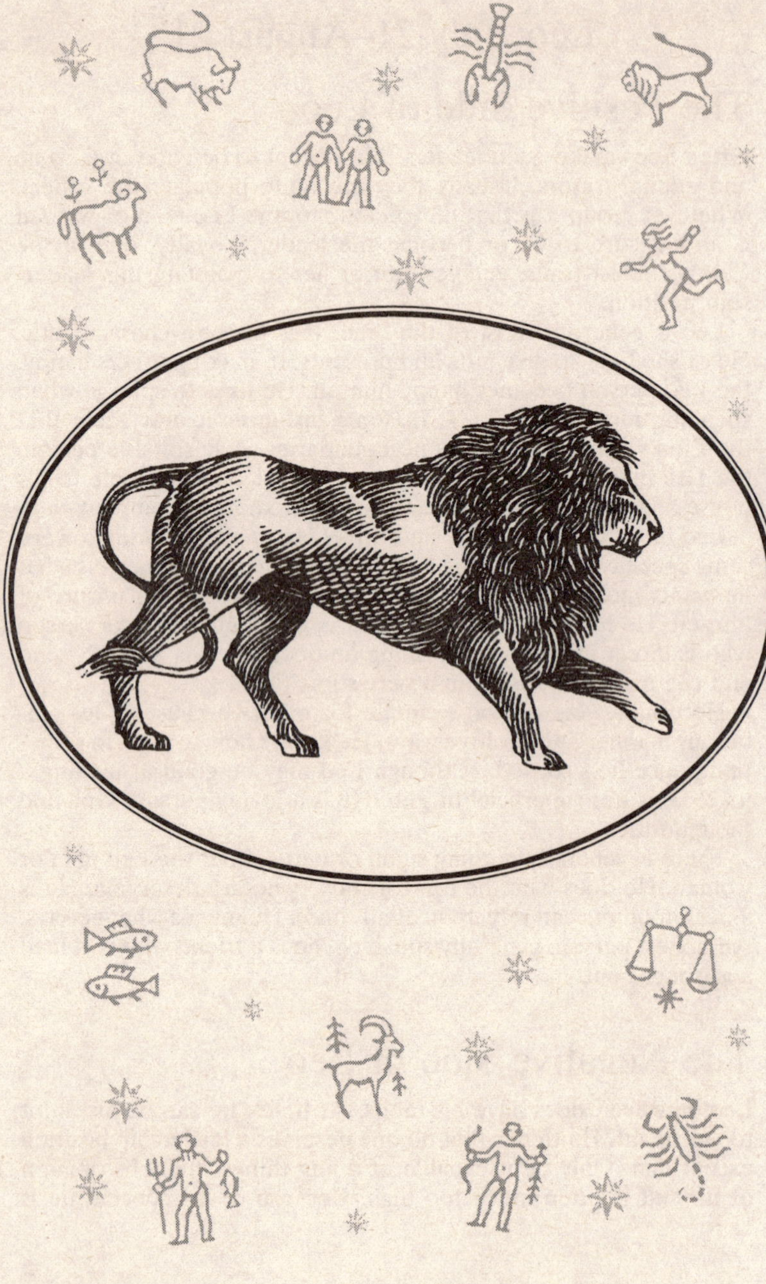

sometimes rather unpopular with a good many people. Some Leos are too materialistic; they can only think in terms of money and profit.

Some Leos enjoy lording it over others—at home or at their place of business. What is more, they feel they have the right to. Egocentric to an impossible degree, this sort of Leo cares little about how others think or feel. He can be rude and cutting.

Virgo: August 22–September 22

The Positive Side of Virgo

The person born under the sign of Virgo is generally a busy person. He knows how to arrange and organize things. He is a good planner. Above all, he is practical and is not afraid of hard work.

Often called the sign of the Harvester, Virgo knows how to attain what he desires. He sticks with something until it is finished. He never shirks his duties, and can always be depended upon. The Virgo person can be thoroughly trusted at all times.

The man or woman born under this sign tries to do everything to perfection. He doesn't believe in doing anything halfway. He always aims for the top. He is the sort of a person who is always learning and constantly striving to better himself—not because he wants more money or glory, but because it gives him a feeling of accomplishment.

The Virgo man or woman is a very observant person. He is sensitive to how others feel, and can see things below the surface of a situation. He usually puts this talent to constructive use.

It is not difficult for the Virgo to be open and earnest. He believes in putting his cards on the table. He is never secretive or underhanded. He's as good as his word. The Virgo person is generally plainspoken and down to earth. He has no trouble in expressing himself.

The Virgo person likes to keep up to date on new developments in his particular field. Well-informed, generally, he sometimes has a keen interest in the arts or literature. What he knows, he knows well. His ability to use his critical faculties is well-developed and sometimes startles others because of its accuracy.

Virgos adhere to a moderate way of life; they avoid excesses. Virgo is a responsible person and enjoys being of service.

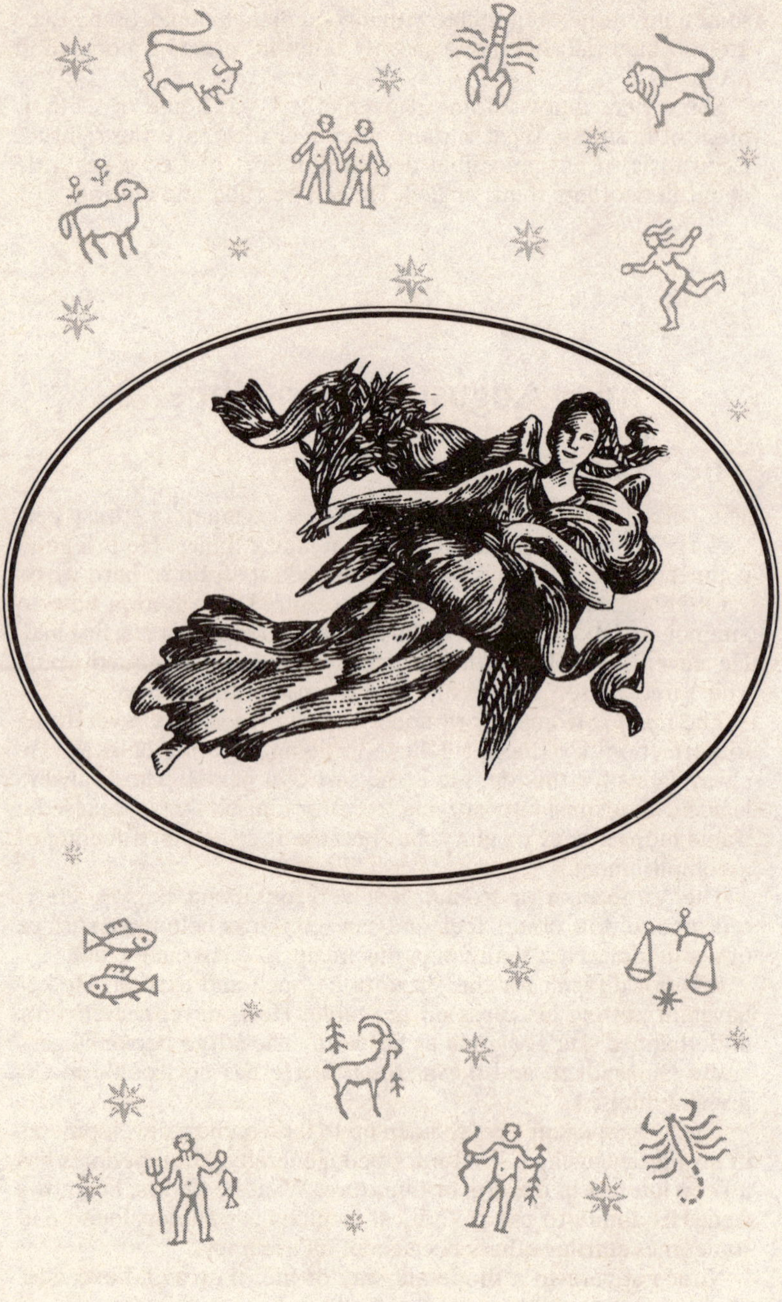

The Negative Side of Virgo

Sometimes a Virgo person is too critical. He thinks that only he can do something the way it should be done. Whatever anyone else does is inferior. He can be rather annoying in the way he quibbles over insignificant details. In telling others how things should be done, he can be rather tactless and mean.

Some Virgos seem rather emotionless and cool. They feel emotional involvement is beneath them. They are sometimes too tidy, too neat. With money they can be rather miserly. Some Virgos try to force their opinions and ideas on others.

Libra: September 23–October 22

The Positive Side of Libra

Libras love harmony. It is one of their most outstanding character traits. They are interested in achieving balance; they admire beauty and grace in things as well as in people. Generally speaking, they are kind and considerate people. Libras are usually very sympathetic. They go out of their way not to hurt another person's feelings. They are outgoing and do what they can to help those in need.

People born under the sign of Libra almost always make good friends. They are loyal and amiable. They enjoy the company of others. Many of them are rather moderate in their views; they believe in keeping an open mind, however, and weighing both sides of an issue fairly before making a decision.

Alert and intelligent, Libra, often known as the Lawgiver, is always fair-minded and tries to put himself in the position of the other person. They are against injustice; quite often they take up for the underdog. In most of their social dealings, they try to be tactful and kind. They dislike discord and bickering, and most Libras strive for peace and harmony in all their relationships.

The Libra man or woman has a keen sense of beauty. They appreciate handsome furnishings and clothes. Many of them are artistically inclined. Their taste is usually impeccable. They know how to use color. Their homes are almost always attractively arranged and inviting. They enjoy entertaining people and see to it that their guests always feel at home and welcome.

Libra gets along with almost everyone. He is well-liked and socially much in demand.

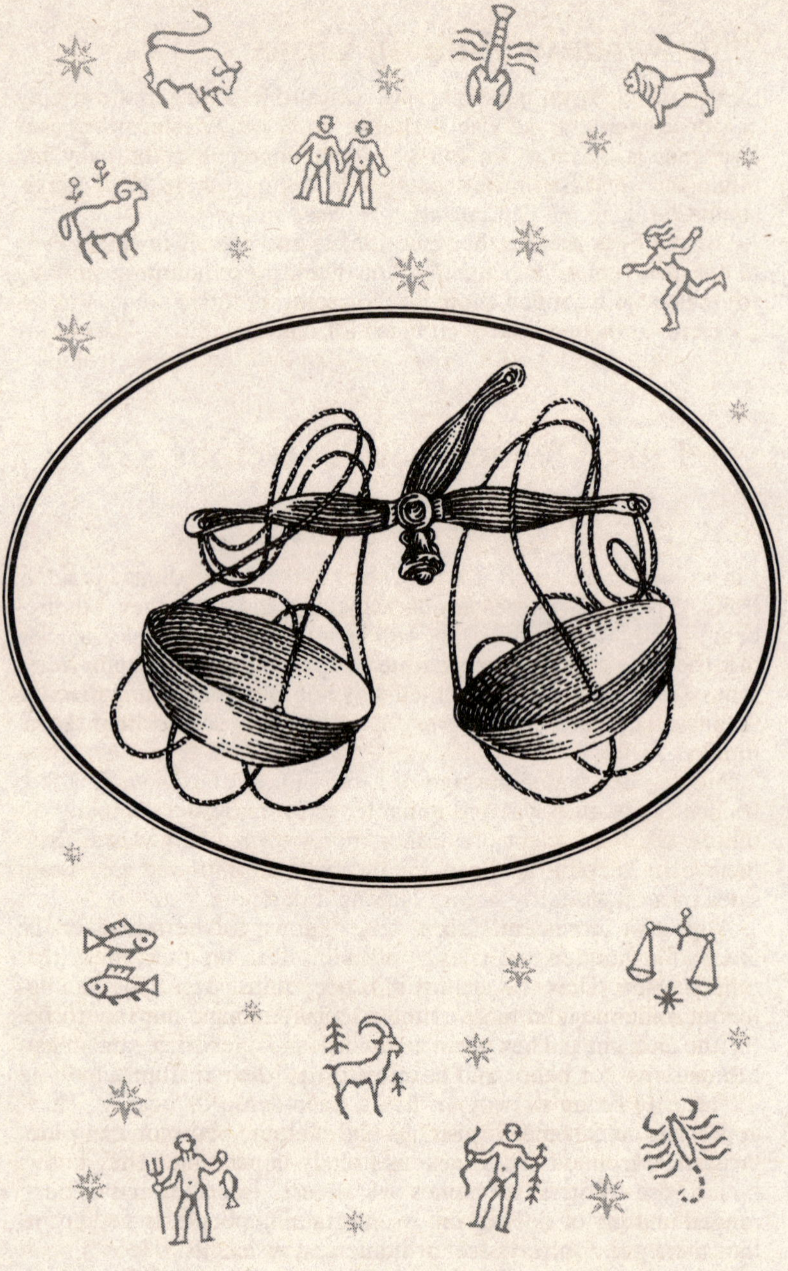

The Negative Side of Libra

Some people born under this sign tend to be rather insincere. So eager are they to achieve harmony in all relationships that they will even go so far as to lie. Many of them are escapists. They find facing the truth an ordeal and prefer living in a world of make-believe.

In a serious argument, some Libras give in rather easily even when they know they are right. Arguing, even about something they believe in, is too unsettling for some of them.

Libras sometimes care too much for material things. They enjoy possessions and luxuries. Some are vain and tend to be jealous.

Scorpio: October 23–November 22

The Positive Side of Scorpio

The Scorpio man or woman generally knows what he or she wants out of life. He is a determined person. He sees something through to the end. Scorpio is quite sincere, and seldom says anything he doesn't mean. When he sets a goal for himself he tries to go about achieving it in a very direct way.

The Scorpion is brave and courageous. They are not afraid of hard work. Obstacles do not frighten them. They forge ahead until they achieve what they set out for. The Scorpio man or woman has a strong will.

Although Scorpio may seem rather fixed and determined, inside he is often quite tender and loving. He can care very much for others. He believes in sincerity in all relationships. His feelings about someone tend to last; they are profound and not superficial.

The Scorpio person is someone who adheres to his principles no matter what happens. He will not be deterred from a path he believes to be right.

Because of his many positive strengths, the Scorpion can often achieve happiness for himself and for those that he loves.

He is a constructive person by nature. He often has a deep understanding of people and of life, in general. He is perceptive and unafraid. Obstacles often seem to spur him on. He is a positive person who enjoys winning. He has many strengths and resources; challenge of any sort often brings out the best in him.

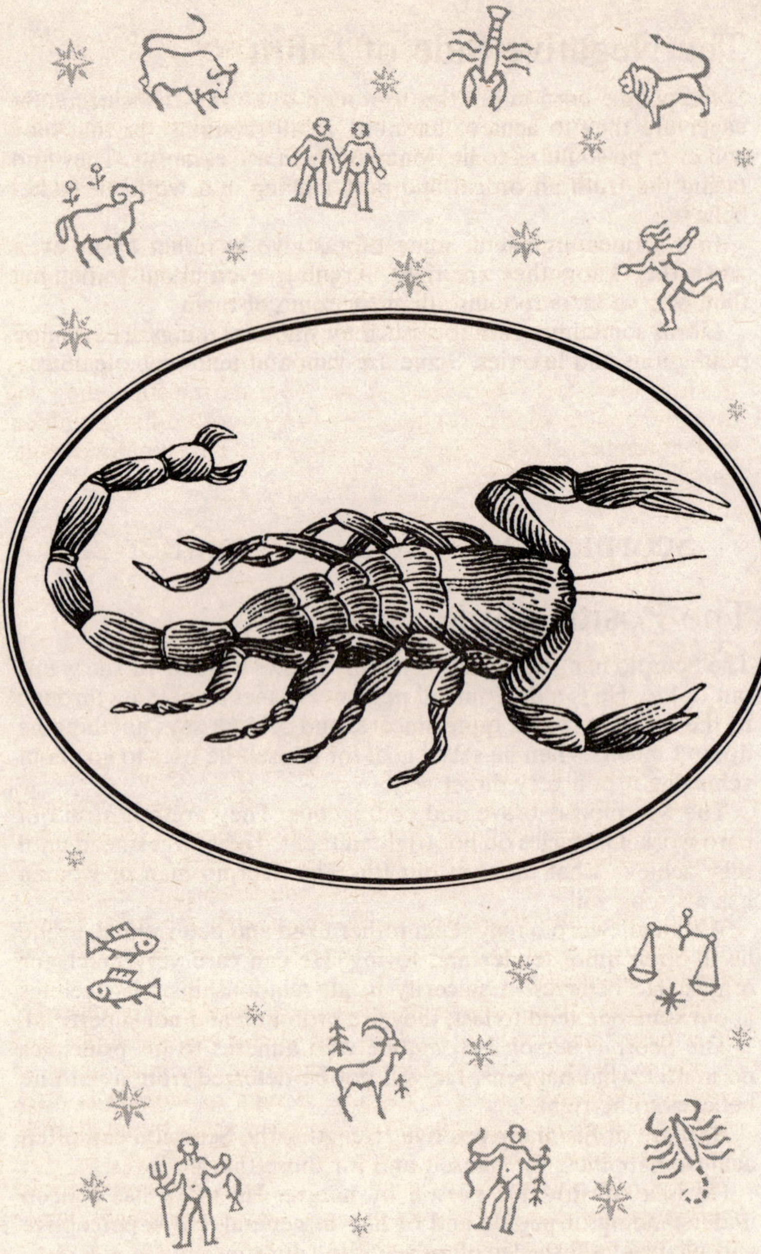

The Negative Side of Scorpio

The Scorpio person is sometimes hypersensitive. Often he imagines injury when there is none. He feels that others do not bother to recognize him for his true worth. Sometimes he is given to excessive boasting in order to compensate for what he feels is neglect.

Scorpio can be proud, arrogant, and competitive. They can be sly when they put their minds to it and they enjoy outwitting persons or institutions noted for their cleverness.

Their tactics for getting what they want are sometimes devious and ruthless. They don't care too much about what others may think. If they feel others have done them an injustice, they will do their best to seek revenge. The Scorpion often has a sudden, violent temper; and this person's interest in sex is sometimes quite unbalanced or excessive.

Sagittarius: November 23–December 20

The Positive Side of Sagittarius

People born under this sign are honest and forthright. Their approach to life is earnest and open. Sagittarius is often quite adult in his way of seeing things. They are broad-minded and tolerant people. When dealing with others the person born under the sign of the Archer is almost always open and forthright. He doesn't believe in deceit or pretension. His standards are high. People who associate with Sagittarius generally admire and respect his tolerant viewpoint.

The Archer trusts others easily and expects them to trust him. He is never suspicious or envious and almost always thinks well of others. People always enjoy his company because he is so friendly and easygoing. The Sagittarius man or woman is often good-humored. He can always be depended upon by his friends, family, and co-workers.

The person born under this sign of the Zodiac likes a good joke every now and then. Sagittarius is eager for fun and laughs, which makes him very popular with others.

A lively person, he enjoys sports and outdoor life. The Archer is fond of animals. Intelligent and interesting, he can begin an

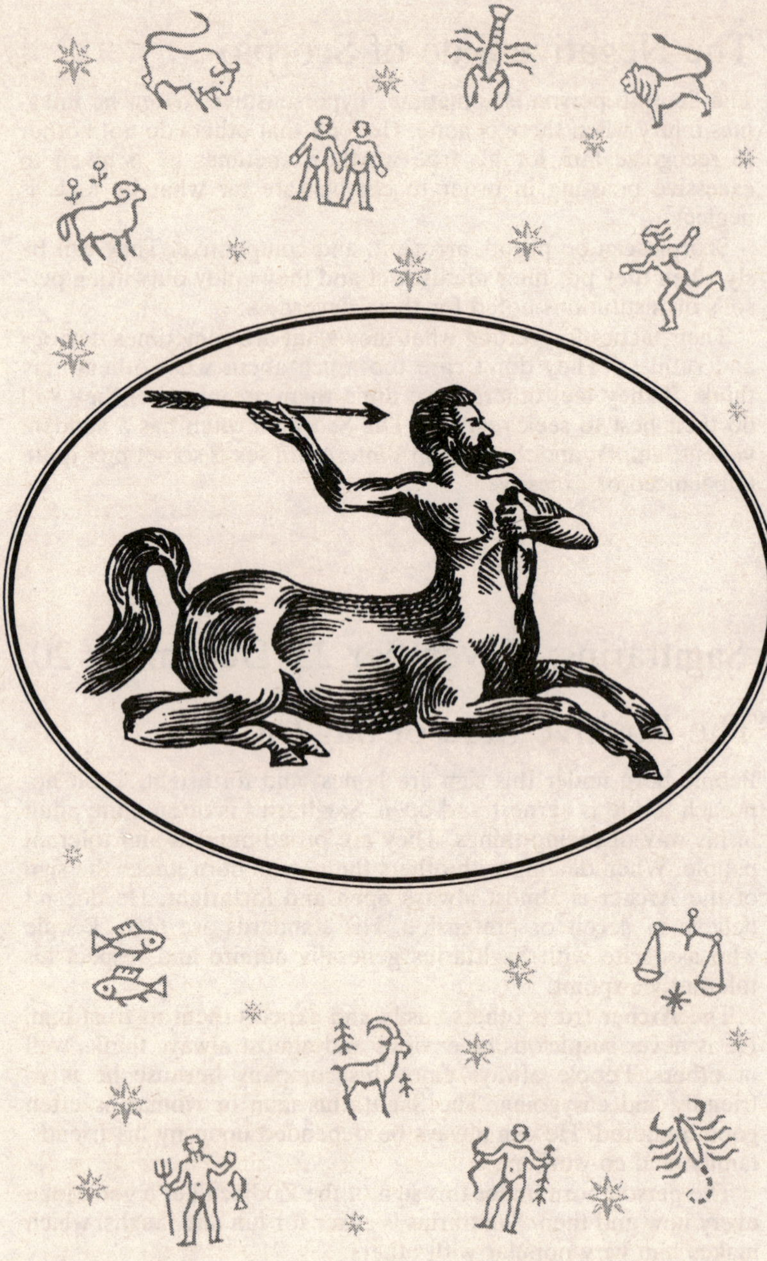

animated conversation with ease. He likes exchanging ideas and discussing various views.

He is not selfish or proud. If someone proposes an idea or plan that is better than his, he will immediately adopt it. Imaginative yet practical, he knows how to put ideas into practice.

The Archer enjoys sport and games, and it doesn't matter if he wins or loses. He is a forgiving person, and never sulks over something that has not worked out in his favor.

He is seldom critical, and is almost always generous.

The Negative Side of Sagittarius

Some Sagittarius are restless. They take foolish risks and seldom learn from the mistakes they make. They don't have heads for money and are often mismanaging their finances. Some of them devote much of their time to gambling.

Some are too outspoken and tactless, always putting their feet in their mouths. They hurt others carelessly by being honest at the wrong time. Sometimes they make promises which they don't keep. They don't stick close enough to their plans and go from one failure to another. They are undisciplined and waste a lot of energy.

Capricorn: December 21–January 19

The Positive Side of Capricorn

The person born under the sign of Capricorn, known variously as the Mountain Goat or Sea Goat, is usually very stable and patient. He sticks to whatever tasks he has and sees them through. He can always be relied upon and he is not averse to work.

An honest person, Capricorn is generally serious about whatever he does. He does not take his duties lightly. He is a practical person and believes in keeping his feet on the ground.

Quite often the person born under this sign is ambitious and knows how to get what he wants out of life. The Goat forges ahead and never gives up his goal. When he is determined about something, he almost always wins. He is a good worker—a hard worker. Although things may not come easy to him, he will not complain, but continue working until his chores are finished.

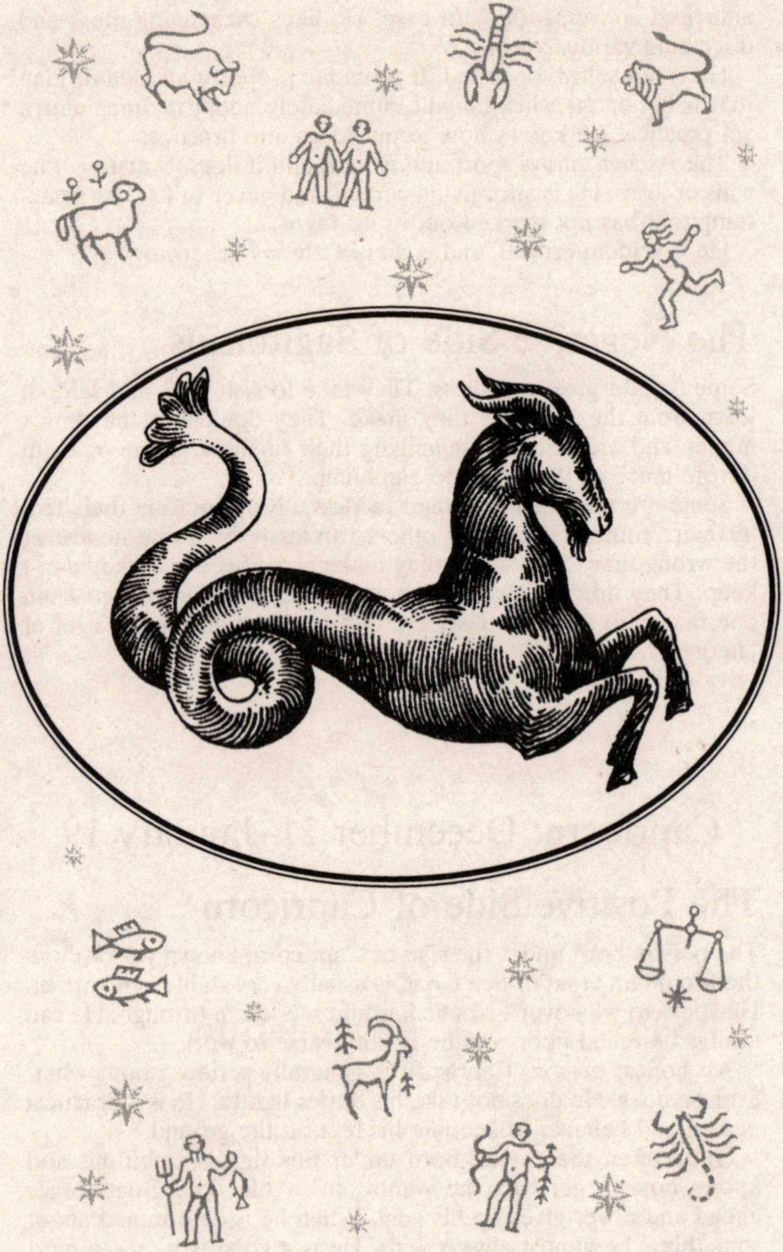

He is usually good at business matters and knows the value of money. He is not a spendthrift and knows how to put something away for a rainy day; he dislikes waste and unnecessary loss.

Capricorn knows how to make use of his self-control. He can apply himself to almost anything once he puts his mind to it. His ability to concentrate sometimes astounds others. He is diligent and does well when involved in detail work.

The Capricorn man or woman is charitable, generally speaking, and will do what is possible to help others less fortunate. As a friend, he is loyal and trustworthy. He never shirks his duties or responsibilities. He is self-reliant and never expects too much of the other fellow. He does what he can on his own. If someone does him a good turn, then he will do his best to return the favor.

The Negative Side of Capricorn

Like everyone, Capricorn, too, has faults. At times, the Goat can be overcritical of others. He expects others to live up to his own high standards. He thinks highly of himself and tends to look down on others.

His interest in material things may be exaggerated. The Capricorn man or woman thinks too much about getting on in the world and having something to show for it. He may even be a little greedy.

He sometimes thinks he knows what's best for everyone. He is too bossy. He is always trying to organize and correct others. He may be a little narrow in his thinking.

Aquarius: January 20–February 18

The Positive Side of Aquarius

The Aquarius man or woman is usually very honest and forthright. These are his two greatest qualities. His standards for himself are generally very high. He can always be relied upon by others. His word is his bond.

Aquarius is perhaps the most tolerant of all the Zodiac personalities. He respects other people's beliefs and feels that everyone is entitled to his own approach to life.

He would never do anything to injure another's feelings. He is never unkind or cruel. Always considerate of others, the Water

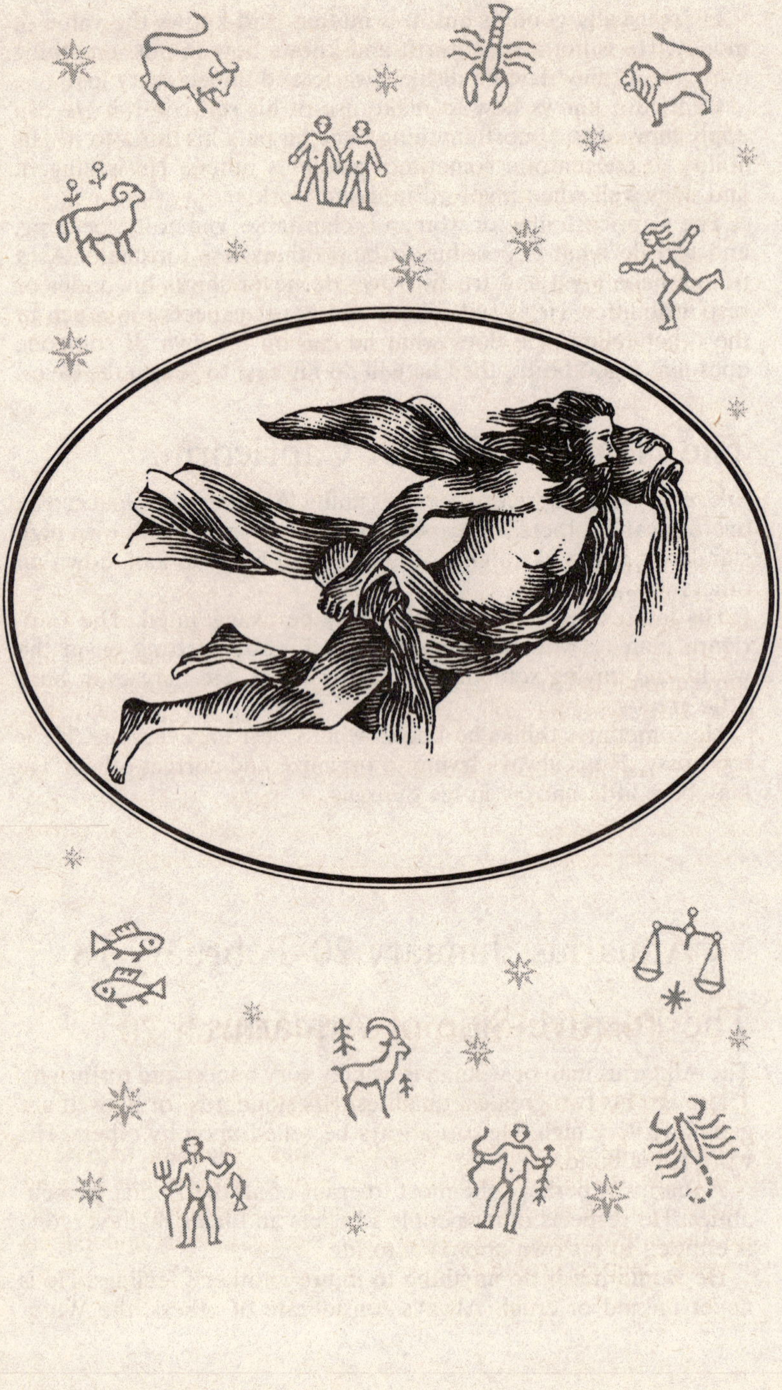

Bearer is always willing to help a person in need. He feels a very strong tie between himself and all the other members of mankind.

The person born under this sign, called the Water Bearer, is almost always an individualist. He does not believe in teaming up with the masses, but prefers going his own way. His ideas about life and mankind are often quite advanced. There is a saying to the effect that the average Aquarius is fifty years ahead of his time.

Aquarius is community-minded. The problems of the world concern him greatly. He is interested in helping others no matter what part of the globe they live in. He is truly a humanitarian sort. He likes to be of service to others.

Giving, considerate, and without prejudice, Aquarius have no trouble getting along with others.

The Negative Side of Aquarius

Aquarius may be too much of a dreamer. He makes plans but seldom carries them out. He is rather unrealistic. His imagination has a tendency to run away with him. Because many of his plans are impractical, he is always in some sort of a dither.

Others may not approve of him at all times because of his unconventional behavior. He may be a bit eccentric. Sometimes he is so busy with his own thoughts that he loses touch with the realities of existence.

Some Aquarius feel they are more clever and intelligent than others. They seldom admit to their own faults, even when they are quite apparent. Some become rather fanatic in their views. Their criticism of others is sometimes destructive and negative.

Pisces: February 19–March 20

The Positive Side of Pisces

Known as the sign of the Fishes, Pisces has a sympathetic nature. Kindly, he is often dedicated in the way he goes about helping others. The sick and the troubled often turn to him for advice and assistance. Possessing keen intuition, Pisces can easily understand people's deepest problems.

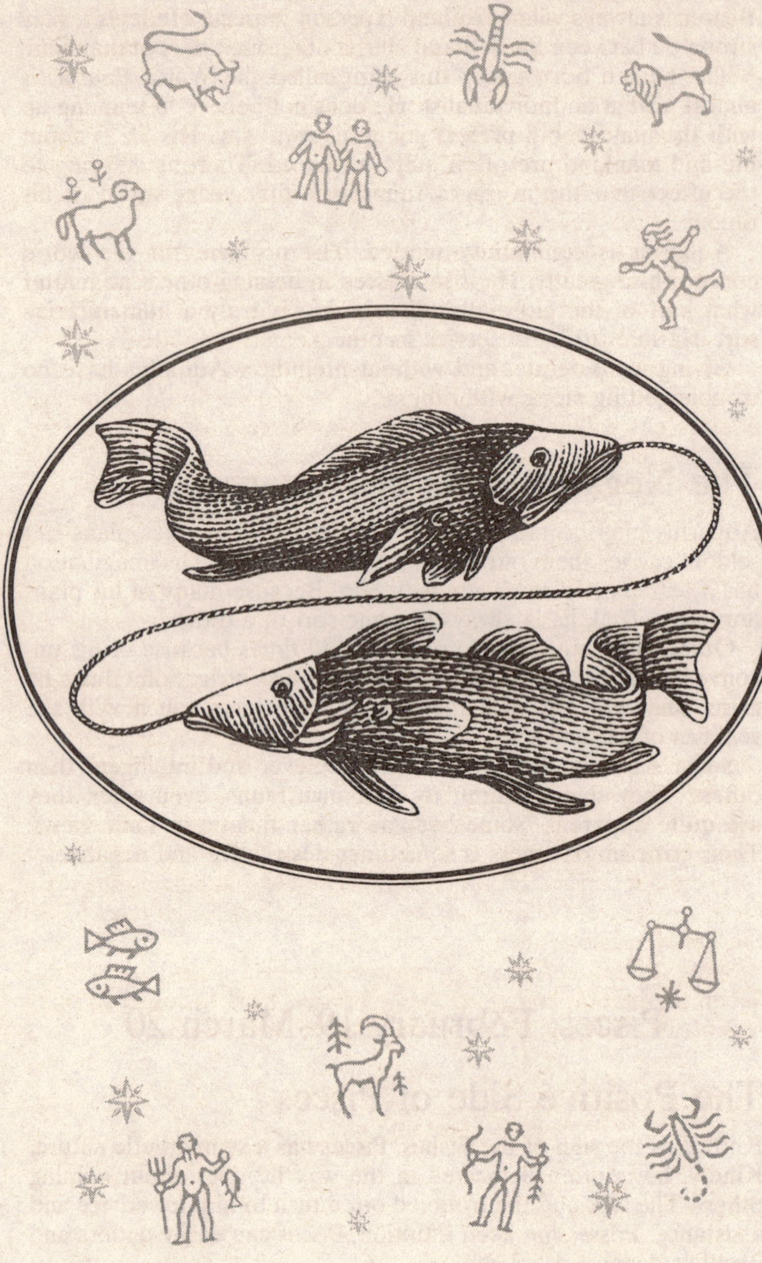

He is very broad-minded and does not criticize others for their faults. He knows how to accept people for what they are. On the whole, he is a trustworthy and earnest person. He is loyal to his friends and will do what he can to help them in time of need. Generous and good-natured, he is a lover of peace; he is often willing to help others solve their differences. People who have taken a wrong turn in life often interest him and he will do what he can to persuade them to rehabilitate themselves.

He has a strong intuitive sense and most of the time he knows how to make it work for him. Pisces is unusually perceptive and often knows what is bothering someone before that person, himself, is aware of it. The Pisces man or woman is an idealistic person, basically, and is interested in making the world a better place in which to live. Pisces believes that everyone should help each other. He is willing to do more than his share in order to achieve cooperation with others.

The person born under this sign often is talented in music or art. He is a receptive person; he is able to take the ups and downs of life with philosophic calm.

The Negative Side of Pisces

Some Pisces are often depressed; their outlook on life is rather glum. They may feel that they have been given a bad deal in life and that others are always taking unfair advantage of them. Pisces sometimes feel that the world is a cold and cruel place. The Fishes can be easily discouraged. The Pisces man or woman may even withdraw from the harshness of reality into a secret shell of his own where he dreams and idles away a good deal of his time.

Pisces can be lazy. He lets things happen without giving the least bit of resistance. He drifts along, whether on the high road or on the low. He can be lacking in willpower.

Some Pisces people seek escape through drugs or alcohol. When temptation comes along they find it hard to resist. In matters of sex, they can be rather permissive.

Sun Sign Personalities

ARIES: Hans Christian Andersen, Pearl Bailey, Marlon Brando, Wernher Von Braun, Charlie Chaplin, Joan Crawford, Da Vinci, Bette Davis, Doris Day, W. C. Fields, Alec Guinness, Adolf Hitler, William Holden, Thomas Jefferson, Nikita Khrushchev, Elton John, Arturo Toscanini, J. P. Morgan, Paul Robeson, Gloria Steinem, Sarah Vaughn, Vincent van Gogh, Tennessee Williams

TAURUS: Fred Astaire, Charlotte Brontë, Carol Burnett, Irving Berlin, Bing Crosby, Salvador Dali, Tchaikovsky, Queen Elizabeth II, Duke Ellington, Ella Fitzgerald, Henry Fonda, Sigmund Freud, Orson Welles, Joe Louis, Lenin, Karl Marx, Golda Meir, Eva Peron, Bertrand Russell, Shakespeare, Kate Smith, Benjamin Spock, Barbra Streisand, Shirley Temple, Harry Truman

GEMINI: Ruth Benedict, Josephine Baker, Rachel Carson, Carlos Chavez, Walt Whitman, Bob Dylan, Ralph Waldo Emerson, Judy Garland, Paul Gauguin, Allen Ginsberg, Benny Goodman, Bob Hope, Burl Ives, John F. Kennedy, Peggy Lee, Marilyn Monroe, Joe Namath, Cole Porter, Laurence Olivier, Harriet Beecher Stowe, Queen Victoria, John Wayne, Frank Lloyd Wright

CANCER: "Dear Abby," Lizzie Borden, David Brinkley, Yul Brynner, Pearl Buck, Marc Chagall, Princess Diana, Babe Didrikson, Mary Baker Eddy, Henry VIII, John Glenn, Ernest Hemingway, Lena Horne, Oscar Hammerstein, Helen Keller, Ann Landers, George Orwell, Nancy Reagan, Rembrandt, Richard Rodgers, Ginger Rogers, Rubens, Jean-Paul Sartre, O. J. Simpson

LEO: Neil Armstrong, James Baldwin, Lucille Ball, Emily Brontë, Wilt Chamberlain, Julia Child, William J. Clinton, Cecil B. De Mille, Ogden Nash, Amelia Earhart, Edna Ferber, Arthur Goldberg, Alfred Hitchcock, Mick Jagger, George Meany, Annie Oakley, George Bernard Shaw, Napoleon, Jacqueline Onassis, Henry Ford, Francis Scott Key, Andy Warhol, Mae West, Orville Wright

VIRGO: Ingrid Bergman, Warren Burger, Maurice Chevalier, Agatha Christie, Sean Connery, Lafayette, Peter Falk, Greta Garbo, Althea Gibson, Arthur Godfrey, Goethe, Buddy Hackett, Michael Jackson, Lyndon Johnson, D. H. Lawrence, Sophia Loren, Grandma Moses, Arnold Palmer, Queen Elizabeth I, Walter Reuther, Peter Sellers, Lily Tomlin, George Wallace

LIBRA: Brigitte Bardot, Art Buchwald, Truman Capote, Dwight D. Eisenhower, William Faulkner, F. Scott Fitzgerald, Gandhi, George Gershwin, Micky Mantle, Helen Hayes, Vladimir Horowitz, Doris Lessing, Martina Navratalova, Eugene O'Neill, Luciano Pavarotti, Emily Post, Eleanor Roosevelt, Bruce Springsteen, Margaret Thatcher, Gore Vidal, Barbara Walters, Oscar Wilde

SCORPIO: Vivien Leigh, Richard Burton, Art Carney, Johnny Carson, Billy Graham, Grace Kelly, Walter Cronkite, Marie Curie, Charles de Gaulle, Linda Evans, Indira Gandhi, Theodore Roosevelt, Rock Hudson, Katherine Hepburn, Robert F. Kennedy, Billie Jean King, Martin Luther, Georgia O'Keeffe, Pablo Picasso, Jonas Salk, Alan Shepard, Robert Louis Stevenson

SAGITTARIUS: Jane Austen, Louisa May Alcott, Woody Allen, Beethoven, Willy Brandt, Mary Martin, William F. Buckley, Maria Callas, Winston Churchill, Noel Coward, Emily Dickinson, Walt Disney, Benjamin Disraeli, James Doolittle, Kirk Douglas, Chet Huntley, Jane Fonda, Chris Evert Lloyd, Margaret Mead, Charles Schulz, John Milton, Frank Sinatra, Steven Spielberg

CAPRICORN: Muhammad Ali, Isaac Asimov, Pablo Casals, Dizzy Dean, Marlene Dietrich, James Farmer, Ava Gardner, Barry Goldwater, Cary Grant, J. Edgar Hoover, Howard Hughes, Joan of Arc, Gypsy Rose Lee, Martin Luther King, Jr., Rudyard Kipling, Mao Tse-tung, Richard Nixon, Gamal Nasser, Louis Pasteur, Albert Schweitzer, Stalin, Benjamin Franklin, Elvis Presley

AQUARIUS: Marian Anderson, Susan B. Anthony, Jack Benny, John Barrymore, Mikhail Baryshnikov, Charles Darwin, Charles Dickens, Thomas Edison, Clark Gable, Jascha Heifetz, Abraham Lincoln, Yehudi Menuhin, Mozart, Jack Nicklaus, Ronald Reagan, Jackie Robinson, Norman Rockwell, Franklin D. Roosevelt, Gertrude Stein, Charles Lindbergh, Margaret Truman

PISCES: Edward Albee, Harry Belafonte, Alexander Graham Bell, Chopin, Adelle Davis, Albert Einstein, Golda Meir, Jackie Gleason, Winslow Homer, Edward M. Kennedy, Victor Hugo, Mike Mansfield, Michelangelo, Edna St. Vincent Millay, Liza Minelli, John Steinbeck, Linus Pauling, Ravel, Renoir, Diana Ross, William Shirer, Elizabeth Taylor, George Washington

The Signs and Their Key Words

		POSITIVE	NEGATIVE
ARIES	self	courage, initiative, pioneer instinct	brash rudeness, selfish impetuosity
TAURUS	money	endurance, loyalty, wealth	obstinacy, gluttony
GEMINI	mind	versatility	capriciousness, unreliability
CANCER	family	sympathy, homing instinct	clannishness, childishness
LEO	children	love, authority, integrity	egotism, force
VIRGO	work	purity, industry, analysis	faultfinding, cynicism
LIBRA	marriage	harmony, justice	vacillation, superficiality
SCORPIO	sex	survival, regeneration	vengeance, discord
SAGITTARIUS	travel	optimism, higher learning	lawlessness
CAPRICORN	career	depth	narrowness, gloom
AQUARIUS	friends	human fellowship, genius	perverse unpredictability
PISCES	confinement	spiritual love, universality	diffusion, escapism

The Elements and Qualities of The Signs

Every sign has both an *element* and a *quality* associated with it. The element indicates the basic makeup of the sign, and the quality describes the kind of activity associated with each.

Element	Sign	Quality	Sign
FIRE	ARIES LEO SAGITTARIUS	CARDINAL	ARIES LIBRA CANCER CAPRICORN
EARTH	TAURUS VIRGO CAPRICORN	FIXED	TAURUS LEO SCORPIO AQUARIUS
AIR	GEMINI LIBRA AQUARIUS	MUTABLE	GEMINI VIRGO SAGITTARIUS PISCES
WATER	CANCER SCORPIO PISCES		

Signs can be grouped together according to their element and quality. Signs of the same element share many basic traits in common. They tend to form stable configurations and ultimately harmonious relationships. Signs of the same quality are often less harmonious, but they share many dynamic potentials for growth as well as profound fulfillment.

Further discussion of each of these sign groupings is provided on the following pages.

The Fire Signs

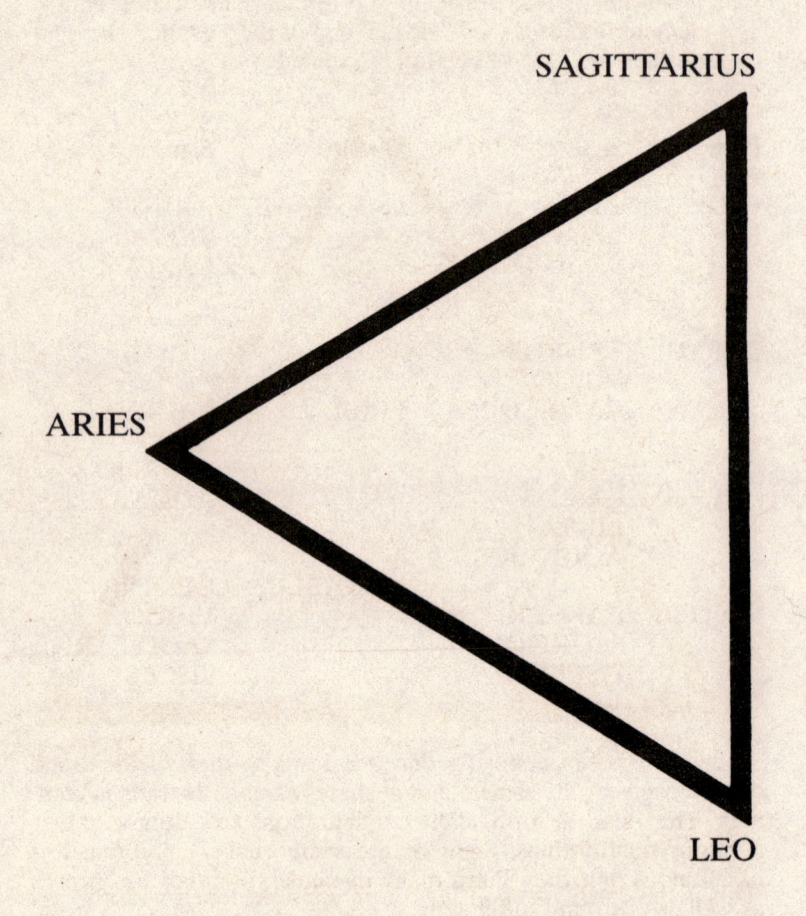

```
        SAGITTARIUS


ARIES


        LEO
```

This is the fire group. On the whole these are emotional, volatile types, quick to anger, quick to forgive. They are adventurous, powerful people and act as a source of inspiration for everyone. They spark into action with immediate exuberant impulses. They are intelligent, self-involved, creative, and idealistic. They all share a certain vibrancy and glow that outwardly reflects an inner flame and passion for living.

The Earth Signs

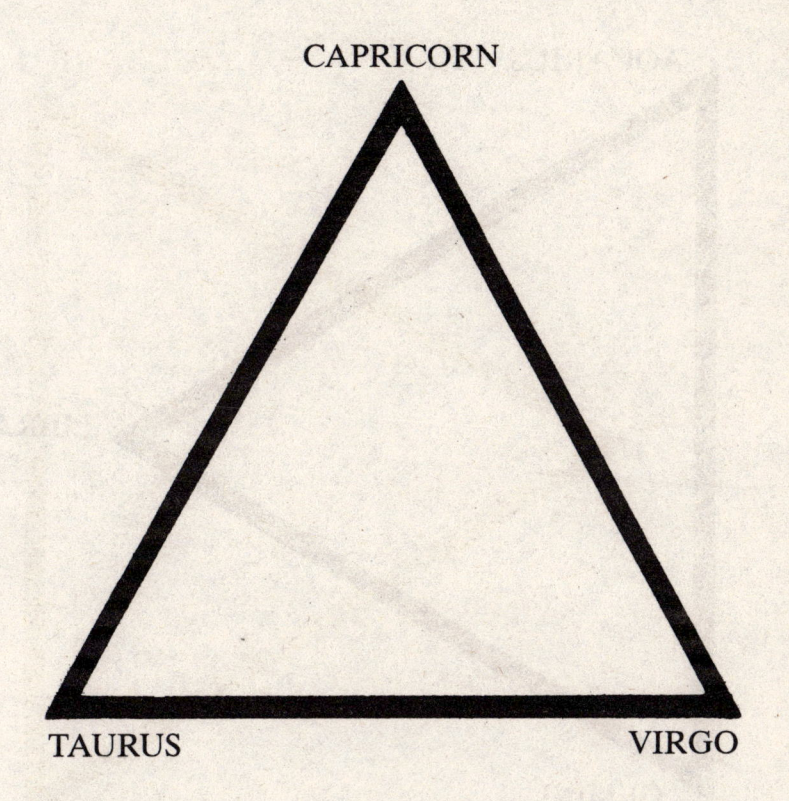

```
        CAPRICORN


TAURUS              VIRGO
```

This is the earth group. They are in constant touch with the material world and tend to be conservative. Although they are all capable of spartan self-discipline, they are earthy, sensual people who are stimulated by the tangible, elegant, and luxurious. The thread of their lives is always practical, but they do fantasize and are often attracted to dark, mysterious, emotional people. They are like great cliffs overhanging the sea, forever married to the ocean but always resisting erosion from the dark, emotional forces that thunder at their feet.

The Air Signs

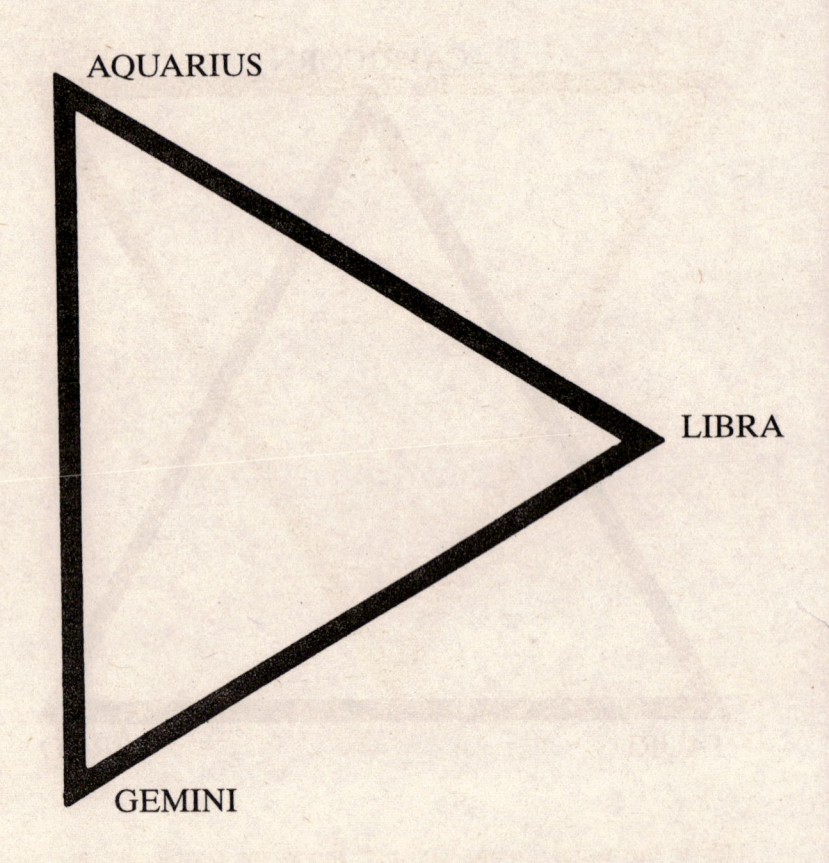

```
        AQUARIUS


                          LIBRA


        GEMINI
```

This is the air group. They are light, mental creatures desirous of contact, communication, and relationship. They are involved with people and the forming of ties on many levels. Original thinkers, they are the bearers of human news. Their language is their sense of word, color, style, and beauty. They provide an atmosphere suitable and pleasant for living. They add change and versatility to the scene, and it is through them that we can explore new territory of human intelligence and experience.

The Water Signs

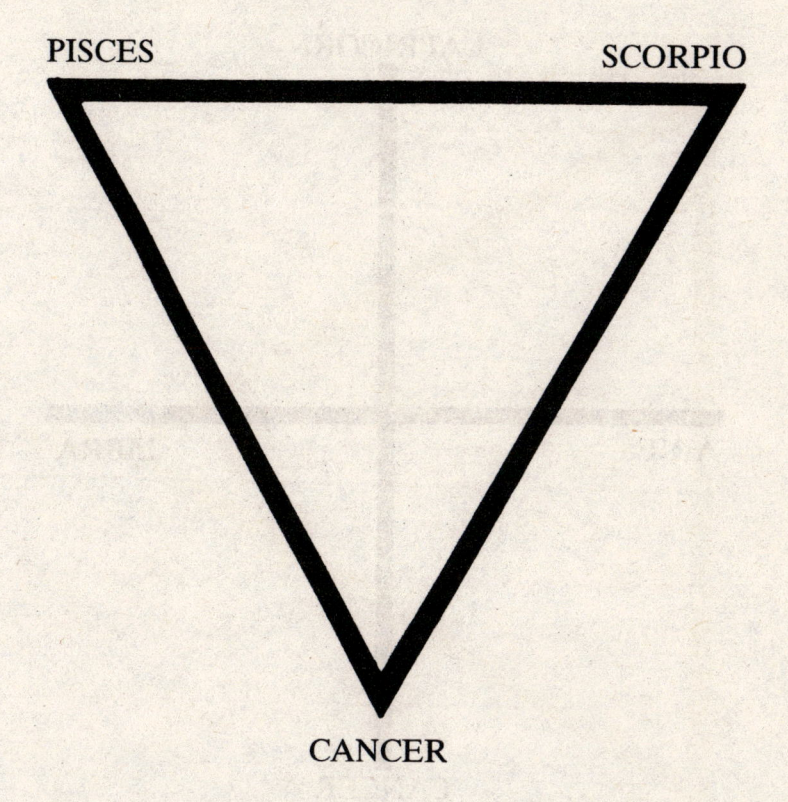

```
PISCES                    SCORPIO




              CANCER
```

This is the water group. Through the water people, we are all joined together on emotional, nonverbal levels. They are silent, mysterious types whose magic hypnotizes even the most determined realist. They have uncanny perceptions about people and are as rich as the oceans when it comes to feeling, emotion, or imagination. They are sensitive, mystical creatures with memories that go back beyond time. Through water, life is sustained. These people have the potential for the depths of darkness or the heights of mysticism and art.

The Cardinal Signs

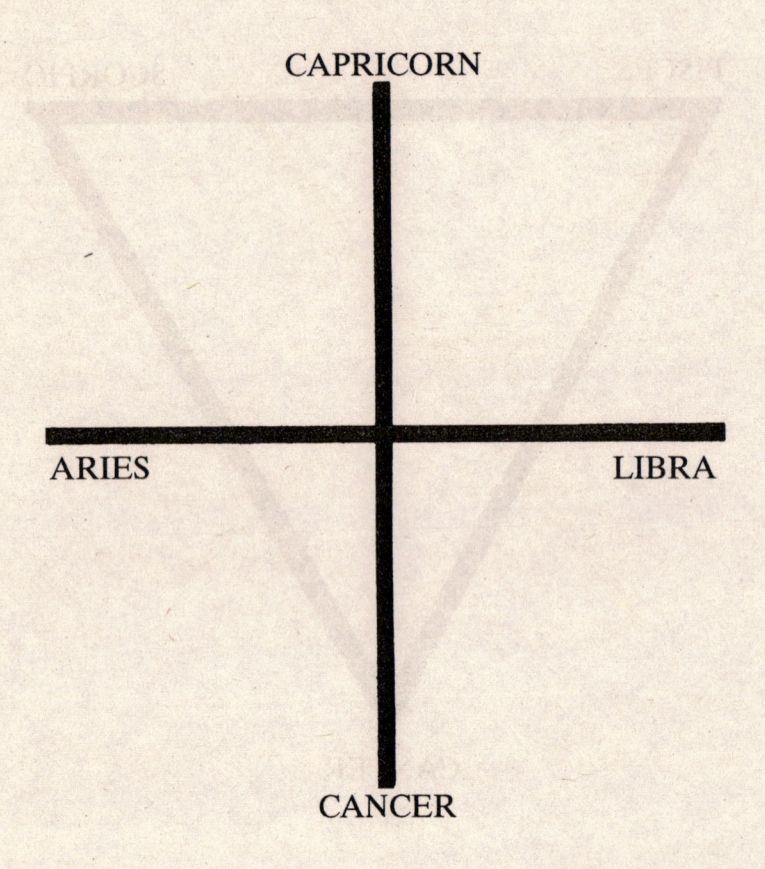

```
                CAPRICORN
                    |
                    |
                    |
    ARIES ——————————+—————————— LIBRA
                    |
                    |
                    |
                 CANCER
```

Put together, this is a clear-cut picture of dynamism, activity, tremendous stress, and remarkable achievement. These people know the meaning of great change since their lives are often characterized by significant crises and major successes. This combination is like a simultaneous storm of summer, fall, winter, and spring. The danger is chaotic diffusion of energy; the potential is irrepressible growth and victory.

The Fixed Signs

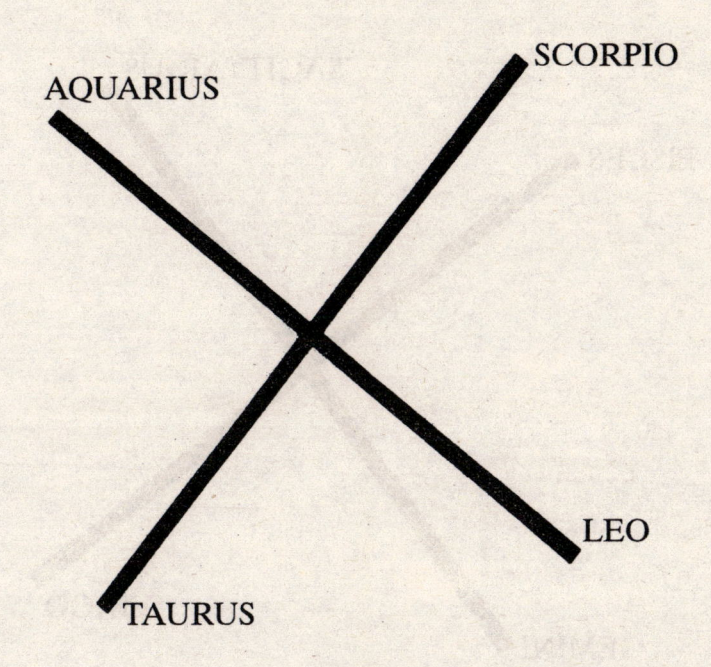

SCORPIO
AQUARIUS
LEO
TAURUS

Fixed signs are always establishing themselves in a given place or area of experience. Like explorers who arrive and plant a flag, these people claim a position from which they do not enjoy being deposed. They are staunch, stalwart, upright, trusty, honorable people, although their obstinacy is well-known. Their contribution is fixity, and they are the angels who support our visible world.

The Mutable Signs

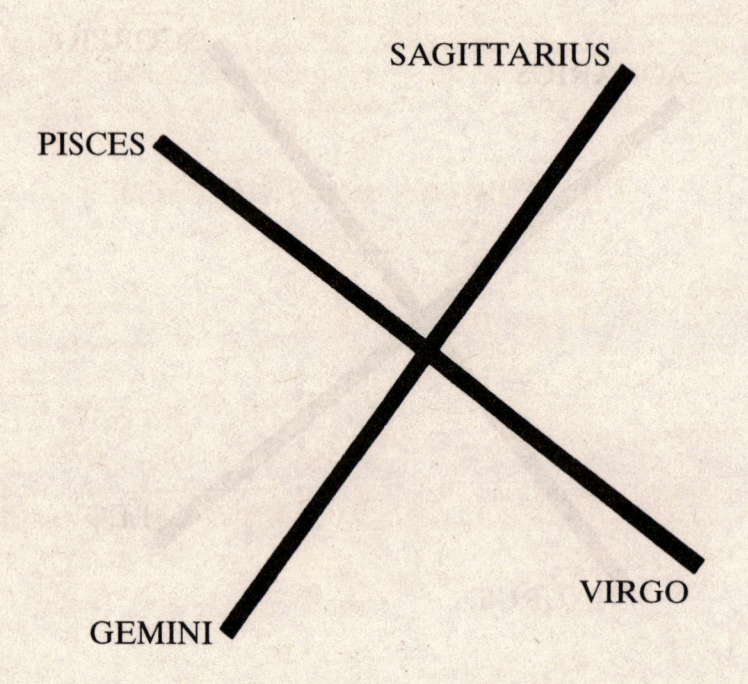

```
              SAGITTARIUS
PISCES

           X

                    VIRGO
   GEMINI
```

Mutable people are versatile, sensitive, intelligent, nervous, and deeply curious about life. They are the translators of all energy. They often carry out or complete tasks initiated by others. Combinations of these signs have highly developed minds; they are imaginative and jumpy and think and talk a lot. At worst their lives are a Tower of Babel. At best they are adaptable and ready creatures who can assimilate one kind of experience and enjoy it while anticipating coming changes.

THE PLANETS OF THE SOLAR SYSTEM

This section describes the planets of the solar system. In astrology, both the Sun and the Moon are considered to be planets. Because of the Moon's influence in our day-to-day lives, the Moon is described in a separate section following this one.

The Planets and the Signs They Rule

The signs of the Zodiac are linked to the planets in the following way. Each sign is governed or ruled by one or more planets. No matter where the planets are located in the sky at any given moment, they still rule their respective signs, and when they travel through the signs they rule, they have special dignity and their effects are stronger.

Following is a list of the planets and the signs they rule. After looking at the list, read the definitions of the planets and see if you can determine how the planet ruling *your* Sun sign has affected your life.

SIGNS	RULING PLANETS
Aries	Mars, Pluto
Taurus	Venus
Gemini	Mercury
Cancer	Moon
Leo	Sun
Virgo	Mercury
Libra	Venus
Scorpio	Mars, Pluto
Sagittarius	Jupiter
Capricorn	Saturn
Aquarius	Saturn, Uranus
Pisces	Jupiter, Neptune

Characteristics of the Planets

The following pages give the meaning and characteristics of the planets of the solar system. They all travel around the Sun at different speeds and different distances. Taken with the Sun, they all distribute individual intelligence and ability throughout the entire chart.

The planets modify the influence of the Sun in a chart according to their own particular natures, strengths, and positions. Their positions must be calculated for each year and day, and their function and expression in a horoscope will change as they move from one area of the Zodiac to another.

We start with a description of the sun.

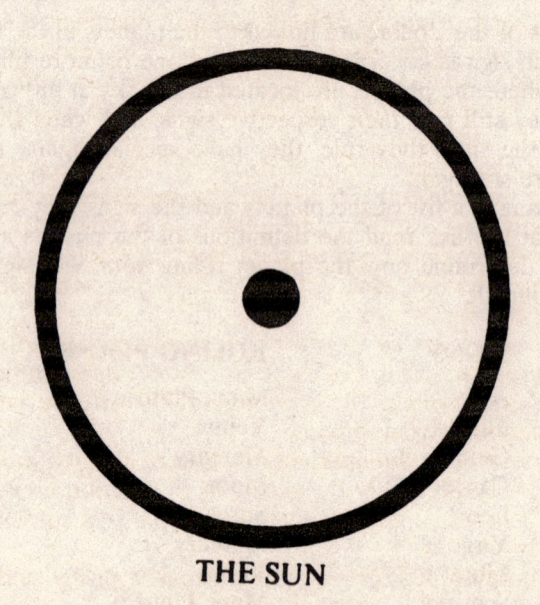

THE SUN

SUN

This is the center of existence. Around this flaming sphere all the planets revolve in endless orbits. Our star is constantly sending out its beams of light and energy without which no life on Earth would be possible. In astrology it symbolizes everything we are trying to become, the center around which all of our activity in life will always revolve. It is the symbol of our basic nature and describes the natural and constant thread that runs through everything that we do from birth to death on this planet.

To early astrologers, the Sun seemed to be another planet because it crossed the heavens every day, just like the rest of the bodies in the sky.

It is the only star near enough to be seen well—it is, in fact, a dwarf star. Approximately 860,000 miles in diameter, it is about ten times as wide as the giant planet Jupiter. The next nearest star is nearly 300,000 times as far away, and if the Sun were located as far away as most of the bright stars, it would be too faint to be seen without a telescope.

Everything in the horoscope ultimately revolves around this singular body. Although other forces may be prominent in the charts of some individuals, still the Sun is the total nucleus of being and symbolizes the complete potential of every human being alive. It is vitality and the life force. Your whole essence comes from the position of the Sun.

You are always trying to express the Sun according to its position by house and sign. Possibility for all development is found in the Sun, and it marks the fundamental character of your personal radiations all around you.

It is the symbol of strength, vigor, wisdom, dignity, ardor, and generosity, and the ability for a person to function as a mature individual. It is also a creative force in society. It is consciousness of the gift of life.

The underdeveloped solar nature is arrogant, pushy, undependable, and proud, and is constantly using force.

MERCURY

Mercury is the planet closest to the Sun. It races around our star, gathering information and translating it to the rest of the system. Mercury represents your capacity to understand the desires of your own will and to translate those desires into action.

In other words it is the planet of mind and the power of communication. Through Mercury we develop an ability to think, write, speak, and observe—to become aware of the world around us. It colors our attitudes and vision of the world, as well as our capacity to communicate our inner responses to the outside world. Some people who have serious disabilities in their power of verbal communication have often wrongly been described as people lacking intelligence.

Although this planet (and its position in the horoscope) indicates your power to communicate your thoughts and perceptions to the world, intelligence is something deeper. Intelligence is distributed throughout all the planets. It is the relationship of the planets to each other that truly describes what we call intelligence. Mercury rules speaking, language, mathematics, draft and design, students, messengers, young people, offices, teachers, and any pursuits where the mind of man has wings.

VENUS

Venus is beauty. It symbolizes the harmony and radiance of a rare and elusive quality: beauty itself. It is refinement and delicacy, softness and charm. In astrology it indicates grace, balance, and the aesthetic sense. Where Venus is we see beauty, a gentle drawing in of energy and the need for satisfaction and completion. It is a special touch that finishes off rough edges. It is sensitivity, and affection, and it is always the place for that other elusive phenomenon: love. Venus describes our sense of what is beautiful and loving. Poorly developed, it is vulgar, tasteless, and self-indulgent. But its ideal is the flame of spiritual love—Aphrodite, goddess of love, and the sweetness and power of personal beauty.

MARS

Mars is raw, crude energy. The planet next to Earth but outward from the Sun is a fiery red sphere that charges through the horoscope with force and fury. It represents the way you reach out for new adventure and new experience. It is energy and drive, initiative, courage, and daring. It is the power to start something and see it through. It can be thoughtless, cruel and wild, angry and hostile, causing cuts, burns, scalds, and wounds. It can stab its way through a chart, or it can be the symbol of healthy spirited adventure, well-channeled constructive power to begin and keep up the drive. If you have trouble starting things, if you lack the get-up-and-go to start the ball rolling, if you lack aggressiveness and self-confidence, chances are there's another planet influencing your Mars. Mars rules soldiers, butchers, surgeons, salesmen—any field that requires daring, bold skill, operational technique, or self-promotion.

JUPITER

This is the largest planet of the solar system. Scientists have recently learned that Jupiter reflects more light than it receives from the Sun. In a sense it is like a star itself. In astrology it rules good luck and good cheer, health, wealth, optimism, happiness, success, and joy. It is the symbol of opportunity and always opens the way for new possibilities in your life. It rules exuberance, enthusiasm, wisdom, knowledge, generosity, and all forms of expansion in general. It rules actors, statesmen, clerics, professional people, religion, publishing, and the distribution of many people over large areas.

Sometimes Jupiter makes you think you deserve everything, and you become sloppy, wasteful, careless and rude, prodigal and lawless, in the illusion that nothing can ever go wrong. Then there is the danger of overconfidence, exaggeration, undependability, and overindulgence.

Jupiter is the minimization of limitation and the emphasis on spirituality and potential. It is the thirst for knowledge and higher learning.

SATURN

Saturn circles our system in dark splendor with its mysterious rings, forcing us to be awakened to whatever we have neglected in the past. It will present real puzzles and problems to be solved, causing delays, obstacles, and hindrances. By doing so, Saturn stirs our own sensitivity to those areas where we are laziest.

Here we must patiently develop *method*, and only through painstaking effort can our ends be achieved. It brings order to a horoscope and imposes reason just where we are feeling least reasonable. By creating limitations and boundary, Saturn shows the consequences of being human and demands that we accept the changing cycles inevitable in human life. Saturn rules time, old age, and sobriety. It can bring depression, gloom, jealousy, and greed, or serious acceptance of responsibilities out of which success will develop. With Saturn there is nothing to do but face facts. It rules laborers, stones, granite, rocks, and crystals of all kinds.

THE OUTER PLANETS: URANUS, NEPTUNE, PLUTO

Uranus, Neptune, Pluto are the outer planets. They liberate human beings from cultural conditioning, and in that sense are the lawbreakers. In early times it was thought that Saturn was the last planet of the system—the outer limit beyond which we could never go. The discovery of the next three planets ushered in new phases of human history, revolution, and technology.

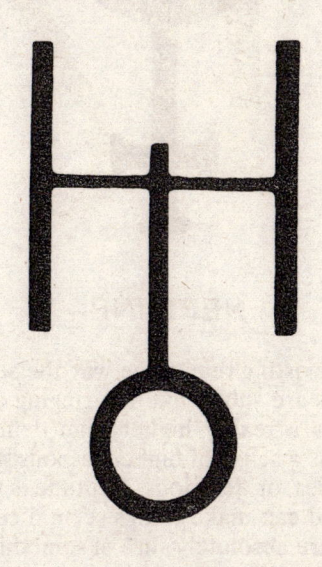

URANUS

Uranus rules unexpected change, upheaval, revolution. It is the symbol of total independence and asserts the freedom of an individual from all restriction and restraint. It is a breakthrough planet and indicates talent, originality, and genius in a horoscope. It usually causes last-minute reversals and changes of plan, unwanted separations, accidents, catastrophes, and eccentric behavior. It can add irrational rebelliousness and perverse bohemianism to a personality or a streak of unaffected brilliance in science and art. It rules technology, aviation, and all forms of electrical and electronic advancement. It governs great leaps forward and topsy-turvy situations, and *always* turns things around at the last minute. Its effects are difficult to predict, since it rules sudden last-minute decisions and events that come like lightning out of the blue.

NEPTUNE

Neptune dissolves existing reality the way the sea erodes the cliffs beside it. Its effects are subtle like the ringing of a buoy's bell in the fog. It suggests a reality higher than definition can usually describe. It awakens a sense of higher responsibility often causing guilt, worry, anxieties, or delusions. Neptune is associated with all forms of escape and can make things seem a certain way so convincingly that you are absolutely sure of something that eventually turns out to be quite different.

It is the planet of illusion and therefore governs the invisible realms that lie beyond our ordinary minds, beyond our simple factual ability to prove what is "real." Treachery, deceit, disillusionment, and disappointment are linked to Neptune. It describes a vague reality that promises eternity and the divine, yet in a manner so complex that we cannot really fathom it at all. At its worst Neptune is a cheap intoxicant; at its best it is the poetry, music, and inspiration of the higher planes of spiritual love. It has dominion over movies, photographs, and much of the arts.

PLUTO

Pluto lies at the outpost of our system and therefore rules finality in a horoscope—the final closing of chapters in your life, the passing of major milestones and points of development from which there is no return. It is a final wipeout, a closeout, an evacuation. It is a distant, subtle but powerful catalyst in all transformations that occur. It creates, destroys, then recreates. Sometimes Pluto starts its influence with a minor event or insignificant incident that might even go unnoticed. Slowly but surely, little by little, everything changes, until at last there has been a total transformation in the area of your life where Pluto has been operating. It rules mass thinking and the trends that society first rejects, then adopts, and finally outgrows.

Pluto rules the dead and the underworld—all the powerful forces of creation and destruction that go on all the time beneath, around, and above us. It can bring a lust for power with strong obsessions.

It is the planet that rules the metamorphosis of the caterpillar into a butterfly, for it symbolizes the capacity to change totally and forever a person's lifestyle, way of thought, and behavior.

THE MOON IN EACH SIGN

The Moon is the nearest planet to the Earth. It exerts more observable influence on us from day to day than any other planet. The effect is very personal, very intimate, and if we are not aware of how it works it can make us quite unstable in our ideas. And the annoying thing is that at these times we often see our own instability but can do nothing about it. A knowledge of what can be expected may help considerably. We can then be prepared to stand strong against the Moon's negative influences and use its positive ones to help us to get ahead. Who has not heard of going with the tide?

The Moon reflects, has no light of its own. It reflects the Sun— the life giver—in the form of vital movement. The Moon controls the tides, the blood rhythm, the movement of sap in trees and plants. Its nature is inconstancy and change so it signifies our moods, our superficial behavior—walking, talking, and especially thinking. Being a true reflector of other forces, the Moon is cold, watery like the surface of a still lake, brilliant and scintillating at times, but easily ruffled and disturbed by the winds of change.

The Moon takes about 27⅓ days to make a complete transit of the Zodiac. It spends just over 2¼ days in each sign. During that time it reflects the qualities, energies, and characteristics of the sign and, to a degree, the planet which rules the sign. When the Moon in its transit occupies a sign incompatible with our own birth sign, we can expect to feel a vague uneasiness, perhaps a touch of irritableness. We should not be discouraged nor let the feeling get us down, or, worse still, allow ourselves to take the discomfort out on others. Try to remember that the Moon has to change signs within 55 hours and, provided you are not physically ill, your mood will probably change with it. It is amazing how frequently depression lifts with the shift in the Moon's position. And, of course, when the Moon is transiting a sign compatible or sympathetic to yours, you will probably feel some sort of stimulation or just be plain happy to be alive.

In the horoscope, the Moon is such a powerful indicator that competent astrologers often use the sign it occupied at birth as the birth sign of the person. This is done particularly when the Sun is on the cusp, or edge, of two signs. Most experienced astrologers, however, coordinate both Sun and Moon signs by reading and confirming from one to the other and secure a far more accurate and personalized analysis.

For these reasons, the Moon tables which follow this section (see pages 86–92) are of great importance to the individual. They show the days and the exact times the Moon will enter each sign of the Zodiac for the year. Remember, you have to adjust the indicated times to local time. The corrections, already calculated for most of the main cities, are at the beginning of the tables. What follows now is a guide to the influences that will be reflected to the Earth by the Moon while it transits each of the twelve signs. The influence is at its peak about 26 hours after the Moon enters a sign. As you read the daily forecast, check the Moon sign for any given day and glance back at this guide.

MOON IN ARIES
This is a time for action, for reaching out beyond the usual self-imposed limitations and faint-hearted cautions. If you have plans in your head or on your desk, put them into practice. New ventures, applications, new jobs, new starts of any kind—all have a good chance of success. This is the period when original and dynamic impulses are being reflected onto Earth. Such energies are extremely vital and favor the pursuit of pleasure and adventure in practically every form. Sick people should feel an improvement. Those who are well will probably find themselves exuding confidence and optimism. People fond of physical exercise should find their bodies growing with tone and well-being. Boldness, strength, determination should characterize most of your activities with a readiness to face up to old challenges. Yesterday's problems may seem petty and exaggerated—so deal with them. Strike out alone. Self-reliance will attract others to you. This is a good time for making friends. Business and marriage partners are more likely to be impressed with the man and woman of action. Opposition will be overcome or thrown aside with much less effort than usual. CAUTION: Be dominant but not domineering.

MOON IN TAURUS
The spontaneous, action-packed person of yesterday gives way to the cautious, diligent, hardworking "thinker." In this period ideas will probably be concentrated on ways of improving finances. A great deal of time may be spent figuring out and going over schemes and plans. It is the right time to be careful with detail.

People will find themselves working longer than usual at their desks. Or devoting more time to serious thought about the future. A strong desire to put order into business and financial arrangements may cause extra work. Loved ones may complain of being neglected and may fail to appreciate that your efforts are for their ultimate benefit. Your desire for system may extend to criticism of arrangements in the home and lead to minor upsets. Health may be affected through overwork. Try to secure a reasonable amount of rest and relaxation, although the tendency will be to "keep going" despite good advice. Work done conscientiously in this period should result in a solid contribution to your future security. CAUTION: Try not to be as serious with people as the work you are engaged in.

MOON IN GEMINI

The humdrum of routine and too much work should suddenly end. You are likely to find yourself in an expansive, quicksilver world of change and self-expression. Urges to write, to paint, to experience the freedom of some sort of artistic outpouring, may be very strong. Take full advantage of them. You may find yourself finishing something you began and put aside long ago. Or embarking on something new which could easily be prompted by a chance meeting, a new acquaintance, or even an advertisement. There may be a yearning for a change of scenery, the feeling to visit another country (not too far away), or at least to get away for a few days. This may result in short, quick journeys. Or, if you are planning a single visit, there may be some unexpected changes or detours on the way. Familiar activities will seem to give little satisfaction unless they contain a fresh element of excitement or expectation. The inclination will be toward untried pursuits, particularly those that allow you to express your inner nature. The accent is on new faces, new places. CAUTION: Do not be too quick to commit yourself emotionally.

MOON IN CANCER

Feelings of uncertainty and vague insecurity are likely to cause problems while the Moon is in Cancer. Thoughts may turn frequently to the warmth of the home and the comfort of loved ones. Nostalgic impulses could cause you to bring out old photographs and letters and reflect on the days when your life seemed to be much more rewarding and less demanding. The love and understanding of parents and family may be important, and, if it is not forthcoming, you may have to fight against bouts of self-pity. The cordiality of friends and the thought of good times with them that are sure to be repeated will help to restore you to a happier frame of mind. The desire to be alone may follow minor setbacks or rebuffs at this time, but solitude is unlikely to help. Better to get on the telephone or visit someone. This period often causes peculiar dreams and upsurges of imaginative thinking which can be helpful to authors of occult and mystical works. Preoccupation with the personal world of simple human needs can overshadow any material strivings. CAUTION: Do not spend too much time thinking—seek the company of loved ones or close friends.

MOON IN LEO
New horizons of exciting and rather extravagant activity open up. This is the time for exhilarating entertainment, glamorous and lavish parties, and expensive shopping sprees. Any merrymaking that relies upon your generosity as a host has every chance of being a spectacular success. You should find yourself right in the center of the fun, either as the life of the party or simply as a person whom happy people like to be with. Romance thrives in this heady atmosphere and friendships are likely to explode unexpectedly into serious attachments. Children and younger people should be attracted to you and you may find yourself organizing a picnic or a visit to a fun-fair, the movies, or the beach. The sunny company and vitality of youthful companions should help you to find some unsuspected energy. In career, you could find an opening for promotion or advancement. This should be the time to make a direct approach. The period favors those engaged in original research. CAUTION: Bask in popularity, not in flattery.

MOON IN VIRGO
Off comes the party cap and out steps the busy, practical worker. He wants to get his personal affairs straight, to rearrange them, if necessary, for more efficiency, so he will have more time for more work. He clears up his correspondence, pays outstanding bills, makes numerous phone calls. He is likely to make inquiries, or sign up for some new insurance and put money into gilt-edged investment. Thoughts probably revolve around the need for future security—to tie up loose ends and clear the decks. There may be a tendency to be "finicky," to interfere in the routine of others, particularly friends and family members. The motive may be a genuine desire to help with suggestions for updating or streamlining their affairs, but these will probably not be welcomed. Sympathy may be felt for less fortunate sections of the community and a flurry of some sort of voluntary service is likely. This may be accompanied by strong feelings of responsibility on several fronts and health may suffer from extra efforts made. CAUTION: Everyone may not want your help or advice.

MOON IN LIBRA

These are days of harmony and agreement and you should find yourself at peace with most others. Relationships tend to be smooth and sweet-flowing. Friends may become closer and bonds deepen in mutual understanding. Hopes will be shared. Progress by cooperation could be the secret of success in every sphere. In business, established partnerships may flourish and new ones get off to a good start. Acquaintances could discover similar interests that lead to congenial discussions and rewarding exchanges of some sort. Love, as a unifying force, reaches its optimum. Marriage partners should find accord. Those who wed at this time face the prospect of a happy union. Cooperation and tolerance are felt to be stronger than dissension and impatience. The argumentative are not quite so loud in their bellowings, nor as inflexible in their attitudes. In the home, there should be a greater recognition of the other point of view and a readiness to put the wishes of the group before selfish insistence. This is a favorable time to join an art group. CAUTION: Do not be too independent—let others help you if they want to.

MOON IN SCORPIO

Driving impulses to make money and to economize are likely to cause upsets all around. No area of expenditure is likely to be spared the ax, including the household budget. This is a time when the desire to cut down on extravagance can become near fanatical. Care must be exercised to try to keep the aim in reasonable perspective. Others may not feel the same urgent need to save and may retaliate. There is a danger that possessions of sentimental value will be sold to realize cash for investment. Buying and selling of stock for quick profit is also likely. The attention turns to organizing, reorganizing, tidying up at home and at work. Neglected jobs could suddenly be done with great bursts of energy. The desire for solitude may intervene. Self-searching thoughts could disturb. The sense of invisible and mysterious energies in play could cause some excitability. The reassurance of loves ones may help. CAUTION: Be kind to the people you love.

MOON IN SAGITTARIUS

These are days when you are likely to be stirred and elevated by discussions and reflections of a religious and philosophical nature. Ideas of faraway places may cause unusual response and excitement. A decision may be made to visit someone overseas, perhaps a person whose influence was important to your earlier character development. There could be a strong resolution to get away from present intellectual patterns, to learn new subjects, and to meet more interesting people. The superficial may be rejected in all its forms. An impatience with old ideas and unimaginative contacts could lead to a change of companions and interests. There may be an upsurge of religious feeling and metaphysical inquiry. Even a new insight into the significance of astrology and other occult studies is likely under the curious stimulus of the Moon in Sagittarius. Physically, you may express this need for fundamental change by spending more time outdoors: sports, gardening, long walks appeal. CAUTION: Try to channel any restlessness into worthwhile study.

MOON IN CAPRICORN

Life in these hours may seem to pivot around the importance of gaining prestige and honor in the career, as well as maintaining a spotless reputation. Ambitious urges may be excessive and could be accompanied by quite acquisitive drives for money. Effort should be directed along strictly ethical lines where there is no possibility of reproach or scandal. All endeavors are likely to be characterized by great earnestness, and an air of authority and purpose which should impress those who are looking for leadership or reliability. The desire to conform to accepted standards may extend to sharp criticism of family members. Frivolity and unconventional actions are unlikely to amuse while the Moon is in Capricorn. Moderation and seriousness are the orders of the day. Achievement and recognition in this period could come through community work or organizing for the benefit of some amateur group. CAUTION: Dignity and esteem are not always self-awarded.

MOON IN AQUARIUS

Moon in Aquarius is in the second last sign of the Zodiac where ideas can become disturbingly fine and subtle. The result is often a mental "no-man's land" where imagination cannot be trusted with the same certitude as other times. The dangers for the individual are the extremes of optimism and pessimism. Unless the imagination is held in check, situations are likely to be misread, and rosy conclusions drawn where they do not exist. Consequences for the unwary can be costly in career and business. Best to think twice and not speak or act until you think again. Pessimism can be a cruel self-inflicted penalty for delusion at this time. Between the two extremes are strange areas of self-deception which, for example, can make the selfish person think he is actually being generous. Eerie dreams which resemble the reality and even seem to continue into the waking state are also possible. CAUTION: Look for the fact and not just for the image in your mind.

MOON IN PISCES

Everything seems to come to the surface now. Memory may be crystal clear, throwing up long-forgotten information which could be valuable in the career or business. Flashes of clairvoyance and intuition are possible along with sudden realizations of one's own nature, which may be used for self-improvement. A talent, never before suspected, may be discovered. Qualities not evident before in friends and marriage partners are likely to be noticed. As this is a period in which the truth seems to emerge, the discovery of false characteristics is likely to lead to disenchantment or a shift in attachments. However, when qualities are accepted, it should lead to happiness and deeper feeling. Surprise solutions could bob up for old problems. There may be a public announcement of the solving of a crime or mystery. People with secrets may find someone has "guessed" correctly. The secrets of the soul or the inner self also tend to reveal themselves. Religious and philosophical groups may make some interesting discoveries. CAUTION: Not a time for activities that depend on secrecy.

NOTE: When you read your daily forecasts, use the Moon Sign Dates that are provided in the following section of Moon Tables. Then you may want to glance back here for the Moon's influence in a given sign.

MOON TABLES

CORRECTION FOR NEW YORK TIME, FIVE HOURS WEST OF GREENWICH

Atlanta, Boston, Detroit, Miami, Washington, Montreal, Ottawa, Quebec, Bogota, Havana, Lima, Santiago .. Same time
Chicago, New Orleans, Houston, Winnipeg, Churchill, Mexico City .... Deduct 1 hour
Albuquerque, Denver, Phoenix, El Paso, Edmonton, Helena .... Deduct 2 hours
Los Angeles, San Francisco, Reno, Portland, Seattle, Vancouver .... Deduct 3 hours
Honolulu, Anchorage, Fairbanks, Kodiak .... Deduct 5 hours
Nome, Samoa, Tonga, Midway .... Deduct 6 hours
Halifax, Bermuda, San Juan, Caracas, La Paz, Barbados .... Add 1 hour
St. John's, Brasilia, Rio de Janeiro, Sao Paulo, Buenos Aires, Montevideo .... Add 2 hours
Azores, Cape Verde Islands .... Add 3 hours
Canary Islands, Madeira, Reykjavik .... Add 4 hours
London, Paris, Amsterdam, Madrid, Lisbon, Gibraltar, Belfast, Rabat .... Add 5 hours
Frankfurt, Rome, Oslo, Stockholm, Prague, Belgrade .... Add 6 hours
Bucharest, Beirut, Tel Aviv, Athens, Istanbul, Cairo, Alexandria, Cape Town, Johannesburg .... Add 7 hours
Moscow, Leningrad, Baghdad, Dhahran, Addis Ababa, Nairobi, Teheran, Zanzibar .... Add 8 hours
Bombay, Calcutta, Sri Lanka .... Add 10 ½ hours
Hong Kong, Shanghai, Manila, Peking, Perth ...... Add 13 hours
Tokyo, Okinawa, Darwin, Pusan .... Add 14 hours
Sydney, Melbourne, Port Moresby, Guam .... Add 15 hours
Auckland, Wellington, Suva, Wake .... Add 17 hours

2001 MOON SIGN DATES— NEW YORK TIME

JANUARY		FEBRUARY		MARCH	
Day Moon Enters		Day Moon Enters		Day Moon Enters	
1. Aries	5:15 pm	1. Taurus		1. Gemini	10:37 pm
2. Aries		2. Gemini	3:57 pm	2. Gemini	
3. Aries		3. Gemini		3. Gemini	
4. Taurus	1:58 am	4. Cancer	7:01 pm	4. Cancer	3:25 am
5. Taurus		5. Cancer		5. Cancer	
6. Gemini	6:45 am	6. Leo	7:22 pm	6. Leo	5:31 am
7. Gemini		7. Leo		7. Leo	
8. Cancer	8:10 am	8. Virgo	6:36 pm	8. Virgo	5:45 am
9. Cancer		9. Virgo		9. Virgo	
10. Leo	7:45 am	10. Libra	6:47 pm	10. Libra	5:48 am
11. Leo		11. Libra		11. Libra	
12. Virgo	7:27 am	12. Scorp.	9:52 pm	12. Scorp.	7:44 am
13. Virgo		13. Scorp.		13. Scorp.	
14. Libra	9:06 am	14. Scorp.		14. Sagitt.	1:18 pm
15. Libra		15. Sagitt.	5:03 am	15. Sagitt.	
16. Scorp.	2:03 pm	16. Sagitt.		16. Capric.	11:03 pm
17. Scorp.		17. Capric.	4:00 pm	17. Capric.	
18. Sagitt.	10:37 pm	18. Capric.		18. Capric.	
19. Sagitt.		19. Capric.		19. Aquar.	11:37 am
20. Sagitt.		20. Aquar.	4:55 am	20. Aquar.	
21. Capric.	9:58 am	21. Aquar.		21. Aquar.	
22. Capric.		22. Pisces	5:46 pm	22. Pisces	0:29 am
23. Aquar.	10:44 pm	23. Pisces		23. Pisces	
24. Aquar.		24. Pisces		24. Aries	11:45 am
25. Aquar.		25. Aries	5:21 am	25. Aries	
26. Pisces	11:40 am	26. Aries		26. Taurus	8:52 pm
27. Pisces		27. Taurus	3:07 pm	27. Taurus	
28. Aries	11:36 pm	28. Taurus		28. Taurus	
29. Aries				29. Gemini	4:02 am
30. Aries				30. Gemini	
31. Taurus	9:22 am			31. Cancer	9:24 am

Summer time to be considered where applicable.

2001 MOON SIGN DATES—
NEW YORK TIME

APRIL		MAY		JUNE	
Day Moon Enters		Day Moon Enters		Day Moon Enters	
1. Cancer		1. Virgo	9:17 pm	1. Libra	
2. Leo	12:55 pm	2. Virgo		2. Scorp.	9:57 am
3. Leo		3. Libra	11:51 am	3. Scorp.	
4. Virgo	2:48 pm	4. Libra		4. Sagitt.	3:59 pm
5. Virgo		5. Libra		5. Sagitt.	
6. Libra	3:58 pm	6. Scorp.	3:02 am	6. Sagitt.	
7. Libra		7. Scorp.		7. Capric.	0:24 am
8. Scorp.	6:02 pm	8. Sagitt.	8:06 am	8. Capric.	
9. Scorp.		9. Sagitt.		9. Aquar.	11:21 am
10. Sagitt.	10:48 pm	10. Capric.	4:11 pm	10. Aquar.	
11. Sagitt.		11. Capric.		11. Pisces	11:54 pm
12. Sagitt.		12. Capric.		12. Pisces	
13. Capric.	7:22 am	13. Aquar.	3:21 am	13. Pisces	
14. Capric.		14. Aquar.		14. Aries	12:04 pm
15. Aquar.	7:12 pm	15. Pisces	4:02 pm	15. Aries	
16. Aquar.		16. Pisces		16. Taurus	9:40 pm
17. Aquar.		17. Pisces		17. Taurus	
18. Pisces	8:08 am	18. Aries	3:42 am	18. Taurus	
19. Pisces		19. Aries		19. Gemini	3:43 am
20. Aries	8:19 pm	20. Taurus	12:30 pm	20. Gemini	
21. Aries		21. Taurus		21. Cancer	6:42 am
22. Aries		22. Gemini	6:13 pm	22. Cancer	
23. Taurus	3:57 am	23. Gemini		23. Leo	7:56 am
24. Taurus		24. Cancer	9:43 pm	24. Leo	
25. Gemini	10:12 am	25. Cancer		25. Virgo	8:59 am
26. Gemini		26. Cancer		26. Virgo	
27. Cancer	2:50 pm	27. Leo	0:13 am	27. Libra	11:12 am
28. Cancer		28. Leo		28. Libra	
29. Leo	6:26 pm	29. Virgo	2:39 am	29. Scorp.	3:30 pm
30. Leo		30. Virgo		30. Scorp.	
		31. Libra	5:42 am		

Summer time to be considered where applicable.

2001 MOON SIGN DATES— NEW YORK TIME

JULY
Day Moon Enters
1. Sagitt.   10:14 pm
2. Sagitt.
3. Sagitt.
4. Capric.   7:23 am
5. Capric.
6. Aquar.   6:34 pm
7. Aquar.
8. Aquar.
9. Pisces   7:06 am
10. Pisces
11. Aries   7:37 pm
12. Aries
13. Aries
14. Taurus   6:14 am
15. Taurus
16. Gemini   1:27 pm
17. Gemini
18. Cancer   4:57 pm
19. Cancer
20. Leo   5:44 pm
21. Leo
22. Virgo   5:30 pm
23. Virgo
24. Libra   6:09 pm
25. Libra
26. Scorp.   9:18 pm
27. Scorp.
28. Scorp.
29. Sagitt. 3:45 am
30. Sagitt.
31. Capric. 1:17 pm

AUGUST
Day Moon Enters
1. Capric.
2. Capric.
3. Aquar.   0:54 am
4. Aquar.
5. Pisces   1:31 pm
6. Pisces
7. Pisces
8. Aries   2:06 am
9. Aries
10. Taurus   1:24 pm
11. Taurus
12. Gemini   10:00 pm
13. Gemini
14. Gemini
15. Cancer   2:56 am
16. Cancer
17. Leo   4:26 am
18. Leo
19. Virgo   3:54 am
20. Virgo
21. Libra   3:20 am
22. Libra
23. Scorp.   4:51 am
24. Scorp.
25. Sagitt. 10:00 am
26. Sagitt.
27. Capric. 7:03 pm
28. Capric.
29. Capric.
30. Aquar.   6:49 am
31. Aquar.

SEPTEMBER
Day Moon Enters
1. Pisces   7:33 pm
2. Pisces
3. Pisces
4. Aries   7:59 am
5. Aries
6. Taurus   7:19 pm
7. Taurus
8. Taurus
9. Gemini   4:42 am
10. Gemini
11. Cancer   11:10 am
12. Cancer
13. Leo   2:17 pm
14. Leo
15. Virgo   2:40 pm
16. Virgo
17. Libra   2:01 pm
18. Libra
19. Scorp.   2:28 pm
20. Scorp.
21. Sagitt. 6:03 pm
22. Sagitt.
23. Sagitt.
24. Capric. 1:49 am
25. Capric.
26. Aquar.   1:06 pm
27. Aquar.
28. Aquar.
29. Pisces   1:51 am
30. Pisces

Summer time to be considered where applicable.

2001 MOON SIGN DATES— NEW YORK TIME

OCTOBER
Day Moon Enters
1. Aries 2:09 pm
2. Aries
3. Aries
4. Taurus 1:02 am
5. Taurus
6. Gemini 10:13 am
7. Gemini
8. Cancer 5:20 pm
9. Cancer
10. Leo 9:55 pm
11. Leo
12. Virgo 11:59 pm
13. Virgo
14. Virgo
15. Libra 0:27 am
16. Libra
17. Scorp. 1:04 am
18. Scorp.
19. Sagitt. 3:48 am
20. Sagitt.
21. Capric. 10:12 am
22. Capric.
23. Aquar. 8:27 pm
24. Aquar.
25. Aquar.
26. Pisces 8:57 am
27. Pisces
28. Aries 9:16 pm
29. Aries
30. Aries
31. Taurus 7:49 am

NOVEMBER
Day Moon Enters
1. Taurus
2. Gemini 4:14 pm
3. Gemini
4. Cancer 10:45 pm
5. Cancer
6. Cancer
7. Leo 3:35 am
8. Leo
9. Virgo 6:50 am
10. Virgo
11. Libra 8:54 am
12. Libra
13. Scorp. 10:46 am
14. Scorp.
15. Sagitt. 1:52 pm
16. Sagitt.
17. Capric. 7:41 pm
18. Capric.
19. Capric.
20. Aquar. 4:56 am
21. Aquar.
22. Pisces 4:53 pm
23. Pisces
24. Pisces
25. Aries 5:22 am
26. Aries
27. Taurus 4:07 pm
28. Taurus
29. Taurus
30. Gemini 0:05 am

DECEMBER
Day Moon Enters
1. Gemini
2. Cancer 5:31 am
3. Cancer
4. Leo 9:17 am
5. Leo
6. Virgo 12:12 pm
7. Virgo
8. Libra 2:58 pm
9. Libra
10. Scorp. 6:10 pm
11. Scorp.
12. Sagitt. 10:31 pm
13. Sagitt.
14. Sagitt.
15. Capric. 4:49 am
16. Capric.
17. Aquar. 1:44 pm
18. Aquar.
19. Aquar.
20. Pisces 1:10 am
21. Pisces
22. Aries 1:46 pm
23. Aries
24. Aries
25. Taurus 1:13 pm
26. Taurus
27. Gemini 9:40 am
28. Gemini
29. Cancer 2:41 pm
30. Cancer
31. Leo 5:10 pm

Summer time to be considered where applicable.

2001 PHASES OF THE MOON—
NEW YORK TIME

New Moon	First Quarter	Full Moon	Last Quarter
Dec. 25 ('00)	Jan. 2	Jan. 9	Jan. 16
Jan. 24	Feb. 1	Feb. 8	Feb. 14
Feb. 23	March 2	March 9	March 16
March 24	April 1	April 7	April 15
April 23	April 30	May 7	May 15
May 22	May 29	June 5	June 13
June 21	June 27	July 5	July 13
July 20	July 27	Aug. 4	Aug. 12
Aug. 18	Aug. 25	Sept. 2	Sept. 10
Sept. 17	Sept. 24	Oct. 2	Oct. 9
Oct. 16	Oct. 23	Nov. 1	Nov. 8
Nov. 15	Nov. 22	Nov. 30	Dec. 7
Dec. 14	Dec. 22	Dec. 30	Jan. 5 ('02)

Each phase of the Moon lasts approximately seven to eight days, during which the Moon's shape gradually changes as it comes out of one phase and goes into the next.

There will be a solar eclipse during the New Moon phase on December 25, at year's end 2000, and then on June 21 and December 14 of the year 2001.

There will be a lunar eclipse during the Full Moon phase on January 9, July 5, and December 30.

2001 FISHING GUIDE

	Good	Best
January	2-6-7-8-10-11-12-24	9-16
February	7-8-9-10-15	1-5-6-11-23
March	3-6-7-8-9-10-16-25	11-12
April	5-6-11-30	1-7-8-9-10-15-23
May	8-9-10-15-23-29	4-5-6-7
June	4-5-6-9-14-21	3-7-8-28
July	2-3-4-7-8-13	5-6-20-27
August	3-4-5-19-25-30-31	1-2-6-7-12
September	1-4-5-10-17	2-3-24-29-30
October	1-2-3-24-29-30-31	4-5-10-16
November	2-3-4-8-15-22-27-30	1-28-29
December	1-2-7-14-22-27-28-29	3-30-31

2001 PLANTING GUIDE

	Aboveground Crops	**Root Crops**
January	4-5-27-28	15-16-17-18-22-23
February	1-5-6-23-24-28	11-12-13-14-18-19
March	1-4-5-27-28	11-12-13-17-18-22-23
April	1-7-24-28-29	8-9-10-14-15-19-20
May	4-5-6-25-26	11-12-16-17-21-22
June	1-2-3-22-28-29-30	7-8-12-13-17-18
July	1-25-26-27-28	6-10-11-15-19
August	1-2-21-22-23-24-28-29	6-7-11-12-15-16
September	18-19-20-21-24-25-29-30	3-7-8-12
October	17-18-22-23-27-28	4-5-9-10-15
November	18-19-23-24-28-29	1-5-6-12-13-14
December	15-16-20-21-26	3-9-10-11-12-31

	Pruning	**Weeds and Pests**
January	17-18	11-12-13-19-20
February	13-14	8-9-10-16-20-21-22
March	13-22-23	15-16-20-21
April	9-10-19-20	11-12-16-17-21-22
May	16-17	9-13-14-18-19
June	12-13	6-10-11-15-16-19-20
July	10-11-19	7-8-12-13-17
August	6-7-15-16	4-8-9-13-14-17-18
September	3-12	5-6-9-10-14-15-16
October	9-10	3-7-8-11-12-13-14
November	5-6-14	3-4-7-8-9-10
December	3-11-12-30	1-5-6-7-13

MOON'S INFLUENCE OVER PLANTS

Centuries ago it was established that seeds planted when the Moon is in signs and phases called Fruitful will produce more growth than seeds planted when the Moon is in a Barren sign.

Fruitful Signs: Taurus, Cancer, Libra, Scorpio, Capricorn, Pisces
Barren Signs: Aries, Gemini, Leo, Virgo, Sagittarius, Aquarius
Dry Signs: Aries, Gemini, Sagittarius, Aquarius

Activity	Moon In
Mow lawn, trim plants	**Fruitful sign:** 1st & 2nd quarter
Plant flowers	**Fruitful sign:** 2nd quarter; best in Cancer and Libra
Prune	**Fruitful sign:** 3rd & 4th quarter
Destroy pests; spray	**Barren sign:** 4th quarter
Harvest potatoes, root crops	**Dry sign:** 3rd & 4th quarter; Taurus, Leo, and Aquarius

MOON'S INFLUENCE OVER YOUR HEALTH

ARIES	Head, brain, face, upper jaw
TAURUS	Throat, neck, lower jaw
GEMINI	Hands, arms, lungs, shoulders, nervous system
CANCER	Esophagus, stomach, breasts, womb, liver
LEO	Heart, spine
VIRGO	Intestines, liver
LIBRA	Kidneys, lower back
SCORPIO	Sex and eliminative organs
SAGITTARIUS	Hips, thighs, liver
CAPRICORN	Skin, bones, teeth, knees
AQUARIUS	Circulatory system, lower legs
PISCES	Feet, tone of being

Try to avoid work being done on that part of the body when the Moon is in the sign governing that part.

MOON'S INFLUENCE OVER DAILY AFFAIRS

The Moon makes a complete transit of the Zodiac every 27 days 7 hours and 43 minutes. In making this transit the Moon forms different aspects with the planets and consequently has favorable or unfavorable bearings on affairs and events for persons according to the sign of the Zodiac under which they were born.

When the Moon is in conjunction with the Sun it is called a New Moon; when the Moon and Sun are in opposition it is called a Full Moon. From New Moon to Full Moon, first and second quarter—which takes about two weeks—the Moon is increasing or waxing. From Full Moon to New Moon, third and fourth quarter, the Moon is decreasing or waning.

Activity	Moon In
Business: buying and selling new, requiring public support	Sagittarius, Aries, Gemini, Virgo 1st and 2nd quarter
meant to be kept quiet	3rd and 4th quarter
Investigation	3rd and 4th quarter
Signing documents	1st & 2nd quarter, Cancer, Scorpio, Pisces
Advertising	2nd quarter, Sagittarius
Journeys and trips	1st & 2nd quarter, Gemini, Virgo
Renting offices, etc.	Taurus, Leo, Scorpio, Aquarius
Painting of house/apartment	3rd & 4th quarter, Taurus, Scorpio, Aquarius
Decorating	Gemini, Libra, Aquarius
Buying clothes and accessories	Taurus, Virgo
Beauty salon or barber shop visit	1st & 2nd quarter, Taurus, Leo, Libra, Scorpio, Aquarius
Weddings	1st & 2nd quarter

CANCER

CANCER

Character Analysis

Cancer is generally rather sensitive. He or she is quite often a generous person by nature, and is willing to help almost anyone in need. He is emotional and often feels sorry for people less fortunate than he. He could never refuse to answer someone's call for help. It is because of his sympathetic nature that others take advantage of him now and again.

In spite of his willingness to help others, the Cancer man or woman may seem difficult to approach by anyone not well acquainted with their character. On the whole, he seems subdued and reserved. Others may feel there is a wall between them and Cancer, although this may not be the case at all. The person born under this sign, which is ruled by the Moon, is careful not to let others hurt him. He has learned through hard experience that protection of some sort is necessary in order to get along in life. The person who wins his confidence and is able to get beyond this barrier will find the Moon Child a warm and loving person.

With his family and close friends, he is a very faithful and dependable person. In his quiet way, he can be affectionate and loving. He is generally not one given to demonstrative behavior. He can be fond of someone without telling them so a dozen times a day. With people he is close to, Cancer is more open about his own need for affection, and he enjoys being pampered by his loved ones. He likes to feel wanted and protected.

When he has made up his mind about something, he sticks to it, and is generally a very constant person. He knows how to hold his ground. He never wavers. People who don't know him may think him weak and easily managed, because he is so quiet and modest, but this is far from true. He can take a lot of punishment for an idea or a cause he believes in. For Cancer, right is right. In order to protect himself, the person born under this sign will sometimes put up a pose as someone bossy and domineering. Sometimes he is successful in fooling others with his brash front. People who have known him for a while, however, are seldom taken in.

Many people born under this sign of the Crab are shy and seemingly lacking in confidence. They know their own minds, though, even if they do not seem to. He responds to kindness and encouragement. He will be himself with people he trusts. A good person can bring out the best in the Crab. Disagreeable or unfeeling people can send him scurrying back into his shell. He is a person who does not appreciate sharp criticism. Some Crabs are worriers. They are very concerned about what others may think of them. This may bother them so much that they develop a deep feeling of inferiority. Sometimes this reaches the point where he is so unsure of himself in some matters that he allows himself to be influenced by someone who has a stronger personality. Also, some Crabs may be afraid that people will talk behind his back if he doesn't comply with their wishes. However, this does not stop him from doing what he feels is right. The cultivated Cancer learns to think for himself and has no fear of disapproval.

The Cancer man or woman is most himself at home. The person born under this sign is a real lover of domesticity. He likes a place where he can relax and feel properly sheltered. Cancers like things to stay as they are; they are not fond of changes of any sort. They are not very adaptable people. When visiting others or going to unfamiliar places, they are not likely to feel very comfortable. They are not the most talkative people at a party. In the comfort of their own homes, however, they blossom and bloom.

The Cancer man or woman sticks by the rules, whatever the game. He is not a person who would ever think of going against an established grain. He is conventional and moderate in almost all things. In a way he likes the old-fashioned things. However, in spite of this, he is interested in new things and does what he can to keep up with the times. In a way, he has two sides to his character. He is seldom forgetful. He has a memory like an elephant and can pick out any detail from the past with no trouble at all. He often reflects on things that have happened. He prefers the past to the future, which sometimes fills him with a feeling of apprehension.

This fourth sign of the Zodiac is a motherly one. Even the Cancer man has something maternal about him. He is usually kind and considerate, ready to help and protect. Others are drawn to Cancer because of these gentle qualities. People in trouble often turn to him for advice and sympathy. People find him easy to confide in.

The Cancer person in general is very forgiving. He almost never holds a grudge. Still, it would not be wise to anger him. Treat him fairly and he will treat you the same. He does not appreciate people who lose patience with him. Cancer is usually proud of his mind and does not like to be considered unintelligent. Even if others feel that he is somewhat slow in some areas, he would rather not have this opinion expressed in his presence. He's not a person to be played with; he can tell when someone is treating him like a fool.

Quite often people born under this sign are musically inclined. Some of them have a deep interest in religious matters. They are apt to be interested in mystical matters, as well. Although they are fascinated by these things, they may be somewhat afraid of being overwhelmed if they go into them too deeply. In spite of this feeling of apprehension, Moon Children try to satisfy their curiosity in these matters.

Health

For the person born under the sign of Cancer, the stomach is the weak point. Chances are that Cancer is easily susceptible to infection. Sometimes his health is affected by nervousness. He can be quite a worrier. Even little things eat at him from time to time, which is apt to lower his resistance to infectious illnesses. He is often upset by small matters.

A Cancer as a child is sometimes sickly and weak. His physique during this period of growth can be described in most cases as fragile. Some develop into physically strong adults, others may have the remnants of childhood ailments with them for a good part of their adult lives. They are frightened of being sick. Illness is a word they would rather not mention. Pain is also a thing they fear.

They are given to quick-changing moods at times, which often has an effect on their overall health. Worry or depression can have a subliminal effect on their general health. Usually their illnesses are not as serious as they imagine them to be. They sometimes find it easy to feel sorry for themselves.

On the whole, the Cancer man or woman is a quiet person. He is not one to brag or push his weight around. However, let it not be thought that he lacks the force that others have. He can be quite purposeful and energetic when the situation calls for it. However, when it comes to tooting their own horn, they can be somewhat shy and reticent. They may lack the get-up-and-go that others have when it comes to pushing their personal interests ahead.

Some Cancers are quite aware of the fact that they are not what one would call sturdy in physique or temperament. Some may go through life rather painfully trying to cover up the weak side of their nature.

Sons and daughters of the Moon may not be very vigorous or active. As a rule, they are not too fond of physical exercise, and they have a weakness for rich and heavy foods. As a result, in later life they could end up overweight. Some Cancers have trouble with their kidneys and intestines. Others digest their food poorly. The wise Cancer man or woman, however, adheres to a strict and well-balanced diet with plenty of fresh fruit and vegetables. Moreover, they see to it that they properly exercise daily. The Cancer man or woman who learns to cut down on rich foods and worry often lives to a ripe old age.

Occupation

Cancer generally has no trouble at all establishing himself in the business world. He has all those qualities that make one a success professionally. He is careful with his equipment as well as his money. He is patient and he knows how to persevere. Any job where he has a chance to use his mind instead of his body is usually a job in which he has no trouble succeeding. He can work well with people—especially people situated in dire straits. Welfare work is the kind of occupation in which he usually excels. He can really be quite a driving person if his job calls for it. Cancer is surprisingly resourceful. In spite of his retiring disposition, he is capable of accomplishing some very difficult tasks.

Cancer can put on an aggressive front, and in some cases it can carry him far. Quite often he is able to develop leadership qualities and make good use of them. He knows how to direct his energy so that he never becomes immediately exhausted. He'll work away at a difficult chore gradually, seldom approaching anything head-on. By working at something obliquely he often finds advantages along the way that are not apparent to others. In spite of his cautious approach, Cancer is often taxed by work that is too demanding of his energy. He may put up a good front of being strong and courageous while actually he is at the end of his emotional rope. Risks sometimes frighten the Crab. It is often fear that exhausts him. The possible dangers in the world of business set him to worrying.

Cancer does not boast about what he is going to do. He or she just quietly goes ahead and does it. Quite often he accomplishes more than others in this quiet way.

The person born under this sign enjoys helping others. By nature, he is quite a sympathetic individual. He does not like to see others suffer or do without. He is willing to make sacrifices for someone he trusts and cares for. Cancer's maternal streak works wonders with children. People born under the fourth sign of the Zodiac often make excellent teachers. They understand young people well and do what they can to help them grow up properly.

Cancers also are fairly intuitive. In business or financial matters, they often make an important strike by playing a strong hunch. In some cases they are able to rely almost entirely on their feelings rather than on reason.

Water attracts the Cancer person. Often they have connections with the oceans through their professions. Cancer homemakers experimenting in the kitchen often are very successful creating new drinks and blending liquid recipes. Overseas trade and commerce also appeal.

The average Cancer has many choices as far as a career is concerned. There are many things that he can do well once he puts his mind to it. In the arts he is quite likely to do well. The Cancer man or woman has a way with beauty, harmony, and creativity. Basically, he is a very capable person in many things; it depends on which of his talents he wants to develop to a professional point. He has a rich imagination and sometimes can make use of it in the area of painting, music, or sculpture.

When working for someone else, Cancer can always be depended upon. He makes a loyal and conscientious employee.

It is important for Cancer to select a job that is well suited to his talents and temperament. Although he may feel that earning money is important, Cancer eventually comes to the point where he realizes that it is even more important to enjoy the work he is doing. He should have a position that allows him to explore the recesses of his personality and to develop. When placed in the wrong job, the Cancer man or woman might wish they were somewhere else.

Cancers know the value of money. They are not the sort of people who go throwing money around recklessly. Cancer is honest and expects others to be the same. He is quite modest in most things and deplores unnecessary display. Cancers have a genius for making money and for investing or saving it.

Security is important to the person born under this sign. He'll always see to it that he has something put away for that inevitable rainy day. He is also a hard worker and is willing to put in long hours for the money it brings him. Financial success is usually the result of his own perseverance and industry. Through his own need for security, it is often easy for Cancer to sympathize with those of like dispositions. He is a helpful person. If he sees someone trying to do his best to get ahead—and still not succeeding—he is quite apt to put aside his own interests temporarily to help another.

Sometimes Cancer worries about money even when he has it. Even the wealthy Cancer can never be too secure. It would be better for him to learn how to relax and not to let his worries undermine his health. Financial matters often cause him considerable concern—even when it is not necessary.

Home and Family

Cancers are usually great home lovers. They are very domestic by nature; home for them spells security. Cancer is a family person. He respects those who are related to him. He feels a great responsibility toward all the members of his family. There is usually a very strong tie between Cancer and his mother that lasts through his whole life. Something a Cancer will not tolerate is for someone to speak ill of a member of his family. This for him is a painful and deep insult. He has a great respect for his family and family traditions. Quite often Cancer is well-acquainted with his family tree. If he happens to have a relative who has been quite successful in life, he is proud of the fact. Once he is home for the weekend, he generally stays there.

Cancer is sentimental about old things and habits. He is apt to have many things stored away from years ago. Something that was dear to his parents will probably be dear to him as well.

Many Cancers travel near and far from time to time. But no matter what their destination, they are always glad to be back where they feel they belong.

The home of a Cancer is usually quite comfortable and tastefully furnished. Cancer men and women are romantic, which is usually reflected in the way their house is arranged.

The Cancer child is always attached to his home and family. He may not care to go out and play with other children very much but enjoys it when his friends come to his house.

The maternal nature of the Cancer person comes out when he gives a party. He is a very attentive host and worries over a guest like a mother hen—anxious to see that they are comfortable and lack nothing. He does his best to make others happy and at home, and he is admired and loved for that. People who visit are usually deeply impressed by their outgoing ways. The Cancer host prepares unusual and delicious snacks for visitors. Cancer is very concerned about them and sees to it that they are well-fed while visiting.

Homebodies that they are, Cancers generally do what they can to make their home a comfortable and interesting place for themselves as well as for others. They feel very flattered when a visitor pays them a compliment on their home.

Children play a very important part in the lives of people born under this sign. Cancers fuss over their youngsters and give them the things they feel that they need. They generally like to have large families. They see to it that their children are well provided for and that they have the chances in life that their parents never had. The best mother of the Zodiac is usually someone born under the sign of Cancer. They have a strong protective nature. They usually have a strong sense of duty, and when their children are in difficulty they do everything they can to set matters right. Children, needless to say, are fond of their Cancer parent, and respond lovingly to make the parent-child relationship a harmonious one.

Social Relationships

Cancer may seem rather retiring and quiet, and this gives people the impression that he is not too warm or sympathetic. However, most Moon Children are very sensitive and loving. Their ability to understand and sympathize with others is great. Cancer likes to have close friends—people who love and understand him as well as he tries to love and understand them. He wants to be well-liked—to be noticed by people who he feels should like him. If he does not get the attention and affection he feels he is entitled to, he is apt to become sullen and difficult to deal with.

The Cancer man or woman has strong powers of intuition and can generally sense when he has met a person who is likely to turn into a good friend. Cancer suffers greatly if ever he should lose a friend. To him friendships are sacred. Sometimes Cancer sets friends on too high a pedestal. He or she is apt to feel crestfallen when he discovers that they have feet of clay. He is often romantic in his approach to friendship and is likely to seek people out for sentimental reasons rather than for practical ones.

Cancer is a very sensitive person and sometimes this contributes to making a friendship unsatisfactory. He sometimes makes the wrong interpretation of a remark that is made by a friend or acquaintance. He imagines something injurious behind a very innocent remark. He sometimes feels that people who profess to be his friends laugh at him cruelly behind his back. He has to be constantly reassured of a friend's sincerity, especially in the beginning of a relationship. If he wants to have the wide circle of friends he desires, Cancer must learn to curb these persecution fantasies.

Love and Marriage

The Cancer man or woman has to have love in their life, otherwise their existence is a dull and humdrum affair. When they love someone, Cancer will do everything in their power to make a lover happy. They are not afraid to sacrifice in order to make an important relationship work. To his loved one he is likely to seem uncertain and moody. Cancer is usually very influenced by the impression he has of his lover. They may even be content to let their romance partner have his or her own way in the relationship. He may not make many demands but be willing to follow those of his loved one. At times he may feel that he is not really loved, and draw away somewhat from the relationship. Sometimes it takes a lot of coaxing before he can be won over to the fact that he is indeed loved for himself alone.

Cancer is often possessive about people as well as material objects. This often makes the relationship difficult to accept for his partner.

His standards are sometimes impossibly high and because of this he is difficult to please. The Cancer man or woman is interested in finding someone with whom he can spend the rest of his life. He or she is not interested in any fly-by-night romance.

Romance and the Cancer Woman

The Cancer woman is sincere in her approach to love. Her feelings run deep. Still, she's moody, tempestuous, and changeable. She is so sensitive in romance that her lover may find her difficult to understand at times. The Moon Child knows exactly the sort of man she is looking for. If she can find him, she'll never let him go.

The trouble is she frequently goes through a lot of men in her search for the perfect lover. She surrenders completely to her emotions. She can experience the whole melodrama of falling in love, longing to be with her man, then being desolate when parted from him. If she does find her ideal mate, she will take to marriage for the rest of her life without looking back or even at another man. If she can't marry the man of her dreams, or even live with him, she might carry a torch for the rest of her days. That is the tenacity of the Cancer woman's pure devotion to the man she loves.

Marriage is a union suited to the Crab's temperament, which needs a safe haven in which her feelings can be nurtured. She longs for permanence in a relationship, and usually is not fond of flings or meaningless romantic adventures. Because her emotions are so deep, she can easily feel wronged by a minor slight. Once she imagines she has been hurt, she can retreat rapidly and withdraw deep within herself to brood. It may be quite a while before she comes out of her shell. She desires a man who is protective and affectionate, someone who can understand and cope with her moods so that she does not feel threatened.

As a Moon Child, Cancer is very temperamental. She'll soar to the heights of ecstasy, then plunge into the depths of despondency all with dazzling speed. She'll sparkle like champagne, then fizzle out before the high wears off. Such marked changes of personality can be bewildering to a lover who may have done nothing to provoke them. Reason and logic will not coax her out of a bad mood. Only patient love will work. And if do you not have staying power or refined sensibilities, then you don't stand the ghost of a chance with the Cancer woman.

Cancer's intuition is usually right on. She can size up a situation instinctively, and more times than not she is right. What her gut feelings tell her can be the cause of many a quarrel and the occasion for nagging her mate about a myriad of things. Because she is possessive, there can be discord. And she more she loves, the more possessive and jealous she can become. The demands she is likely to make can be overbearing at times. But as long as she is reassured and appreciated, all will be well.

The Cancer woman makes a devoted wife and mother who will do everything to keep her family together. The only danger is that she may transfer all her love to the children, making her man feel useless and left out. As long as her man participates fully in family life, there will be harmony and affection.

Romance and the Cancer Man

The Cancer man may come on as the reserved type. It can be difficult for some women to understand him. Generally, he is a very loving person, but sometimes he will not let his sensitive side show. He is afraid of being rejected or hurt, so he tries to keep his true feelings hidden until he knows that the intended object of his affections is capable of taking him seriously.

For him, love is a serious business. And he is so serious about love that you might say he lives for love—to give it and to receive it. True to the symbol of the sign of Cancer, which is the Crab, he feels his way very carefully in any romantic alliance. He is not going to make any rash mistakes. But even if it's only a brief affair, the Cancer man will treat his lover as the only woman in the world. When he is convinced that you, too, are serious, then this sensuous idealist is all yours.

You must never play around with his feelings. Like the Crab, the Cancer man pretends to be tough and invulnerable on the outside, but on the inside he is so soft it hurts. He is perhaps the most sensitive person you have ever met. Your Moon Child is highly emotive and moody, reflecting the Moon's quick changeability and shifts of temperament. And, like his ruler the Moon, he is terribly responsive to the vibes coming from his lover. It's all or nothing with him, so jealousy and possessiveness can become a problem. He needs to be constantly reassured that you love him.

If you love him, tell him so often. And show him that you love him, not only with physical love but also with thoughtfully chosen fine gifts no matter how small. He is sentimental. He will treasure everything you give him. He will keep mementos of your happy moments together, especially souvenirs of the occasion when he became sure you would be the love his life.

When deeply in love, the Cancer man does everything in his power to hold the woman of his choice. He is very affectionate and may be extravagant from time to time with the woman he loves. He will lavish gifts upon you and will see that you never lack anything you desire to make your home life together warm and cozy.

Marriage is something the Cancer man sets as a goal early in his life. He wants to settle down with someone who will mother him to some extent. Often he looks for a woman who has the same qualities as his mother, especially if his early childhood revolved around his mother's central role in the family. The remembrance of things maternal makes him feel truly loved and secure.

The Cancer man is an attentive father. He is fond of large families. Sometimes his love for the children may be too possessive, and he can stifle their independence with smothering ways.

Woman—Man

CANCER WOMAN
ARIES MAN

Although it's possible that you could find happiness with a man born under the sign of the Ram, it's uncertain as to how long that happiness would last.

An Aries who has made his mark in the world and is somewhat steadfast in his outlooks and attitudes could be quite a catch for you. On the other hand, men under this sign are often swift-footed and quick-minded. Their industrious mannerisms may fail to impress you, especially if you feel that much of their get-up-and-go often leads nowhere.

When it comes to a fine romance, you want someone with a nice, broad shoulder to lean on. You are likely to find a relationship with someone who doesn't like to stay put for too long somewhat upsetting.

Aries may have a little trouble in understanding you, too, at least in the beginning of the relationship. He may find you too shy and moody. Aries speak their minds and can criticize at the drop of a hat.

You may find a Ram too demanding. He may give you the impression that he expects you to be at his beck and call. You have a barrelful of patience at your disposal and he may try every last bit of it. He is apt not to be as thorough as you are in everything that he does. In order to achieve success or a goal quickly, he will overlook small but important details—and regret it when it is far too late.

Being married to an Aries does not mean that you'll have a secure and safe life as far as finances are concerned. Not all Aries are rash with cash, but they lack that sound head you have for putting away something for that inevitable rainy day. He'll do his best, however, to see that you're adequately provided for, even though his efforts may leave something to be desired as far as you're concerned.

With an Aries mate, you'll find yourself constantly among people. Aries generally have many friends—and you may not heartily approve of them all. Rams are more interested in interesting people than they are in influential ones. Although there can be a family squabble from time to time, you are stable enough to take it all in your stride. Your love of permanence and a harmonious home life will help you to take the bitter with the sweet.

Aries men love children. They make wonderful fathers. Kids take to them like ducks to water. Their quick minds and behavior appeal to the young.

CANCER WOMAN
TAURUS MAN

Some Taurus men are strong and silent. They do all they can to protect and provide for the women they love. The Taurus man will never let you down. He's steady, sturdy, and reliable. He's pretty honest and practical, too. He says what he means and means what he says. He never indulges in deceit and will always put his cards on the table.

Taurus is very affectionate. Being loved, appreciated, and understood is very important for his well-being. Like you, he is also looking for peace, harmony, and security in his life. If you both work toward these goals together, they are easily attained.

If you should marry a Taurus, you can be sure that the wolf will never darken your door. They are notoriously good providers and do everything they can to make their families comfortable and happy.

He'll appreciate the way you have of making a home warm and inviting. Good meals and the evening papers are essential ingredients in making your Taurus husband happy at the end of the workday. Although he may be a big lug of a guy, he's fond of gentleness and soft things. If you puff up his pillow and tuck him in at night, he won't complain.

You probably won't complain about his friends. Taurus tends to seek out friends who are successful or prominent. You admire people, too, who work hard and achieve what they set out for. It helps to reassure your way of life and the way you look at things.

The Taurus man doesn't care too much for change. He's a stay-at-home of the first degree. Chances are that the house you move into after you're married will be the house you'll live in for the rest of your life.

You'll find that the man born under the sign of the Bull is easy to get along with. It's unlikely that you'll have many quarrels or arguments.

Although he'll be gentle and tender with you, your Taurus man is far from being a sensitive type. He's a man's man. Chances are he loves sports like fishing and football. He can be earthy as well as down to earth.

Taurus love their children very much but try hard not to spoil them. They believe in children staying in their places. They make excellent disciplinarians. Your children will be polite and respectful. They may find their Taurus father a little gruff, but as they grow older they'll learn to understand him.

CANCER WOMAN
GEMINI MAN

Gemini men, in spite of their charm and dashing manner, may unnerve you. They seem to lack the common sense you set so much store in. Their tendency to start something, then out of boredom never finish it, may exasperate you.

You may be inclined to interpret a Gemini's jumping from here to there as childish or neurotic. A man born under the sign of the Twins will seldom stay put. If you should take it upon yourself to try and make him sit still, he will resent it.

On the other hand, the Gemini man may think you're a slow-poke, someone far too interested in security and material things. He's attracted to things that sparkle and dazzle. You, with your practical way of looking at things, are likely to seem a little dull and uninteresting to this gadabout. If you're looking for a life of security and permanence—and what Cancer isn't—then you'd better look elsewhere for your Mr. Right.

Chances are you'll be taken in by his charming ways and facile wit—few women can resist Gemini magic. But after you've seen through his live-for-today, gossamer facade, you'll most likely be very happy to turn your attention to someone more stable, even if he is not as interesting. You want a man who is there when you need him. You need someone on whom you can fully rely. Keeping track of a Gemini's movements will make you dizzy. Still, you are a patient woman, most of the time, and you are able to put up with something contrary if you feel that in the end it will prove well worth the effort.

A successful and serious Gemini could make you a very happy woman, perhaps, if you gave him half a chance. Although you may think that he has holes in his head, the Gemini man generally has a good brain and can make good use of it when he wants. Some Geminis who have learned the importance of being consistent have risen to great heights professionally. Once you can convince yourself that not all Twins are witless grasshoppers, you'll find you've come a long way in trying to understand them.

Life with a Gemini man can be more fun than a barrel of clowns. You'll never have a chance to experience a dull moment. He lacks your sense when it comes to money, however. You should see to it that you handle the budgeting and bookkeeping.

In ways, Gemini is like a child himself. Perhaps that is why a Gemini father can get along so well with his own children, indeed with most of the younger generation.

CANCER WOMAN
CANCER MAN
You'll find the man born under the same sign as you easy to get along with. You're both sensitive and sensible people. You'll see eye-to-eye on most things. He'll share your interest in security and practicality.

Cancer men are always hard workers. They are very interested in making successes of themselves in business and socially. Like you, he's a conservative person who has a great deal of respect for tradition. He's a man you can depend on come rain or come shine. He'll never shirk his responsibilities as provider and will always see to it that you never want.

The Cancer man is not the type that rushes headlong into romance. Neither are you, for that matter. Courtship between the two of you will be a sensible and thorough affair. It may take months before you even get to that holding-hands stage of romance. One thing you can be sure of: he'll always treat you like a lady. He'll have great respect and consideration for your feelings. Only when he is sure that you approve of him as someone to love, will he reveal the warmer side of his nature. His coolness, like yours, is just a front. Beneath it lies a very affectionate heart.

Although he may seem restless or moody at times, on the whole the Cancer man is very considerate and kind. His standards are extremely high. He is looking for a partner who can measure up to his ideals—a partner like you.

Marriage means a lot to the Cancer male. He's very interested in settling down with someone who has the same attitudes and outlooks as he has. He's a man who loves being at home. He'll be a faithful husband. Cancers never pussyfoot around after they have made their marriage vows. They do not take their marriage responsibilities lightly. They see to it that everything in this relationship is just the way it should be. Between the two of you, your home will be well managed, bills will be paid on time, there will be adequate insurance on everything of value, and there will be money in the bank. When retirement time rolls around, you both should be very well off.

The Cancer man has a great respect for family. You'll most likely be seeing a lot of his mother during your marriage, just as he'll probably be seeing a lot of yours. He'll do his best to get along with your relatives; he'll treat them with the kindness and concern you think they deserve. He'll expect you to be just as considerate with his relatives.

Cancer is a very good father. He's very patient and understanding, especially when the children are young and dependent and need his protection.

CANCER WOMAN
LEO MAN
To know a man born under the sign of the Lion is not necessarily to love him—even though the temptation may be great. When he fixes most women with his leonine double-whammy, it causes their hearts to throb and their minds to soar.

But with you, the sensible Cancer, it takes more than a regal strut and roar to win you over. There is no denying that Leo has a way with women, even practical Cancers. If he sweeps you off your feet, it may be hard for you to scramble upright again. Still, you are no pushover for romantic charm when you feel there may be no security behind it.

He'll wine you and dine you in the fanciest places. He'll croon to you under the moon and shower you with diamonds if he can get ahold of them. Still, it would be wise to find out just how long that shower is going to last before consenting to be his wife.

Lions in love are hard to ignore, let alone brush off. Once mesmerized by this romantic powerhouse, you may find yourself doing things you never dreamed of. Leos can be vain pussycats when involved romantically. They like to be cuddled and petted, tickled under the chin, and told how wonderful they are. This may not be your cup of tea. Still, when you're romantically dealing with a Lion, you'll instinctively do the things that make him purr.

Although he may be big and magnanimous while trying to win you, he'll let out a blood-curdling roar if he thinks he's not getting the tender love and care he feels is his due. If you keep him well supplied with affection, you can be sure his eyes will never stray and his heart will never wander.

Leo men often tend to be authoritarian. They are born to lord it over others in one way or another, it seems. If he is the top banana of his firm, he'll most likely do everything he can to stay on top. If he's not number one, he's most likely working on it and will be sitting on the throne before long. You'll have more security than you can use if he is in a position to support you in the manner to which he feels you should be accustomed. He's apt to be too lavish, though, at least by your standards.

You'll always have plenty of friends when you have a Leo for a mate. He's a natural born friend-maker and entertainer. He loves to kick up his heels at a party.

As fathers, Leos may go from one extreme to another with their children. Leos either lavish too much attention on the youngsters or demand too much from them.

CANCER WOMAN
VIRGO MAN
The Virgo man is often a quiet, respectable type who sets great store in conservative behavior and levelheadedness. He'll admire you for your practicality and tenacity—perhaps even more than for your good looks. The Virgo man is seldom bowled over by glamour. When looking for someone to love, he always turns to a serious, reliable woman.

He'll be far from a Valentino while dating. In fact, you may wind up making all the passes. Once he gets his motor running, however, he can be warm and wonderful to the right lover.

The Virgo man is gradual about love. Chances are your romance with him will start out looking like an ordinary friendship. Once he's sure that you are no fly-by-night flirt and have no plans of taking him for a ride, he'll open up and rain sunshine all over your heart.

The Virgo man takes his time about romance. It may be many years before he seriously considers settling down. Virgos are often middle-aged when they make their first marriage vows. They hold out as long as they can for the woman who perfectly measures up to their ideals.

He may not have many names in his little black book; in fact, he may not even have a little black book. He's not interested in playing the field; leave that to the more flamboyant signs. The Virgo man is so particular that he may remain romantically inactive for a long period of time. The mate he chooses has to be perfect or it's no go.

With your surefire perseverance, you'll be able to make him listen to reason, as far as romance is concerned. Before long, you'll find him returning your love. He's no block of ice and will respond to what he considers to be the right feminine flame.

Once your love life with Virgo starts to bubble, don't give it a chance to die down. The Virgo man will never give a woman a second chance at winning his heart. If there should ever be a bad break between you, forget about picking up the pieces. With him, it's one strike and you're out.

Once married, he'll stay that way—even if it hurts. He's too conscientious to back out of a legal deal of any sort. He'll always be faithful and considerate. He's as neat as a pin and will expect you to be the same.

If you marry a Virgo man, keep your kids spic-and-span, at least by the time he gets home from work. He likes children to be clean and polite.

CANCER WOMAN
LIBRA MAN

Cancers are apt to find Libra men too wrapped up in their own private dreams to be romantically interesting. He's a difficult man to bring back down to earth, at times. Although he may be very careful about weighing both sides of an argument, he may never really come to a reasonable decision about anything. Decisions, large and small, are capable of giving Libra the willies. Don't ask him why. He probably doesn't know.

If you are looking for permanence and constancy in a love relationship, you may find him a puzzlement. One moment he comes on hard and strong with declarations of his love; the next moment you find he's left you like yesterday's mashed potatoes. It does no good to wonder what went wrong. Chances are nothing, really. It's just one of Libra's strange ways.

On the other hand, you'll probably admire his way with harmony and beauty. If you're all decked out in your fanciest gown, you'll receive a ready compliment and one that's really deserved. Libras don't pass out compliments to all and sundry. If something strikes him as distasteful, he'll remain silent. He's tactful.

He may not seem as ambitious as you would like your lover or husband to be. Where you have a great interest in getting ahead, Libra is often content just to drift along. It is not that he is lazy or shiftless. Material gain generally means little to him. He is more interested in aesthetic matters. If he is in love with you, however, he'll do everything in his power to make you happy.

You may have to give him a good nudge now and again to get him to recognize the light of reality. On the whole, he'll enjoy the company of his artistic dreams when you're not around. If you love your Libra, don't be too harsh or impatient with him. Try to understand him.

Libras are peace-loving people. They hate any kind of confrontation that might lead to an argument. Some of them will do almost anything to keep the peace—even tell a little lie.

If you find yourself involved with a man born under this sign, either temporarily or permanently, you'd better take over the task of managing his money. It's for his own good. Money will never interest a Libra as much as it should. He often has a tendency to be generous when he shouldn't be.

Don't let him see the materialistic side of your nature too often. It might frighten him off.

Libra makes a gentle and understanding father. He's careful not to spoil children or to demand too much from them. He believes that discipline should be a matter of gentle guidance.

CANCER WOMAN
SCORPIO MAN

Some people have a hard time understanding the man born under the sign of Scorpio. Few, however, are able to resist his fiery charm. When angered, he can act like an overturned wasps' nest; his sting can leave an almost permanent mark. If you find yourself interested in a Scorpion, you'd better learn how to keep on his good side.

The Scorpio man can be quite blunt when he chooses; at times, he'll seem like a brute to you. He's touchy—more so than you—and it can get on your nerves after a while. When you feel like you can't take it anymore, you'd better tiptoe away from the scene rather than chance an explosive confrontation. He's capable of giving you a sounding-out that will make you pack your bags and go back to Mother for good.

If he finds fault with you, he'll let you know. He might misinterpret your patience and think it a sign of indifference. Still and all, you are the kind of woman who can adapt to almost any sort of relationship or circumstance if you put your heart and mind to it.

Scorpio men are perceptive and intelligent. In some respects, they know how to use their brains more effectively than most. They believe in winning in whatever they do; second place holds no interest for them. In business, they usually achieve the position they want through drive and use of intellect.

Your interest in home life is not likely to be shared by him. No matter how comfortable you've managed to make the house, it will have little influence on making him aware of his family responsibilities. He does not like to be tied down, generally, and would rather be out on the battlefield of life, belting away for what he feels is a just and worthy cause. Don't try to keep the home fires burning too brightly while you wait for him to come home from work; you may run out of firewood.

The Scorpio man is passionate in all things—including love. Most women are easily attracted to him, and the Cancer woman is no exception, at least before she knows what she might be getting into. If you are swept off your feet by a Scorpio man, soon you find you are dealing with a carton of romantic fireworks. The Scorpio man is passionate with a capital P, make no mistake about that.

Scorpio men are straight to the point. They can be as sharp as a razor blade and just as cutting. Always manage to stay out of his line of fire; if you don't, it could cost you your love life.

Scorpio men like large families. They love children but they do not always live up to the role of the responsible, nurturing father.

CANCER WOMAN
SAGITTARIUS MAN
Sagittarius men are not easy to catch. They get cold feet whenever visions of the altar enter the romance. You'll most likely be attracted to Sagittarius because of his exuberant nature. He's lots of laughs and easy to get along with. But as soon as the relationship begins to take on a serious hue, you may feel let down.

Sagittarius are full of bounce, perhaps too much bounce to suit you. They are often hard to pin down; they dislike staying put. If he ever has a chance to be on the move, he'll go without so much as a how-do-you-do. Archers are quick people both in mind and spirit. If ever they do make mistakes, it's because of their zip. They leap before they look.

If you offer him good advice, he probably will not follow it. Sagittarius like to rely on their own wits and ways whenever possible.

His up-and-at-'em manner about most things is likely to drive you up the wall at times. And your cautious, deliberate manner is likely to make him seem impatient. He will tease when you're accompanying him on a hike or jogging through the park. He can't abide a slowpoke.

At times you'll find him too much like a kid—too breezy. Don't mistake his youthful zest for premature senility. Sagittarius are equipped with first-class brainpower and know how to use it well. They are often full of good ideas and drive. Generally, they are very broad-minded people and very much concerned with fair play and equality.

In the romance department, he's quite capable of loving you wholeheartedly while treating you like a good buddy. His hail-fellow-well-met manner in the arena of love is likely to scare off a dainty damsel. However, a woman who knows that his heart is in the right place won't mind it too much if, once in a while, he pats her on the back instead of giving her a gentle embrace.

He's not very much of a homebody. He's got ants in his pants and enjoys being on the move. Humdrum routine, especially at home, bores him silly. At the drop of a hat, he may ask you to dine out for a change. He's a past master in the instant-surprise department. He'll love keeping you guessing. His friendly, candid nature will win him many friends. He'll expect his friends to be yours, and vice versa.

Sagittarius is a good father when youngsters are old enough for rough-and-tumble sports. But with infants, Sagittarius may be all thumbs and feel helpless.

CANCER WOMAN
CAPRICORN MAN

The Capricorn man is often not the romantic lover that attracts most women. Still, with his reserve and calm, he is capable of giving his heart completely once he has found the right partner. The Cancer woman who is thorough and deliberate can appreciate these same qualities in the average Capricorn man. He is slow and sure about most things—love included.

He doesn't believe in flirting and would never lead a heart on a merry chase just for the game of it. If you win his trust, he'll give you his heart on a platter. Quite often, it is the woman who has to take the lead when romance is in the air. As long as he knows you're making the advances in earnest, he won't mind—in fact, he'll probably be grateful. Don't get to thinking he's all cold fish; he isn't. While some Capricorns are indeed quite capable of expressing passion, others often have difficulty displaying affection. He should have no trouble in this area, however, once he has found a patient and understanding mate.

The Capricorn man is very interested in getting ahead. He's ambitious and usually knows how to apply himself well to whatever task he undertakes. He's far from being a spendthrift. Like you, he knows how to handle money with extreme care. You, with your knack for putting pennies away for that rainy day, should have no difficulty in understanding his way with money. Capricorn thinks in terms of future security. He saves to make sure that he and his wife have something to fall back on when they reach retirement age. There's nothing wrong with that; in fact, it's a plus quality.

The Capricorn man will want to handle household matters efficiently. Most Cancers have no trouble in doing this. If he should check up on you from time to time, don't let it irritate you. Once you assure him that you can handle this area to his liking, he'll leave it all up to you.

Although he's a hard man to catch when it comes to marriage, once he's made that serious step, he's likely to become possessive. Capricorns need to know that they have the support of their women in whatever they do, every step of the way.

The Capricorn man likes to be liked. He may seem like a dull, reserved person. But underneath it all, he's often got an adventurous nature that has never had the chance to express itself. He may be a real daredevil in his heart of hearts. The right woman, the affectionate and adoring woman, can bring out that hidden zest in his nature.

Although he may not understand his children fully, Capricon will be a loving and dutiful father, raising his children with strong codes of honor and allegiance.

CANCER WOMAN
AQUARIUS MAN

You may find the Aquarius man the most broad-minded man you have ever met. On the other hand, you may find him the most impractical. Oftentimes, he's more of a dreamer than a doer. If you don't mind putting up with a man whose heart and mind are as wide as the universe and whose head is almost always up in the clouds, then start dating that Aquarius who has somehow captured your fancy. Maybe you, with your good sense, can bring him back down to earth when he gets too starry-eyed.

He's no dope, make no mistake about that. He can be busy making some very complicated and idealistic plans when he's got that out-to-lunch look in his eyes. But more than likely, he'll never execute them. After he's shared one or two of his progressive ideas with you, you'll think he's a nut. But don't go jumping to conclusions. There's a saying that Aquarius are a half-century ahead of everybody else in the thinking department.

If you decide to say yes to his will you marry me, you'll find out how right his zany whims are on or about your 50th anniversary. Maybe the waiting will be worth it. Could be that you have an Einstein on your hands—and heart.

Life with an Aquarius won't be one of total despair if you can learn to temper his airiness with your down-to-earth practicality. He won't gripe if you do. The Aquarius man always maintains an open mind. He'll entertain the ideas and opinions of everybody, though he may not agree with all of them.

Don't go tearing your hair out when you find that it's almost impossible to hold a normal conversation with your Aquarius friend at times. He's capable of answering a casual question with an imposing intellectual response. But always try to keep in mind that he means well.

His broad-mindedness doesn't stop when it comes to you and your personal freedom. You won't have to give up any of your hobbies or projects after you're married. In fact, he'll encourage you to continue your interests.

He'll be a kind and generous husband. He'll never quibble over petty things. Keep track of the money you both spend. He can't. Money burns a hole in his pocket.

You'll have plenty of chances to put your legendary patience to good use during your relationship with an Aquarius. At times, you may feel like tossing in the towel, but you'll never call it quits.

Aquarius is a good family man and father. He understands children as much as he loves them.

CANCER WOMAN
PISCES MAN

The Pisces man is perhaps the man you've been looking all over for, high and low—the man you thought didn't exist. As a lover, he'll be attentive and faithful.

The Pisces man is very sensitive and very romantic. Still, he is a reasonable person. He may wish on the moon, yet he's got enough good sense to know that it isn't made of green cheese.

He'll be very considerate of your every wish and whim. He will do his best to be a very compatible mate. The Pisces man is great for showering the object of his affection with all kinds of little gifts and tokens of his affection. He's just the right mixture of dreamer and realist that pleases most women.

When it comes to earning bread and butter, the strong Pisces man will do all right in the world. Quite often they are capable of rising to very high positions. Some do very well as writers or psychiatrists. He'll be as patient and understanding with you as you are with him.

One thing a Pisces man dislikes is pettiness. Anyone who delights in running another into the ground is almost immediately crossed off his list of possible mates. If you have even small grievances with any of your friends, don't tell him about them. He will be quite disappointed in you if you complain and criticize.

If you fall in love with a weak Pisces man, don't give up your job at the office before you get married. Better still: hang onto it a good while after the honeymoon; you may need it.

A funny thing about the man born under the sign of the Fishes is that he can be content almost anywhere. This is perhaps because he is inner-directed and places little value on some exterior things. In a shack or a palace, the Pisces man is capable of making the best of all possible adjustments. He won't kick up a fuss if the roof leaks or if the fence is in sad need of repair. He's got more important things on his mind. Still and all, the Pisces man is not lazy or aimless. It's important to understand that material gain is never a direct goal for him.

Pisces men have a way with the sick and troubled. He'll offer his shoulder to anyone in the mood for a good cry. He can listen to one hard-luck story after another without seeming to tire. Quite often he knows what is bothering someone before that person, himself, realizes what it is. It's almost intuitive with Pisces, it seems.

Children are often delighted with Pisces men. As fathers, they are never strict or faultfinding. They are encouraging and always permissive with their youngsters.

Man—Woman

CANCER MAN
ARIES WOMAN

The Aries woman may be too bossy and busy for you. Aries are ambitious creatures. They can become impatient with people who are more thorough and deliberate than they are, especially if they feel such people are taking too much time. The Aries woman is a fast worker. Sometimes she's so fast she forgets to look where she's going. When she stumbles or falls, it would be nice if you were there to grab her.

Aries are proud women. They don't like to be told "I told you so" when they err. Criticism can turn them into blocks of ice. Don't begin to think that the Aries woman frequently gets tripped up in her plans. Quite often they are capable of taking aim and hitting the bull's-eye. You'll be flabbergasted at times by their accuracy as well as by their ambition. On the other hand, because of your interest in being sure and safe, you're apt to spot a flaw in your Aries' plans before she does.

You are somewhat slower than Aries in attaining what you have your sights set on. Still, you don't make any mistakes along the way; you're almost always well-prepared.

The Aries woman is sensitive at times. She likes to be handled with gentleness and respect. Let her know that you love her for her brains as well as for her good looks. Never give her cause to become jealous. When your Aries date sees green, you'd better forget about sharing a rosy future together. Handle her with tender love and care and she's yours.

The Aries woman can be giving if she feels her partner is deserving. She is no iceberg; she responds to the proper flame. She needs a man she can look up to and feel proud of. If the shoe fits, put it on. If not, better put your sneakers back on and quietly tiptoe out of her sight. She can cause you heartache if you've made up your mind about her but she hasn't made up hers about you. Aries women are very demanding at times. Some of them are high-strung. They can be difficult if they feel their independence is being hampered.

The cultivated Aries woman makes a wonderful homemaker and hostess. She's clever in decorating and color use. Your house will be tastefully furnished. She'll see to it that it radiates harmony. Friends and acquaintances will love your Aries wife. She knows how to make everyone feel at home and welcome.

Although the Aries woman may not be keen on the responsibilities of motherhood, she is fond of children and the joy they bring.

CANCER MAN
TAURUS WOMAN
A Taurus woman could perhaps understand you better than most women. She is very considerate and loving. She is methodical and thorough in whatever she does. She knows how to take her time in doing things; she is anxious to avoid mistakes. Like you, she is a careful person. She never skips over things that may seem un-

important; she goes over everything with a fine-tooth comb.

Home is very important to the Taurus woman. She is an excellent homemaker. Although your home may not be a palace, it will become, under her care, a comfortable and happy abode. She'll love it when friends drop by for the evening. She is a good cook and enjoys feeding people well. No one will ever go away from your house with an empty stomach.

The Taurus woman is serious about love and affection. When she has taken a tumble for someone, she'll stay by him—for good, if possible. She will try to be practical in romance, to some extent. When she sets her cap for a man, she keeps after him until he's won her. Generally, the Taurus woman is a passionate lover, even though she may appear otherwise at first glance. She is on the lookout for someone who can return her affection fully. Taurus are sometimes given to fits of jealousy and possessiveness. They expect fair play in the area of marriage. When it doesn't happen, they can be bitingly sarcastic and mean.

The Taurus woman is easygoing. She's fond of keeping peace. She won't argue unless she has to. She'll do her best to keep a love relationship on even keel.

Marriage is generally a one-time thing for Taurus. Once they've made the serious step, they seldom try to back out of it. Marriage is for keeps. They are fond of love and warmth. With the right man, they turn out to be ideal wives.

The Taurus woman will respect you for your steady ways; she'll have confidence in your common sense.

Taurus women seldom put up with nonsense from their children. They are not so much strict as concerned. They like their children to be well-behaved and dutiful. Nothing pleases a Taurus mother more than a compliment from a neighbor or teacher about her child's behavior. Although children may inwardly resent the iron hand of a Taurus woman, in later life they are often thankful that they were brought up in such an orderly and conscientious way.

CANCER MAN
GEMINI WOMAN
The Gemini woman may be too much of a flirt ever to take your heart too seriously. Then again, it depends on what kind of mood she's in. Gemini women can change from hot to cold quicker than a cat can wink its eye. Chances are her fluctuations will tire you after a time, and you'll pick up your heart—if it's not already broken into small pieces—and go elsewhere. Women born under the sign of the Twins have the talent of being able to change their

moods and attitudes as frequently as they change their party dresses.

Sometimes, Geminis like to whoop it up. Some of them are good-time gals who love burning the candle to the wick. You'll always see them at parties and gatherings, surrounded by men of all types, laughing gaily or kicking up their heels at every opportunity. Wallflowers, they're not. The next day you may bump into her at the neighborhood library and you'll hardly recognize her for her sensible attire. She'll probably have five or six books under her arm—on five or six different subjects. In fact, she may even work there.

You'll probably find her a dazzling and fascinating creature—for a time, at any rate. Most men do. But when it comes to being serious about love you may find that your sparkling Eve leaves quite a bit to be desired. It's not that she has anything against being serious, it's just that she might find it difficult trying to be serious with you.

At one moment, she'll be capable of praising you for your steadfast and patient ways. The next moment she'll tell you in a cutting way that you're an impossible stick-in-the-mud.

Don't even begin to fathom the depths of her mercurial soul—it's full of false bottoms. She'll resent close investigation anyway, and will make you rue the day you ever took it into your head to try to learn more about her than she feels is necessary. Better keep the relationship fancy free and full of fun until she gives you the go-ahead sign. Take as much of her as she is willing to give; don't ask for more. If she does take a serious interest in you, then she'll come across with the goods.

There will come a time when Gemini will realize that she can't spend her entire life at the ball. The security and warmth you offer are just what she needs for a happy, fulfilled life.

The Gemini mother will be easygoing with her children. She'll probably spoil them and dote on their every whim. Because she has a youthful outlook, she will be a fun playmate for her kids.

**CANCER MAN
CANCER WOMAN**
The Cancer woman needs to be protected from the cold cruel world. She'll love you for your gentle and kind manner. You are the kind of man who can make her feel safe and secure.

You won't have to pull any he-man or heroic stunts to win her heart; she's not interested in things like that. She's more likely to be impressed by your sure, steady ways—the way you have of putting your arm around her and making her feel that she's the only girl in the world. When she's feeling glum and tears begin to well up in her eyes, you'll know how to calm her fears, no matter how silly some of them may seem.

The Moon Child, like you, is inclined to have her ups and downs. Perhaps you can both learn to smooth out the roughed-up spots in each other's life. She'll most likely worship the ground you walk on or place you on a very high pedestal. Don't disappoint her if you can help it. She'll never disappoint you. The Cancer woman will take great pleasure in devoting the rest of her natural life to you. She'll darn your socks, mend your overalls, scrub floors, wash windows, shop, cook, and do anything short of murder in order to please you and to let you know she loves you. Sounds like that legendary old-fashioned girl, doesn't it? Contrary to popular belief, there are still many of them around and the majority of them are Cancers.

Treat your Cancer mate fairly and she'll treat you like a king. There is one thing you should be warned about, though. Never be unkind to your mother-in-law. It will be the only golden rule your Cancer wife will expect you to live up to. Mother is something special for her. You should have no trouble in understanding this, for your mother has a special place in your heart, too. It's always that way with the Cancer-born. They have great respect and love for family ties. It might be a good idea for you both to get to know each other's relatives before tying the marriage knot, because after the wedding bells have rung, you'll be seeing a lot of them.

Of all the signs in the Zodiac, Cancer is the most maternal. In caring for and bringing up children, she knows just how to combine tenderness and discipline. A child couldn't ask for a better mother. Cancer women are sympathetic, affectionate, and patient with children. Both of you will make excellent parents, especially when the children are young. When they grow older you'll most likely be reluctant to let them go out into the world.

**CANCER MAN
LEO WOMAN**
The Leo woman can make most men roar like lions. If any woman in the Zodiac has that indefinable something that can make men lose their heads and find their hearts, it's Leo.

She's got more than a fair share of charm and glamour and she knows how to make the most of her assets, especially when she's in the company of the opposite sex. Jealous men lose either their cool or their sanity when trying to woo a woman born under the sign of the Lion. She likes to kick up her heels and doesn't care who knows it. She often makes heads turn and tongues wag. You don't have to believe any of what you hear—it's most likely just jealous gossip or wishful thinking. Needless to say, other women in her vicinity turn green with envy and will try anything to put her out of commission.

Although this vamp makes the blood rush to your head and makes you momentarily forget all the things you thought were important and necessary in your life, you may feel differently when you come back down to earth and the stars are out of your eyes. You may feel that although this vivacious creature can make you feel wonderful, she just isn't the type you planned to bring home to Mother. Not that your mother might disapprove of your choice—but you might after the shoes and rice are a thing of the past. Although the Leo woman may do her best to be a good wife for you, chances are she'll fall short of your idea of what a good wife should be.

If you're planning on not going as far as the altar with that Leo woman who has you flipping your lid, you'd better be financially equipped for some very expensive dating. Be prepared to shower her with expensive gifts and to take her dining and dancing to the smartest spots in town. Promise her the moon if you're in a position to go that far. Luxury and glamour are two things that are bound to lower a Leo's resistance. She has expensive tastes, and you'd better cater to them if you expect to get to first base with the Lioness.

If you've got an important business deal to clinch and you have doubts as to whether you can swing it or not, bring your Leo along to the business luncheon. Chances are that with her on your arm, you'll be able to win any business battle with both hands tied. She won't have to say or do anything—just be there at your side. The grouchiest oil magnate can be transformed into a gushing, obedient schoolboy if there's a charming Lioness in the room.

Leo mothers are blind to the faults of their children. They make very loving and affectionate mothers and tend to give their youngsters everything under the sun.

CANCER MAN
VIRGO WOMAN

The Virgo woman is particular about choosing her men friends. She's not interested in going out with anybody. She has her own idea of what a boyfriend or prospective husband should be. Perhaps that image has something of you in it.

Generally, she's quiet and correct. She doesn't believe that nonsense has any place in a love affair. She's serious about love and she'll expect you to be. She's looking for a man who has both feet on the ground—someone who can take care of himself as well as her. She knows the value of money and how to get the most out of a dollar. She's far from being a spendthrift. Throwing money around turns her stomach, even when it isn't her money.

She'll most likely be very shy about romancing. Even the simple act of holding hands may make her turn crimson—at least, on the first couple of dates. You'll have to make all the advances, and you'll have to be careful not to make any wrong moves. She's capable of showing anyone who oversteps the boundaries of common decency the door. It may even take quite a long time before she'll accept that goodnight kiss at the front gate. Don't give up. You are perhaps the kind of man who can bring out the warm woman in her.

There is love and tenderness underneath Virgo's seemingly frigid facade. It will take a patient and understanding man to bring it out into the open. She may have the idea that sex is reserved for marriage. Like you, she has a few old-fashioned concepts. And, like you, it's all or nothing. So if you are the right man, gentle and affectionate, you will melt her reserve.

When a Virgo has accepted you as a lover or mate, she won't stint in giving her love in return. You'll be surprised at the transformation your earnest attention can bring about in this quiet kind of woman. When in love, Virgos only listen to their hearts, not to what the neighbors say.

Virgo women are honest about love once they've come to grips with it. They don't appreciate hypocrisy—particularly in this area of life. They will always be true to their hearts—even if it means tossing you over for a new love. But if you convince her that you are earnest about your interest in her, she'll reciprocate your love and affection and never leave you. Do her wrong once, however, and you can be sure she'll call the whole thing off.

Virgo mothers are tender and loving. They know what's good for their children and will always take great pains in bringing them up correctly.

**CANCER MAN
LIBRA WOMAN**
It's a woman's prerogative to change her mind. This wise saying characterizes the Libra woman. Her changes of mind, in spite of her undeniable charm, might drive even a man of your changeable moods up the wall. She's capable of smothering you with love and kisses one day and on the next avoid you like the plague. If you think you're a man of great patience, then perhaps you can tol-

erate her sometime-ness without suffering too much. However, if you own up to the fact that you're a mere mortal who can only take so much, then you'd better fasten your attention on a girl who's somewhat more constant.

But don't get the wrong idea—a love affair with a Libra is not all bad. In fact, it can have an awful lot of pluses to it. Libra women are soft, very feminine, and warm. She doesn't have to vamp all over the place in order to gain a man's attention. Her delicate presence is enough to warm any man's heart. One smile and you're a piece of putty in the palm of her hand.

She can be fluffy and affectionate. On the other hand, her indecision about which dress to wear, what to cook for dinner, or whether or not to redecorate could make you tear your hair out. What will perhaps be more exasperating is her flat denial of the accusation that she cannot make even the simplest decision. The trouble is that she wants to be fair or just in all matters. She'll spend hours weighing both sides of an argument or situation. Don't make her rush into a decision; that would only irritate her.

The Libra woman likes to be surrounded by beautiful things. Money is no object when beauty is concerned. There will always be antiques and objects of art in her apartment. She'll know how to arrange them tastefully, too, to show them off. Women under this sign are fond of beautiful clothes and furnishings. They will run up bills without batting an eye—if given the chance.

Once she's cottoned to you, the Libra woman will do everything in her power to make you happy. She'll wait on you hand and foot when you're sick, bring you breakfast in bed on Sundays, and even read you the funny papers if you're too sleepy to open your eyes. She'll be very thoughtful and devoted. If anyone dares suggest you're not the grandest man in the world, your Libra wife will give that person a good sounding-out.

Libras work wonders with children. Gentle persuasion and affection are all she uses in bringing them up. Her subtlety sets a good example for them to follow.

CANCER MAN
SCORPIO WOMAN

When the Scorpio woman chooses to be sweet, she's apt to give the impression that butter wouldn't melt in her mouth . . . but, of course, it would. When her temper flies, so will everything else that isn't bolted down. She can be as hot as a tamale or as cool as a cucumber when she wants. Whatever mood she's in, you can be sure it's for real. She doesn't believe in poses or hypocrisy.

The Scorpio woman is often seductive and sultry. Her femme

fatale charm can pierce through the hardest of hearts like a laser ray. She doesn't have to look like Mata Hari (many of them resemble the tomboy next door) but once you've looked into those tantalizing eyes, you're a goner.

The Scorpio woman can be a whirlwind of passion. Life with her will not be all smiles and smooth sailing. If you think you can handle a woman who can spit bullets, try your luck. Your stable and steady nature will most likely have a calming effect on her. You're the kind of man she can trust and rely on. But never cross her—even on the smallest thing. If you do, you'd better tell Fido to make room for you in the doghouse—you'll be his guest for the next couple of days.

Generally, the Scorpio woman will keep family battles within the walls of your home. When company visits, she's apt to give the impression that married life with you is one big joyride. It's just her way of expressing her loyalty to you—at least in front of others. She believes that family matters are and should stay private. She certainly will see to it that others have a high opinion of you both.

Although she's an individualist, after she has married she'll put her own interests aside for those of the man she loves. With a woman like this behind you, you can't help but go far. She'll never try to take over your role as boss of the family. She'll give you all the support you need in order to fulfill that role. She won't complain if the going gets rough. She knows how to take the bitter with the sweet. She is a courageous woman. She's as anxious as you are to find that place in the sun for you both. She's as determined a person as you are.

Although Scorpio loves her children, she may not be too affectionate toward them. She'll make a devoted mother, though. She'll be anxious to see them develop their talents. She'll teach the children to be courageous and steadfast.

**CANCER MAN
SAGITTARIUS WOMAN**

The Sagittarius woman is hard to keep track of: first she's here, then she's there. She's a woman with a severe case of itchy feet. She's got to keep on the move.

People generally like her because of her hail-fellow-well-met manner and her breezy charm. She is constantly good-natured and almost never cross. With the female Archer you're likely to strike up a palsy-walsy relationship. You might not be interested in letting it go any farther. She probably won't sulk if you leave it on a friendly basis. Treat her like a kid sister and she'll love it.

She'll probably be attracted to you because of your restful, self-assured manner. She'll need a friend like you to help her over the rough spots in her life. She'll most likely turn to you for advice frequently.

There is nothing malicious about a woman born under this sign. She is full of bounce and good cheer. Her sunshiny disposition can be relied upon even on the rainiest of days. No matter what she says or does, you'll always know that she means well. Sagittarius are sometimes short on tact. Some of them say anything that comes into their heads, no matter what the occasion. Sometimes the words that tumble out of their mouths seem downright cutting and cruel; they mean well but often everything they say comes out wrong. She's quite capable of losing her friends—and perhaps even yours—through a careless slip of the lip. Always remember that she is full of good intentions. Stick with her if you like her and try to help her mend her ways.

She's may not be the quiet, home-loving woman you'd be interested in marrying, but she'll certainly be lots of fun to pal around with. Quite often, Sagittarius women are outdoor types. They're crazy about things like fishing, camping, and mountain climbing. They love the wide open spaces. They are fond of all kinds of animals. Make no mistake about it: this busy little lady is no slouch. She's full of pep and vigor.

She's great company most of the time; she's more fun than a three-ring circus when she's in the right company. You'll like her for her candid and direct manner. On the whole, Sagittarius are very kind and sympathetic women.

If you do wind up marrying this girl-next-door type, you'd better see to it that you take care of all financial matters. Sagittarius often let money run through their fingers like sand.

A Sagittarius mother may smother her children with love on the one hand, then give them all of the freedom they think they need. It can be very confusing.

**CANCER MAN
CAPRICORN WOMAN**

The Capricorn woman may not be the most romantic woman of the Zodiac, but she's far from frigid when she meets the right man. She believes in true love. She doesn't appreciate getting involved in flings. To her, they're just a waste of time. She's looking for a man who means business—in life as well as in love. Although she can be very affectionate with her boyfriend or mate, she tends to let her head govern her heart. That is not to say that she is a cool, calculating cucumber. On the contrary, she just feels she can be more honest about love if she consults her brains first. She wants to size up the situation first before throwing her heart in the ring. She wants to make sure it won't get stepped on.

The Capricorn woman is faithful, dependable, and systematic in just about everything that she undertakes. She is quite concerned with security and sees to it that every penny she spends is spent wisely. She is very economical about using her time, too. She does not believe in whittling away her energy on a scheme that is bound not to pay off.

Ambitious themselves, they are quite often attracted to ambitious men—men who are interested in getting somewhere in life. If a man of this sort wins her heart, she'll stick by him and do all she can to help him get to the top.

The Capricorn woman is almost always diplomatic. She makes an excellent hostess. She can be very influential when your business acquaintances come to dinner.

The Capricorn woman is likely to be very concerned, if not downright proud, about her family tree. Relatives are important to her, particularly if they're socially prominent. Never say a cross word about her family members. That can really go against her grain and she'll punish you by not talking for days.

She's generally thorough in whatever she does: cooking, housekeeping, entertaining. Capricorn women are well-mannered and gracious, no matter what their backgrounds. They seem to have it in their natures to always behave properly.

If you should marry a woman born under this sign, you need never worry about her going on a wild shopping spree. They understand the value of money better than most women. If you turn over your paycheck to her at the end of the week, you can be sure that a good hunk of it will go into the bank and that all the bills will be paid on time.

With children, the Capricorn mother is both loving and correct. She'll see to it that they're polite and respectful and that they honor the codes they are taught when young.

CANCER MAN
AQUARIUS WOMAN

The woman born under the sign of the Water Bearer can be odd and eccentric at times. Some say that this is the source of her mysterious charm. You may think she's just a plain screwball, and you may be right.

Aquarius women often have their heads full of dreams and stars in their eyes. By nature, they are often unconventional; they have their own ideas about how the world should be run. Sometimes their ideas may seem pretty weird—chances are they're just a little bit too progressive. There is a saying that runs: The way the Aquarius thinks, so will the world in fifty years.

If you find yourself falling in love with a woman born under this sign, you'd better fasten your safety belt. It may take some time before you know what she's like and even then, you may have nothing to go on but a string of vague hunches.

She can be like a rainbow: full of dazzling colors. She's like no other girl you've ever known. There is something about her that is definitely charming, yet elusive. You'll never be able to put your finger on it. She seems to radiate adventure and optimism without even trying. She'll most likely be the most tolerant and open-minded woman you've ever encountered.

If you find that she's too much mystery and charm for you to handle—and being a Cancer, chances are you might—just talk it out with her and say that you think it would be better if you called it quits. She'll most likely give you a peck on the cheek and say "Okay, but let's still be friends." Aquarius women are like that. Perhaps you'll both find it easier to get along in a friendship than in a romance.

It is not difficult for her to remain buddy-buddy with an ex-lover. For many Aquarius, the line between friendship and romance is a fuzzy one.

She's not a jealous person and while you're romancing her, she won't expect you to be, either. You'll find her a free spirit most of the time. Just when you think you know her inside out, you'll discover that you don't really know her at all. She's a very sympathetic and warm person. She is often helpful to those in need of assistance and advice.

She'll seldom be suspicious even when she has every right to be. If the man she loves makes a little slip, she's likely to forgive it and forget it.

Aquarius makes a fine mother. Her positive and bighearted qualities are easily transmitted to her children. They will be taught tolerance at an early age.

CANCER MAN
PISCES WOMAN

The Pisces woman places great value on love and romance. She's gentle, kind, and romantic. Like you, she has very high ideals, and will only give her heart to a man who she feels can live up to her expectations.

Many a man dreams of an alluring Pisces woman. You're perhaps no exception. Even though she appears soft and cuddly, she has a sultry, seductive charm that can win the heart of almost any man.

She will not try to wear the pants in the relationship. She'll let you be the brains of the family. She's content to play a behind-the-scenes role in order to help you achieve your goals.

She can be very ladylike and proper. Your business associates and friends will be dazzled by her warmth and femininity. Although she's a charmer, there is a lot more to her than just a pretty exterior. There is a brain ticking away behind that gentle, womanly facade. You may never become aware of it—that is, until you're married to her. It's no cause for alarm, however; she'll most likely never use it against you, only to help you and possibly set you on a more successful path.

If she feels you're botching up your married life through careless behavior or if she feels you could be earning more money than you do, she'll tell you about it. But any wife would.

No one had better dare say one uncomplimentary word about you in her presence. It could set the stage for an emotional scene. Pisces women are maddeningly temperamental and can go to theatrical extremes when expressing their feelings. Their reaction to adversity or frustration can run the gamut from tears to tantrums and back again.

She can do wonders with a house. She is very fond of dramatic and beautiful things. There will always be plenty of fresh-cut flowers around the house. She will choose charming artwork and antiques, if they are affordable.

She'll have an extra special dinner prepared for you when you come home from an important business meeting. Don't dwell on the boring details of the meeting, though. But if you need that big idea, to seal a contract or make a conquest, your Pisces woman is sure to confide a secret that will guarantee your success.

Treat her with tenderness and generosity and your relationship will be an enjoyable one. A bunch of beautiful flowers will never fail to make her eyes light up. See to it that you never forget her birthday or your anniversary. These things are very important to her.

If you are patient and kind, you can keep a Pisces woman happy for a lifetime. She, however, is not without her faults. You may find her lacking in practicality and good old-fashioned stoicism; you may even feel that she uses her tears as a method of getting her own way.

Pisces is a strong, self-sacrificing mother. She will teach her children the value of service to the community while not letting them lose their individuality.

CANCER
LUCKY NUMBERS 2001

Lucky numbers and astrology can be linked through the movements of the Moon. Each phase of the thirteen Moon cycles vibrates with a sequence of numbers for your Sign of the Zodiac over the course of the year. Using your lucky numbers is a fun system that connects you with tradition.

New Moon	First Quarter	Full Moon	Last Quarter
Dec. 25 ('00) **4 3 8 1**	Jan. 2 **1 5 8 0**	Jan. 9 **8 6 4 2**	Jan. 16 **4 9 7 8**
Jan. 24 **1 5 2 7**	Feb. 1 **5 9 3 7**	Feb. 8 **1 1 4 6**	Feb. 14 **8 4 6 1**
Feb. 23 **7 5 8 3**	March 2 **3 6 1 4**	March 9 **4 7 8 2**	March 16 **9 9 4 7**
March 24 **0 7 3 5**	April 1 **8 6 6 9**	April 7 **0 1 4 9**	April 15 **2 6 9 0**
April 23 **7 9 2 5**	April 30 **9 3 6 1**	May 7 **1 6 8 3**	May 15 **6 7 4 9**
May 22 **1 4 2 2**	May 29 **2 5 7 9**	June 5 **5 7 2 5**	June 13 **1 3 4 1**
June 21 **4 8 8 4**	June 27 **1 2 6 2**	July 5 **4 8 3 9**	July 13 **0 3 7 1**
July 20 **1 5 7 1**	July 27 **5 1 0 3**	August 4 **7 2 8 2**	August 12 **4 9 6 9**
August 18 **7 1 5 5**	August 25 **5 7 2 5**	Sept. 2 **6 3 6 8**	Sept. 10 **7 4 8 2**
Sept. 17 **2 5 9 9**	Sept. 24 **6 8 3 6**	Oct. 2 **4 7 2 5**	Oct. 9 **8 3 3 6**
Oct. 16 **7 1 6 8**	Oct. 23 **3 7 0 7**	Nov. 1 **1 3 5 8**	Nov. 8 **3 6 9 2**
Nov. 15 **4 9 2 9**	Nov. 22 **3 1 4 6**	Nov. 30 **8 2 9 9**	Dec. 7 **6 3 7 3**
Dec. 14 **5 9 3 1**	Dec. 22 **9 4 4 7**	Dec. 30 **2 5 5 0**	Jan. 5 ('02) **0 8 6 4**

CANCER
YEARLY FORECAST 2001

*Forecast for 2001 Concerning Business
and Financial Affairs, Job Prospects,
Travel, Health, Romance and Marriage
for Those Born with the Sun
in the Zodiacal Sign of Cancer.
June 21–July 20*

For those born under the influence of the Sun in the zodiacal sign of Cancer, ruled by the changeable and intuitive Moon, this promises to be a positive and deeply satisfying year. Your more confident attitude toward life favors success in work and business matters. You could uncover and develop skills that have been dormant for several years. This feeling of being better able to cope with the practical side of life means that small problems will lose their power to upset you to any significant degree. Cancers who are in business could make some lucrative investments in areas such as the arts and technology. Catering to the masses will probably become an increasingly more important area of your enterprise. Financially, this should be quite a prosperous and stable year. A raise in salary could enable you to salt away significant savings. However, it would be wise to get expert advice before investing any large sums on a long-term basis. This is apt to be a year when you travel less than usual. All the same, a vacation spent with friends can be highly enjoyable. And attraction to more exotic locations could arise during the later months. Health matters look promising, with the possibility of a new treatment curing an old problem. Try to keep up sensible eating and exercising, not least because you might put on a bit too much weight otherwise. Where romance is concerned, single Cancers may meet someone quite outside the usual social circle. Getting to know this person and appreciate their ideas can be both stimulating and romantic. A long-term relationship may enter a new phase as the feelings are rekindled that you had for each other when you first met. A brief separation might occur, which could make you both realize how attached you are to each other. All new starts are favored, whether in a new partnership or within a long-standing relationship.

The year 2001 is likely to find you working harder at business affairs and then reaping the appropriate rewards. You may have to take over a colleague's responsibilities, at least for a while; this could necessitate developing new skills. Dealing with board members and working groups is one area in which you will gain expertise, so that it becomes easier to persuade other people to back you on important decisions. During the first months of the year you might be required to work behind the scenes on a large project. Then it is likely that you will step into the limelight as July progresses, ready to take full credit for all of your hard work. There are unusual and perhaps very lucrative investments to be made in the media, arts, and new technology. It will help to build up contacts in these areas who can tip you off regarding the latest developments. You might need to get your business account checked more carefully than usual since there is a possibility of mistakes being made by the bank. The terms of all large financial transactions should be made as clear as possible in order to guard against misunderstanding on either side. Cancer people who are involved in selling should pay more attention to research and development. Updating and overall improving is bound to boost sales. During the year working practices should be reviewed and overhauled to some extent. Relations between management and employees often require sensitive handling, which is just what Cancer folk are good at doing. It can be a good investment to offer employees better facilities, such as a gym or child-care center, if that will strengthen their loyalty to the company.

Your financial situation looks promising. After a period when you had to meet quite a few big expenses, you can now relax and begin to get more pleasure out of pure self-indulgent spending. Those luxuries will seem all the more precious because they were out of your reach for a while. At the same time, there are almost sure to be good opportunities to save. You might be given a raise at work, or offered extra pay for a period. It would be sensible to bank all extra income, or at least as much of it as you can live without. Joint savings will rise and fall during the year. Coordinating savings efforts with your mate or partner so that at least one of you puts money into your account each week should even things out a bit. As a Cancer you are usually quite cautious when it comes to investing. This year it would certainly be wise to seek the best advice before committing funds for the long term. It is not too soon to start considering your pension, although at first you might be quite bewildered at the variety being offered. This is a good time to start shopping around and considering what would suit you and your retirement expectations. If you are loaning money to a friend, it is a sound idea to write down your agreement and each keep a copy. This may seem fussy and formal, but it can save misunderstandings later on. A small legacy from a distant relative could come as a welcome surprise. Unless you use the money for a specific purpose, it will probably just melt away with little to show for it. Try to be practical with your spare cash as well as splurging on pure pleasure.

Your job prospects this year are likely to improve dramatically, with the possibility of new responsibilities in your present job or a lucrative change of employment if you are looking for new work. You may become more interested in researching purely theoretical aspects of your job, and becoming something of an expert. Cancer people who are casting around in search of a new and more satisfying career could be drawn to advertising or psychology. Opportunities to perform in support of someone who is in the limelight could give you exciting insights into the world of the media and the celebrity lifestyle. Charitable ventures are highlighted. Even if you do not work for a benevolent organization, you may wish to do some fund-raising within your workplace. It is more important than usual that you have a chance to fulfill your personal ethics and ideals through your work. If this is not really possible, you could find it deeply satisfying to offer some hours of volunteer work to an organization dedicated to a cause you support with all your heart.

Although you may not be the greatest traveler as a rule, there are some alluring possibilities for having a great deal of fun this year. A vacation with a few friends could be especially inspiring. Being in a crowd may encourage you to try sports and excursions that are more adventurous than your usual pursuits. A business conference might not at first appeal to you as a way of passing several days, but you can make very useful contacts as well as obtaining important information. This is a good year to take a winter break, or at least start leafing through travel brochures on the long dark evenings. If you decide to head for the winter sun, it would be a good idea to pick a destination that is more exotic than usual, or a more daring form of travel such as overland trekking. A getaway that involves little more than just lying on a beach could boost your self-confidence and give you inspiration for more adventure in the future.

Improvements to your health could come from a new treatment for a problem that has been a minor irritation for years. A new sense of well-being should make life more enjoyable. It would be good to keep up any diet and exercise regime you have been following. If you rest on your laurels, there is a distinct possibility of putting on more weight than is comfortable. Since you are quite likely to be working harder than usual during the year, give some attention to methods of winding down at the end of the day. Relaxation techniques such as breathing exercises, meditation, or yoga can be very helpful. Keep in mind that your body has seasons, during which your energy level fluctuates. Rely on your good Cancer intuition and do not push yourself to perform when you are really longing to rest. From the beginning of the year to February 13, it is best to keep your exercise to a reasonable level and avoid strenuous sports. Use the cycle of the year to build up your muscular power, so that by the end of December you are in topnotch condition.

Romance and relationships can be not only a source of great pleasure but also a certain amount of learning, both for single Cancers and couples. When you closely examine how your expectations of your mate or partner actually match up to reality, you will begin to see where you could be making some unreasonable demands. That could lead you to relax more, so that the relationship begins to go more smoothly. From July 12 until the end of the year, Cancer singles who are looking for a new partner only have to ask in order to get a date. There will be a special charm about you which makes other people want to please you. Just do not forget that you need to give as well as take. The period between September 8 and October 26 needs gentle handling, especially if you are already in an established relationship. Outbursts of anger could spoil an otherwise starred time. The secret is not to brood until you reach a point where you cannot help exploding. Cancer men and women are usually sensitive to loved ones' needs, but a little extra effort to please can oil the wheels of your relationship. Small acts of kindness and shows of affection will make this a year in which you discover the secrets of an enduring harmonious relationship.

CANCER DAILY FORECAST

January–December 2001

JANUARY

1. MONDAY. Fair. As the new year begins, you are apt to be in a rather indecisive mood about love. It is all very well making resolutions to be more assertive, but when the chips are down you must guard against being too willing to compromise. If you are not getting the love you want and need, start looking elsewhere. Think about going on a vacation trip with a group of close friends. You need not plan anything too physical; even a quiet week in the country would be a pleasant break. Today is not the best time to think about personal money matters. Your usual good Cancer sense is not as much in evidence as usual, so savings or budgeting plans might not be realistic.

2. TUESDAY. Variable. As a Cancer you are often happiest working behind the scenes, supporting someone who relishes the limelight. This is very true today. Make the most of your ability to put practical arrangements into place for a colleague who is busy negotiating a business deal. Your financial hunches may seem off the wall to other people, but it would not hurt to follow your instincts if you think you are onto a good investment. Just be cautious about how much money you commit all at once. On the home front, you and your mate or partner may be pulling in different directions. You need to decide if your own ambitions are really as important as keeping the relationship strong and vital.

3. WEDNESDAY. Good. Love of the exotic is featuring more strongly in all aspects of your life. Do not be surprised if you find yourself hungry for ethnic food and eager to experiment with foreign recipes. At least this is one way of learning about distant cultures. It never hurts to set your sights high where love is concerned. You deserve someone who can fulfill your mental aspirations as well as engaging your emotions. Do not hide your light under a bushel. On a practical level, many small daily tasks around the house can be gotten out of the way in record time. Once you set your mind to them, it should be a positive pleasure to make your environment brighter and cleaner.

4. THURSDAY. Challenging. If you want to get the best out of this challenging day, network as much as possible. Use your ability to set people at ease and to persuade colleagues to work together. Close friendships need careful handling; someone near you is determined to take offense. It could be that they are simply looking for an excuse to argue with you, but you should not fall into the trap. There are some situations in which it is fatal to be vague. You need to speak up and give your frank opinion in a work meeting if you are asked for it even though it might not be popular. An evening out on the town with friends is likely to be fun but tiring.

5. FRIDAY. Tricky. A budding friendship with someone who has been training you at work may not be all that it seems. If you feel at all uncomfortable, that is almost certainly a sign that the other person is becoming romantically attracted to you. Do all that you can to let them down gently. Trying to send money to relatives abroad can be not only expensive but less straightforward than it at first appears. Be prepared to spend quite a lot of time checking on the safe arrival of your letter or package. One bonus of dating a new person is that you get introduced to their friends, expanding your own social circle without any extra effort on your part.

6. SATURDAY. Low-keyed. Be extra patient with yourself this morning. You are likely to be feeling rather tired at the end of the week and should not force yourself into any social situation that does not really appeal. Focus on your inner world. Go through old letters and mementos, allowing past memories to fully occupy your mind. In this way much inner healing can take place quietly and with a minimum of tears. A romantic partner may seem ready to go out all the time, whereas you would prefer to stay in on occasion for a cozy evening by the fire. This is a good time to discuss these differences and come to an arrangement that will suit you both in the long term. Do not seem too eager tonight.

7. SUNDAY. Auspicious. This is a great day for children to bring friends home to play. Organize an impromptu party for them, then join in the games yourself. All relationships are strengthened or broken by good communication. Right now you have the chance to sort out lots of minor problems with that special person in your life by spending a couple of hours together and talking it all out. Plans to work around the home could be spoiled by the demands of one or more family members. Dealing with a child's bruised knee or a sister's relationship woes has to take precedence over regular chores. Try not to let the day go by without taking some photos of loved ones and pets.

8. MONDAY. Sparkling. If you are looking for romance, you can make yourself almost irresistible to that special person. Do not have any qualms about turning on the charm and dressing to impress. Keep in mind that all's fair in love and war. As a Cancer you feel more secure with money earning a good rate of return. Right now you should be considering overseas investments, but seek professional advice before you act. Life can be more interesting if you allow your mind to lead you down strange paths. You could add sparkle to your daily existence by signing up for an evening class. Not only will you learn something, but it is a good way to make new friends, too.

9. TUESDAY. Demanding. A certain close relationship is likely to come under the microscope. If you have been hesitating between breaking off the relationship or going on with it, that decision must not be made lightly. Try to weather the current crisis in order to give yourself some extra time to probe your true feelings for this person. A business deal could put you under considerable pressure to act against your basic Cancer instincts. Whatever happens, do not let yourself be talked into a decision that is purely a compromise. All things considered, you deserve to relax this evening. It would be ideal to find time for a hobby that is absorbing enough to make you forget the outside world.

10. WEDNESDAY. Changeable. Sometimes it takes a special kind of courage to keep quiet. If a friend upsets you, but you know they did not mean to do so, there is little point exposing all of your complicated feelings to them. A stiff upper lip can save the matter from blowing up out of all proportion. Taking responsibility for your life involves accepting that only you can reach your desired aims. Although you can lean on other people to a certain extent, all really important work has to be done by you and you alone. When youngsters talk back or refuse to obey, you really have no choice but to be firm with them unless you want them to lose respect for you.

11. THURSDAY. Interesting. Even though it may not be obvious, you have a great deal to contribute to a current work project. Your patience and research skills can be invaluable, so do not let other people steal your thunder. If you have always been interested in your family history, begin now to take steps to find out about it. There can be a great deal of information tucked away in records in local libraries or at newspaper offices. Although normally cautious with money, you may have been exceeding your budget recently with nights out and expensive entertainment. When the bills begin to come in, it might be necessary to be honest with friends and admit that you prefer to stay home more often.

12. FRIDAY. Stressful. The end of the workweek is likely to be a tough time. A job that has not been finished on schedule must now be completed in a real hurry, which could well mean working overtime. For you as a Cancer, friends can be a kind of second family. You are likely to expect their unquestioning support, sometimes forgetting that they have their own issues to deal with. Try to understand that not all friends are willing or even able to let you cry on their shoulder, especially if you need to do so often. Blocked traffic could make traveling tedious this evening. Call home and explain that you might be late or you risk a burnt dinner.

13. SATURDAY. Hectic. Although you may go out this morning feeling quite excited about shopping for an exotic gift, be aware that you might not be able to find the ideal present. And if you do so, it is bound to be very expensive. Keeping up a relationship over a long distance is challenging during the best of times. You are bound to want to spend more time than is possible with that special person, and it can be disappointing when a get-together has to be canceled. Even though Cancer people are not fanatic about keeping fit, a local health club is likely to have facilities that can be quite enjoyable. At least consider stopping by with a friend to check out what is available.

14. SUNDAY. Fulfilling. It can be extremely beneficial to a close relationship when you socialize with mutual friends. Even if there is some tension between you and your mate or partner, it tends to evaporate once you are in a warm and welcoming atmosphere, with the focus of attention no longer on your differences. This is a great day for using your good Cancer intuition. Insights into your emotions are worth writing down so that you do not forget them. Youngsters should be encouraged in all artistic activities. The smallest talent will develop if it is fostered from an early age. This evening favors indulging in an escapist film to your heart's content, with a box of chocolates at your side.

15. MONDAY. Rewarding. Cancer people hoping to sell their home could get a good offer out of the blue. There is no need to hurry with this; make sure all contractual obligations are cleared up before you sign anything. There is no reason you should not aid youngsters' education by helping them at home. Your own special areas of knowledge should very effectively complement what is being taught at school. The end of a work project clears the way for a more interesting period in which you have greater control over what you do and with whom. You have proved your ability to work independently and with a responsible no-nonsense attitude.

16. TUESDAY. Uneasy. It is not always easy getting along with your mate or partner's family. If you allow yourself to focus on real or imagined rudeness, you are hardly paving the way to better understanding. Instead, why not be the one to hold out the olive branch of peace. Cancers who have gardens may feel that there is little to do at this time of year. However, an hour's work outside will probably convince you that winter maintenance is time-consuming if it is not to get out of hand. Taking a day off from work because you feel under the weather is unlikely to make you popular with a co-worker who has to fill in for you. Just be sure you are not exaggerating your symptoms for the sake of a rest.

17. WEDNESDAY. Surprising. The stirring up of deep feelings may take you by surprise, catapulting you into a romantic situation that might be unwanted or even inappropriate. Everyone gets carried away sometimes, and there is nothing too wrong in that. However, it can be difficult extricating yourself from an impulsive entanglement. The lure of foreign lands is often very strong during dark winter days. Cheer yourself up by getting a few travel brochures and planning a real adventure. Children could benefit from a bit of extra coddling. Their fears and worries will soon disappear if you assure them of your enduring love and protection.

18. THURSDAY. Volatile. Today's rather volatile atmosphere makes it difficult to settle down to routine tasks. You might find yourself having to apologize to a teacher or senior staff member, just to keep them from losing their temper. Where love is concerned, you run a real risk of letting an important relationship break up over nothing much at all. It is probably not enough to air hidden resentments that you have been harboring; these have to be worked out on an inner level. Try not to commit yourself to certain social obligations just to impress a new friend. This is unlikely to work anyway, and you could wind up being bored by entertainment that is not your thing at all.

19. FRIDAY. Sensitive. There is apt to be more going on among colleagues than meets the eye. You are bound to pick up snippets of gossip about a possible promotion, but dismiss such rumors for now, or at least until you hear them from a reputable source. Everyone gets occasional inklings that there is more to life than material possessions. As a Cancer you are a sensitive enough person to be aware that such feelings are not easily dismissed. It would help right now to discuss such feelings with a friend who has more religious or philosophical knowledge than you and who could guide your thoughts along positive lines. Take life slow and easy tonight.

20. SATURDAY. Bumpy. It is very important not to let children get you angry and out of control, no matter what the provocation. Even if they interrupt precious time you earmarked for pursuing a favorite hobby, they are not to blame for putting their own needs first. Now more than ever it is vital to keep from saying harsh things to your mate or partner. A cutting remark is never forgotten, even if it was only meant as a joke. This is a great day for getting on with in-depth cleaning around the house. Move furniture that usually stays in one place and there is no saying what might be revealed, from loose change to long-forgotten jewelry.

21. SUNDAY. Promising. On one level this should be a very focused day. However, it is up to you to choose to concentrate on some serious reading or on going out and cutting loose with friends. A quick glance at your financial situation could reveal a more optimistic picture than expected. Your savings should be coming along well, so that at last your future looks more secure than ever before. It is never easy to discuss a future legacy with loved ones, but today an aunt or uncle may be anxious to let you know what they will be leaving to you. This is a chance for you to draw closer to them emotionally. Also be sure that your own will is current.

22. MONDAY. Chancy. Schemes to make quick money rarely if ever work out as promised. Take a long, hard look at anyone offering anything along this line. Decide if they really seem trustworthy. If you have plans to map out for work or pleasure, this is a very promising day to settle down to them. Problems will be more easily solved than usual, especially a work matter since it should be possible to find colleagues to whom to delegate some of your responsibility. This can be a good day for telling youngsters the facts of life, especially if you have been putting off such a discussion for some time. It is likely to be slightly more embarrassing for you than for them.

23. TUESDAY. Delightful. Sometimes it is wise to act on your first impulse. If you have been wondering whether to ask someone for a date, there is only one way to find out if you are going to be lucky. Today is a propitious moment to begin a new plan of exercise. Pledging to go running or to the gym with a friend will help keep you to your word. Friends made while you are away on vacation are often never heard from again, but today you might be delighted to receive a letter from someone you met last year. If there is a possibility of exchanging visits, that could make a nice extra vacation. Spend the evening with the person who means the most to you.

24. WEDNESDAY. Complicated. Although you may imagine that you are getting very close to someone you have been going out with for a while, the relationship is unlikely to be that simple. There may well be aspects of their life they have been hiding from you, and with good reason. Your dreams are likely to stay with you in a haunting kind of a way, making it hard to concentrate. That is a sure sign there is a message for you to decipher that is quite urgent. Where joint finances are concerned, it has never been more important to seek expert advice. After all, your mate or partner's money is at stake as well as your own. Leave the past where it belongs; do not brood over painfully sad memories.

25. THURSDAY. Illuminating. If you are tuned in to your inner world, it should be possible to feel the big shifts that are occurring in two areas. A greater sense of idealism should begin asserting itself, combined with a growing sense of compassion for those who are less well-off than you. You may want to consider volunteering some time to a local charity. Turning your back on a friend in need is not going to help either of you. Even if you have no experience in dealing with their particular problem, you can still give emotional support. Your health could benefit from an alternative remedy such as herbal teas and flower essences, which at least have no negative side effects.

26. FRIDAY. Confusing. Not everyone who is superior to you at work is capable of giving clear orders. It would be sensible to double-check with a colleague if you are told to do things that do not quite make sense. Financially this is a vulnerable time. Major expenses have made quite a dent in your savings, so that the challenge now is to begin building them up once again. Romance could sweep you off your feet. Although this can be an exhilarating feeling, recognize that sooner or later you will come back down to earth. All the same, the person you are so attracted to may remain special even if they do not become a permanent part of your life.

27. SATURDAY. Problematic. Taking up a new sport can be irresistible, but if it involves an element of danger then think again. Seeking thrills for their sake alone is not really your style. You would be better off sticking to gentler activity involving less physical danger. It is said that fools rush in where angels fear to tread, and that seems to be what you are doing if pursuing a romantic partner whose affections are clearly directed elsewhere. This can be a lovely day to go out with good friends. Pick a destination none of you has visited before, preferably where you can relax completely. You do not have to spend a lot of money to have fun; some of the best things in life are free.

28. SUNDAY. Refreshing. This is definitely not a day to stay close to home unless you are absolutely backed into doing so. Get out and about and you will soon feel deeply refreshed. A romantic liaison could take on a whole new life if you spend time alone together enjoying the peace of the countryside or of a local park. Wrap up warm and the weather will be forgotten in the pleasure of being in each other's arms. Cancer people who are in a more introspective mood may want to browse through some good travel pamphlets. You like to travel mentally in the comfort of your own home as much as actually journeying. Remember to keep in touch with friends and family members who live at a distance.

29. MONDAY. Positive. There is a surprising amount you can do to plan a career change. Your aspirations should all fall into place, helping you to realize just what training you need to alter direction and how to go about getting it. Even though you do not always like taking personal responsibility, it may be inevitable to do so when a colleague gets sick. You should soon realize that your good relationships with other people at work are paying off. Use a little imagination to make a tough decision about moving. It does not hurt to know what your dream house would be, even if you are unlikely to be able to afford it. Deciding what you want and do not want is half the battle.

30. TUESDAY. Helpful. It never hurts to have someone in authority who you can turn to at difficult moments. Right now a bank manager or financial adviser can help swing a difficult financial situation to your advantage. Concentrate on improving your health and fitness; you should be amazed at the results in only a few short weeks. You can afford to make quite drastic changes to your diet, cutting out sugar completely if you feel strong-willed enough to do so. Pets may need some extra exercise. Do not just throw on a shabby coat to walk the dog; there is no telling who you might meet. Keep in mind that animals make an ideal talking point, even to a stranger you would like to meet.

31. WEDNESDAY. Encouraging. If you are going on a job interview, speak up and do not attempt to bluff your way. You should make a very positive impression, so aim to be as confident as possible. It is not always easy to know how to help a friend in distress, but right now practical assistance in the form of a loan would get them over a difficult time. You may not yet fully realize how emotional problems can be lessened once money ceases to be a major worry. Youngsters should be doing quite well at school, even beginning to be given responsible tasks. It might also be a good idea to give them jobs to do at home to make them feel more grown-up and capable.

FEBRUARY

1. THURSDAY. Confusing. Your mind is likely to wander far from what you should be concentrating on. This may actually be useful just as long as it does not lead to poor decision-making. Romantically you may not quite know how you feel about a certain new person in your life. Sometimes this person may look like the ideal partner, while at other times you have doubts about getting involved. At the moment it would be best not to jump in at the deep end. Joint finances are almost certainly best left alone; do not get involved now in any new investments. Concentrate on saving, coming up with an agreed policy between you and your mate or partner.

2. FRIDAY. Tricky. Quite a lot of activity at work brings the workweek to a more hectic conclusion than you would like. Business meetings may lead to character clashes, forcing you to smooth ruffled feathers. The temptation with romance is to throw caution to the winds. But even if you think you have been patient for too long, try to hold on little while longer. A too hasty move now would probably prove disastrous. This is a better time for enjoying the company of good friends than for looking for love. An ideal evening out should start at an exotic restaurant where you can dine well and relax thoroughly without trying to make a good impression.

3. SATURDAY. Productive. This ideal day for doing practical work should inspire you to take a fresh look at your home. Put some extra vigor into housework and do-it-yourself tasks designed to revitalize your surroundings. All matters of the heart may seem to be stalled at the moment. It would be unwise to try to kick-start any affair. Love has its own rhythm, which should not be tampered with. Socializing with friends can be surprisingly demanding. You may begin to think about the age group you are usually with. Perhaps it would be stimulating to meet some younger people, since their outlook can be refreshing, and a good balance to any tendency toward cynicism.

4. SUNDAY. Serene. Conditions should be fairly quiet, at least in the sense that the phone will not interrupt what you are trying to do. This is a good time to have a heart-to-heart talk with youngsters and begin to instill them with a more serious sense of responsibility. At the same time, however, do not take the fun out of life by expecting too much too soon. If you are looking for romance, decide whether you would rather fantasize about it or risk meeting an actual person. Although coming to terms with a real live human being can be the hardest part of relating, as long as you feel up to it this could be an excellent day to begin a love affair. A formal social gathering is apt to be your best hunting ground.

5. MONDAY. Challenging. The morning offers the best chance of asserting yourself in a critical work situation. Your judgment could be called into question; stand up to criticism, defend your actions, and prove that you are right. Cancer people who are caring for children should find this a pleasant and rewarding day. Young minds can be exposed to exciting subjects such as space travel and technology; you will probably be amazed by the way youngsters grasp quite complex subjects. Although this is a good time to start thinking about a relaxing break, do not spring the idea on your mate or partner as a surprise because it may well clash with plans they have made independently.

6. TUESDAY. Successful. You should be glad to be given a second chance today to do some in-depth research, since your first attempt was probably rather fumbling. This time around you know better where to look for information and how to retrieve it in order to give a work project just the boost it needs. Old habits die hard, so be easy on yourself if you crave sugar, caffeine, or cigarettes shortly after giving them up. Your body will reeducate itself to do without, but this takes time and patience on your part. It is good to be able to give a friend some useful financial advice based on your own experience. They will feel like they are in the presence of an expert, which is sure to raise your self-esteem.

7. WEDNESDAY. Good. Just by keeping your head down at work and quietly getting on with your job you may be given the chance to make some extra money. A senior staff member is almost sure to notice that it is safe to leave you with responsible tasks, which is an invaluable reputation. Love that has been nourished in secret may burst out into the open, with a declaration that takes you by surprise. Although you will doubtless be flattered, you may decide not to get too involved at this point. Money may seem to be running through your hands like water at the moment. Consider whether you are spending it wisely or frittering it away with little to show as a result.

8. THURSDAY. Chancy. You are at a turning point where an emotional entanglement is concerned. An affair that has been on-again, off-again for several years may no longer offer you much pleasure. It is now time to decide whether you would prefer to end the relationship or go for full commitment. This is not the wisest time to make a major financial decision. You are likely to receive advice to put your money in property, but that is a serious step to take unless you are absolutely sure of being able to manage the accompanying high taxes and costs. There is no point trying to fill the role of counselor for a close friend if they need professional help; gently tell them how to obtain the guidance they require.

9. FRIDAY. Stormy. Even though on the surface you appear to be quite an easygoing person, there are limits to what you are prepared to accept. At the moment you risk getting into trouble by lashing out at an unreasonable employer. Try to rein in your temper; put your grievances in writing once you feel calmer. Close emotional relationships are always somewhat stormy, partly because you get to know each other's weaknesses so well. Unless you want to sever ties with someone who is very dear to you, some extra tolerance is necessary. There could be problems at school that youngsters are keeping to themselves; try to draw them out so that you can help resolve the situation.

10. SATURDAY. Fair. Your usual leisure pursuits may just not seem to satisfy or engage your attention as they used to do. The reason is that you appear to need deeper and more meaningful activity. Although it would be a good idea to get some extra exercise, you will not get much benefit skipping from one thing to another. If you decide to go jogging, do it wholeheartedly rather than giving up to play a game instead. This is a good day to get on the phone to old friends. They will give you the understanding and effortless support that newer acquaintances just cannot match no matter how hard they try. Keep evening plans flexible until the last minute.

11. SUNDAY. Happy. Someone you have long admired is likely to reciprocate your feelings and may finally admit to wanting to spend more time just with you. For this reason it is vital to look your best and prepare yourself for a profoundly romantic encounter. A close relative could come up with a surprising suggestion for making money. Their experience with the media and with a glamour industry may be just what you need to begin a new and unusual area of your life, where large sums of money are thrown around quite casually. Try to find time to do a good turn. Visiting a friend who is in the hospital may not strike you as an ideal weekend pastime, but it will mean a great deal to them.

12. MONDAY. Variable. Group activities at work are apt to be fraught with all kinds of minor problems due to people not communicating clearly. If you are in a position to take responsibility, do your best to make sure everyone issues commands in one-syllable words. It would do children a lot of good to get out more in order to widen their social circle. Do not let them spend too much time at home in front of the television or the computer screen; what they need is creative playtime with friends who will stimulate their minds. If you are worried about keeping physically fit, monitor how much energy you spend on ordinary work around the house; it is good exercise.

13. TUESDAY. Disappointing. As long as you continue yearning for someone who really is not interested in a relationship, then you are inevitably heading for heartache. Why do this to yourself when there are so many other eligible people from whom to choose. No matter how great the temptation, all kinds of gambling should be considered strictly off-limits. Anyone who tries to persuade you otherwise probably stands to gain from your almost certain loss. Sometimes writing down your innermost feelings can be extremely therapeutic. You do not have to show what you write to anyone; just scribble down enough to clarify your thoughts and ease your heart.

14. WEDNESDAY. Uneasy. There is always an element of risk in love because you never really know what you are getting into until it is too late. Right now it would be wise to trust your good Cancer instincts and hold back from a relationship that would probably be extremely stressful. Two sides of your character may well be fighting for supremacy. While part of you just wants to go out and have fun, at the same time you long to delve into the meaning of life and the mysteries of existence. Actually, however, if you adopt the right attitude you should be able to see meaning in even apparently superficial areas of life. Do not allow older friends to turn you against a new acquaintance.

15. THURSDAY. Upsetting. If you hold back feelings that really need to be expressed, you could end up feeling physically ill. For this reason it is vital to take a deep breath and let your colleague or family members know that they are upsetting you on a deep level. Just do so tactfully. This is a good moment to take a second look at ongoing financial problems. Shortage of cash need not be an insoluble difficulty; seek expert advice to see if there are ways your money can be put to better use. There is not much point trying to seduce someone just to prove that you can do it. In fact, you could land yourself in a very awkward situation if you manage to truly arouse their feelings.

16. FRIDAY. Mixed. Put some thought into ways of beautifying your surroundings, particularly if your work environment leaves something to be desired. Even a few plants can bring life and a more relaxed atmosphere into impersonal rooms and offices. Cancer people who are looking for a better job are unlikely to sneak into a rewarding position through the back door. It is thus essential not to try any tricks once you get as far as being interviewed. Promising favors you have no intention of fulfilling is not going to give a good impression of your character. Take some extra care with your health by refusing to get into activities that would stress you to the max.

17. SATURDAY. Pleasurable. This promises to be a highly enjoyable day as you find new pleasure in everyday activities. For a start, shopping for household goods may hold extra interest, especially if you come across some unusual kitchen gadgets. It would not do you any harm to adopt a new exercise program. If you carry on with one certain pattern of exercise for too long, it becomes increasingly less beneficial. If youngsters have been agitating recently for a pet, on a whim you may now be willing to adopt a cat or a dog. This can be a good opportunity for everyone in the family to learn shared responsibility, taking turns feeding and grooming the pet.

18. SUNDAY. Uneven. Today's restless mood is likely to pull you away from home. It would certainly be fun just to get up and go, perhaps to enjoy a lunch in a picturesque setting. If you find yourself mulling over subjects that usually do not bother you, get some books and read a little. It certainly will not hurt to bone up on politics and religion, if only for the sake of being better informed. Close relationships are apt to be rather tricky. Every couple needs time apart in order to appreciate each other more, but keep in mind that your motivation for going off alone can easily be misunderstood by a person who feels lonely or sorry for themselves. Turn down an invitation to go out tonight.

19. MONDAY. Frustrating. As a Cancer you are not normally the sort of person to throw your weight around. Today, however, you could find yourself really getting annoyed at your colleagues. The question is whether they would be better left to get on with what they are doing without the benefit of your advice. A very strict diet may seem like a good idea, and you will probably get off to a flying start. Just remember that Rome was not built in a day; a more cautious approach will help you develop the persistence you really need to drop weight and then to keep it off. An old friend could help you out with business advice as their experience enables you to visualize the solution to a knotty problem.

20. TUESDAY. Disconcerting. The last-minute cancellation of a business trip could upset your plans. However, this may be a blessing in disguise, since problems in the workplace are apt to claim your attention immediately. There is no way you can skimp on learning a new subject. Particularly if you are studying a foreign language, practice and more practice is the only way to thoroughly absorb all that you need to know. Old emotional problems can sometimes be solved simply through meeting a new person who relates to you so differently that past patterns of behavior are no longer relevant. Such a relationship promises you a delightful feeling of freedom.

21. WEDNESDAY. Interesting. Cancer folk tend to have very acute insights into other people, usually without any words being spoken. For this reason it is not out of the question to warn a friend against acting on financial advice, even though it may appear to come from a trustworthy expert. Romance is definitely in the air, with a colleague casting you looks on the sly. Whether or not you respond depends on how attractive you find this person. Conditions favor cleaning out the refrigerator and kitchen cupboards. It is amazing what can accumulate over time. Make room for some new and more exotic ingredients, then try preparing some unusual recipes.

22. THURSDAY. Trying. It can be immensely annoying to have someone point out the flaws in your grand plans for self-improvement. But perhaps it is true you are being unrealistic in trying to cram too much studying into your daily routine. Real self-development happens as much in everyday life as in yoga and meditation. A small health problem is likely to make work seem harder than usual, but at the same time you probably want to get everything finished by the end of the week. However, let colleagues take some responsibilities off your shoulders. Careless handling of precious possessions might result in breakage.

23. FRIDAY. Bumpy. Cut-price flights can be useful from time to time, but not if you are in a hurry to get to your destination. There could well be lengthy delays, and less than adequate service once you board the plane. Cancer men and women who do charity work seem to be finding it less rewarding than formerly. It is too easy to get bogged down in internal politics, so that the principles and good works suffer from bickering. Today a change of scene is in order. It is an ideal time to expand your mental horizons. Visit an art gallery or go to a play; escape the humdrum round of daily routine. A whole new world will open up.

24. SATURDAY. Slow. You may seem to be at cross-purposes with loved ones, who are focused on going out and having lots of fun. However, your inner self demands that you plan a quieter day, concentrating on household tasks while allowing your mind to roam over many deep topics. There could be mechanical problems with your car, probably blocking the flow of oil or of water. It is an ideal time to get it checked out thoroughly in order to ward off defects before they arise. By all means take your health seriously, but do not become obsessive. It is far healthier to enjoy what you do and what you eat rather than stick rigidly to a regime that gives you no pleasure.

25. SUNDAY. Stimulating. This much more lively day is likely to give you more than enough stimulation. You are much in demand socially, with invitations to go to various events pouring in. Just guard against overbooking yourself. Romance with someone a little younger than you is in the cards, but do not let the age difference put you off. When there is true rapport between two people, the years are not a hindrance to love. Ideas to brighten up your home are likely to get you quite excited. Do not hesitate to think up a quite radical color scheme. Your innate good taste will steer you away from anything too wild while getting you off the beaten track.

26. MONDAY. Rewarding. It is not often you get to start the workweek with compliments about your personal efforts, but this could happen today. Research you recently completed may have impressed a senior colleague so much that they want to work more closely with you. Fresh air and exercise will get you going after the rather demanding weekend. Give in to an urge to nap and you will probably just feel more tired. Talking out a problem may be just what a friend needs. Do not worry because you cannot offer them profound advice; what they really require is your sympathy and emotional support. Look for love right in the vicinity of your hardest task.

27. TUESDAY. Beneficial. There are likely to be changes in the way your work is organized, shattering your familiar routine. After the understandable period of insecurity, you will probably find that things are much improved, even though you may be reluctant to stop grumbling long enough to admit this possibility. There has rarely been a better time to invest in a good camera and start capturing loved ones for eternity. It would be wise to buy a couple of photography manuals as well, to pick up hints on taking really stunning pictures. Changing your aims in life is not necessarily the sign of a weak character but is a measure of how much you have grown and developed.

28. WEDNESDAY. Taxing. Although it can be embarrassing to confess in front of colleagues to making a mistake, there is no way you can cover up. At least it will be off your mind and you can begin to take steps to put it right. If you are borrowing money from a friend or family member, write down the exact sum. It can be all too easy to forget even quite a large amount, and you do not want to disagree about it later. New situations can be daunting, but they do not always have to be faced alone. Get a friend or colleague to go with you to a training course that sounds as if it is going to be demanding. You will be able to talk and study with them rather than working yourself into a nervous state.

MARCH

1. THURSDAY. Challenging. A slapdash approach to daily tasks will only irritate you. Your current mood of perfectionism makes you want to do even minor jobs such as putting away breakfast dishes or jotting down a to-do list as well as possible. The mental state that arises from this is worth investigating; you will probably discover that you are seeing the reality around you much more clearly. Certain things might even look totally different. Although keeping fit is likely to be on your mind, sports and vigorous exercise may seem a bit pointless. Instead, try a more rhythmical and gentle pastime such as yoga. It would be wise to listen to a friend's complaints without comment so that you do not get drawn into a disagreement that does not involve you directly.

2. FRIDAY. Lucky. Your guardian angel may seem to have been working overtime. You are apt to realize you made a potentially serious mistake just in time to correct it with no one being the wiser. Resolve to be more careful in the future. Street musicians may play a song that brings back a surge of romantic memories. Instead of walking by in a dream state, make sure you give them a donation. It is time to think about spring cleaning. At the same time, look for hidden corners of your home that could be emptied out to give you more space. Although as a Cancer you dislike throwing anything away, you really do not need to save old newspapers and magazines.

3. SATURDAY. Good. Your emotional life is profound, but it is not always clear to other people what you are feeling. Just make the effort today to tell a special person that you are attracted to them; they will probably be delighted. What is obvious to you is not necessarily clear to everyone. There is nothing to be gained from sulking if loved ones plan an outing that does not appeal to you. Just be a good sport and go along. This is an ideal day to dust off some old cookbooks that include healthy recipes. As long as you are not put off by complicated preparations, you can produce a truly delicious and sophisticated meal that is also good for you. Buy only the freshest ingredients.

4. SUNDAY. Easy. This is the sort of easygoing day that you dream about. Nothing urgent is likely to claim your attention. It should be possible to withdraw into yourself and simply putter around the house. Several small tasks that need finishing off can be completed, whether they involve sewing, easy carpentry, or wielding a paintbrush. The afternoon is energized. You might find yourself standing in front of a full-length mirror taking a critical look at your body. It would not hurt to work on improving your posture, which can make all the difference to the way your clothes hang. Practice balancing a book on your head while walking around the house. Get to bed early tonight.

5. MONDAY. Difficult. No matter how eager you are to start the workweek with vim and vigor, there are apt to be forces working against you. Mostly these forces are in the shape of colleagues who seem determined to make your work twice as hard as need be. Controlling your temper may become your most challenging task. You would really benefit from taking better care of yourself. Your hectic lifestyle is more demanding than you may realize; nor can you miss meals too often without depleting your body's resources. Have the confidence to believe that you can mentor a new colleague; it will be surprising how much you know and how good you are at imparting this knowledge.

6. TUESDAY. Problematic. The early part of the day is the best time to put into action an idealistic project. If you have been planning to join an environmental or political group, do not delay any longer. Otherwise you will probably keep putting it off and all your good intentions will be wasted. Later you may be easily distracted. It will be a problem just keeping a sense of living in the real world, but the last thing you should do is drift off into fantasy. It is fine making plans for increasing your income, but you must follow through with action. Force yourself to apply for a better job; do not be put off by complicated forms or the thought of having to relocate.

7. WEDNESDAY. Profitable. As a Cancer you tend to be at the mercy of your moods. However, this morning it should be very positive to follow your impulses. You are likely to wake up full of energy and raring to go. It may be possible to diversify your skills at work just by keeping an eye on what colleagues do. Then, if someone is absent, you can step in and earn extra money as well as recognition by doing so. Youngsters may be going through a tricky time, needing lots of extra support and understanding. Growing up is not easy; cast your mind back and you will remember what it was like. Financially it is vital to be as cautious as possible, even with small sums.

8. THURSDAY. Stressful. Sometimes it feels as if life is all work and no play. If this is the case right now, do not hesitate to do something about it. You need to strike a balance between earning a decent living and enjoying your leisure hours. Although it is always interesting to meet new people, not all of them will be congenial with your Cancer personality. Joining a club ensures you have interests in common with other people, but that does not mean you will strike up instant friendships. Local travel can be a problem. If you choose to use public transportation, there could be long delays in the service. Use your ingenuity to keep yourself or your youngsters happy while waiting.

9. FRIDAY. Wearing. This busy day at work or at home is likely to wear you out. The way to maximize your energy is by planning your work rather than launching into it without thinking. Problems with a neighbor may come to a head, so that you can no longer ignore them. Before complaining to the authorities, have a chat and see if they even realize that they are upsetting you with noise or untidiness. If you are hanging on to a relationship for fear of being alone, be aware that this situation cannot last. Today may mark the turning point, when the other person also begins to lose interest. Try not to be sad about this situation; nothing lasts forever.

10. SATURDAY. Exciting. Drastic changes in your routine are not usually to your taste, but this weekend you are apt to feel the sudden urge to be spontaneous. Open yourself to the natural flow of life. Forget the shopping and household chores for now and take off where your fancy leads you. Cancer people in charge of youngsters need to keep a sharp eye on them. They are apt to be bursting with energy and mischief, which may well lead them to get into trouble around the neighborhood. Creatively this should be an exciting day. Fresh ideas for expressing yourself through clay, paint, fabric, or words are likely to inspire you. Act now, letting these insights carry you away.

11. SUNDAY. Fair. Work around the house should be given precedence. It would be a good idea to thoroughly clean cupboards and shelves. Also get youngsters to clean up their bedrooms despite the protests. This is a starred day to entertain family members. You should be able to get along better with parents and close relatives, creating a warm and loving atmosphere. Where romance is concerned, it can be a challenge not to let minor disagreements blow up out of all proportion. Keep in mind that if you are actually looking for excuses to argue, there is something wrong between you that needs to be addressed without delay.

12. MONDAY. Favorable. It would be ideal to be able to do some of your work from home. Try to persuade your boss that you would be of more use getting urgent work out of the way by phone or computer, without the normal distractions of the usual working environment. Relatives may be willing to take children off your hands if you and your mate or partner need to get away together. It would certainly help renew your relationship to spend some time as a twosome. All written work is favored. It you are hoping to get poetry or prose into print, concentrate on presenting your work in as professional a manner as possible. First impressions count for a lot.

13. TUESDAY. Disenchanting. You cannot be expected to take responsibility for your friends' lives when your own needs so much organizing. You probably slipped into just such a compliant attitude in the past, being more than willing to help other people. However now is the time to put your foot down. Just tell them they have to rely on themselves for a change. Sometimes it can be quite disillusioning to get involved in an idealistic group. If you do so, you will probably have to come to terms with the fact that people still quarrel and complain no matter how noble the enterprise. You run the risk of getting romantically involved with someone who is not totally trustworthy, so be cautious. Protect yourself from being hurt.

14. WEDNESDAY. Chancy. Hard-earned money should be squirreled away in a safe place, not risked on some dubious enterprise. As a Cancer you do not really have a gambling instinct, so guard against letting yourself be tempted by the promise of a large return on your investment. There is a danger of a close emotional bond being severed if you insist on being demanding. Allow the other person an extra measure of freedom; they need to feel that you trust them completely. The brightest spot of the day is likely to take place in a travel agency. It would do you a lot of good to plan to go off on a creative break such as a museum tour or a whale-watching expedition. Choose your evening companions with care.

15. THURSDAY. Trying. If you are suffering the effects of last night's excess this morning, you have only yourself to blame. It would certainly not hurt to make a resolution that from now on you will be moderate in both eating and drinking. You do not have to deny yourself every pleasure; just know when to stop. Arguments at work could flare up over insignificant matters such as use of the photocopier. Since you have to get along with colleagues, it would be unwise to fan the flames even higher. Although hygiene at home is important, it can be taken too far. Keep a check on yourself to be sure your use of bleach and household cleanser is not becoming a bit obsessive.

16. FRIDAY. Fortunate. It can be immensely helpful to build up a circle of friends who have expertise in a number of different areas. Then when you need help with money or business matters or home repairs, there will always be someone who can give you sound advice. Cancer people who are taking evening classes may be surprised to find the teacher becoming quite friendly. This is not only a boost to your self-confidence but also a door opening into more interesting areas of life. While it may be tempting to reach for the skies with impossible aims, you will be happier in the long run setting your sights on goals that are within reach. For example, why not develop a creative skill to the expert level.

17. SATURDAY. Interesting. Although as a Cancer you tend to be home-loving, from time to time everyone gets the urge to travel. Right now your itchy feet are not going to be satisfied with a day trip, so it is time to start planning a more adventurous getaway later in the year. This is a good day to take youngsters to a museum or other place of cultural interest. Just be sure to pick somewhere that caters to children, and also be alert for signs of boredom. A bad experience at an early age can be off-putting for life. Vary your diet a little more and the benefits will soon show. Instead of sticking to the same old recipes, try something new and better for you.

18. SUNDAY. Tiresome. Probably the best way of coping with this day is to lay low. Your energy is apt to be a little meager. Rather than push yourself to the limits, it would be far wiser to pamper yourself. Quite a nasty disagreement could erupt at home over the different ways you and your mate or partner go about household chores. Keep in mind that compromise is the essence of living together, so neither of you should expect to have everything exactly to your liking. If work is on your mind keep quiet about it, especially if a certain attractive colleague keeps popping up in your thoughts. Do not encourage such daydreams; focus your mind elsewhere.

19. MONDAY. Advantageous. If you are hoping for a change of career, this is a most promising day to start looking. Keep in mind that it can be an enormous help to know people who are able to point you in the right direction. Make a list and start calling around. Love should be smiling upon you. Someone you see virtually every day clearly wants to get to know you better, so give them some encouragement. Your health will probably benefit from a change of daily routine. If you tend to go to bed late and wind up short of sleep, try from now on to keep earlier hours. A mutual friend can help you and your mate or partner with a small financial problem.

20. TUESDAY. Promising. Give your working life a boost by asking if you can take on more direct responsibility. Even if there is not a pay raise in sight yet, if you perform well more money will inevitably follow. Now more than ever it pays to be choosy about the people with whom you associate. It is not hard to pinpoint those who do not contribute much to your life; you will probably be happier if you begin seeing less of them. Take time this afternoon to finish tasks that you had to put aside in favor of more urgent business. You are now able to restart them with fresh energy and renewed enthusiasm. This is an ideal evening to enjoy the company of that special person in your life.

21. WEDNESDAY. Deceptive. Do not allow a travel agent to pull the wool over your eyes. If the arrangements for a long journey seem at all dubious, insist on having them changed. In a training course you only get as much out of it as you put in. Although you may have begun the class with superb confidence, soon enough you have come down to earth and discovered that learning anything worthwhile is never easy. Walking a dog can be an excellent way of getting regular exercise. If you do not own one yourself, offer to take a neighbor's pet to the park or the woods. Allow yourself to relax in front of the television this evening.

22. THURSDAY. Uneven. Refusing to take a hard look at your life and where you are currently headed is not the way to get a sense of direction. Although as a Cancer you tend to ignore the big picture, you need a lifetime game plan just to give you a definite purpose and to keep you on track. For instance, you need to decide if you want to concentrate on developing your career or want to focus on family life. Overseas business connections are very promising but should be checked out thoroughly. It is particularly important to insist on withholding full payment until goods from abroad have been received. Variety is the spice of life, so if you receive an unusual invitation accept with pleasure.

23. FRIDAY. Stormy. Relations with colleagues are heading for a showdown. It is very important not to seethe away silently, only to explode when you can no longer contain your emotions. Find the opportunity to chat informally, so that both sides can state their views calmly. An evening class may not be giving you what you had expected. It is up to you to decide whether it would be advantageous to cut your losses and drop out or hang on and hope it improves. A pet could wander off this evening; a long search will probably ensue because it is likely to stray a long way from home. Bring along a favorite food to tempt them back once located.

24. SATURDAY. Fulfilling. This is an ideal day to go out with friends. Let the wind blow all your troubles away. There is no need to go far; it is much more important just being in good company. Shopping may be extremely useful for picking up bargains, particularly if you are looking for exotic, unusual gifts. Poke around in smaller shops that are off the beaten track. As long as you keep your sense of idealism shining bright, there is much you can do to make the world a better place. It is particularly important that your local neighborhood be safe for youngsters. Getting involved in local politics or a neighborhood watch group can be helpful in this regard.

25. SUNDAY. Excellent. This is an excellent day to being planning a career change. Sit down with your mate or partner and discuss what areas of your current work you enjoy, and what skills you would like to develop further. Honesty is always the best policy where relationships are concerned. If something has been preying on your mind, it is better to confess the matter and then let it fade into the past. An old photograph album could turn up when you are looking for something else. This is bound to spark many happy memories, along with a little sadness as well. Do not be ashamed to shed a tear for what once was. Loved ones deserve a little extra affection this evening.

26. MONDAY. Productive. Roll up your sleeves and prepare to get on with work that normally you would attempt to pass off to someone else. Now, however, there seems to be positive satisfaction in getting your hands dirty and then seeing concrete results. A more active life would do a lot for your level of fitness. It is very well going to the gym or health club once a week, but a more integrated form of daily exercise would be highly beneficial. You may want to walk to work, for example. Although it may seem a bit brash, you are in a good position to give a senior staff member some worthwhile advice. Approach this person in a tactful manner and they might not even realize what is going on.

27. TUESDAY. Opportune. Optimism is not a strong Cancer characteristic. However, when a promising job opportunity comes up today, you will probably be quite confident that you could fit the bill. As long as you get an interview, you should be able to impress those who matter with your positive attitude. It never hurts to give to charity, even to give a bit more than you think you can comfortably afford. If you find your wallet being emptied too much, pick a few favorite charities to donate to on a regular basis. Then you can turn down other requests with a clear conscience. Try not to allow an upset friend to sink into self-pity. Encourage this person to look on the bright side by emphasizing all that is positive in their current situation.

28. WEDNESDAY. Important. As a Cancer you generally have a good intuitive sense. If it is telling you that you can trust someone whose credentials are not very brilliant, do not hesitate to follow this hunch. Romance may creep up on you when you least expect it. A familiar figure in your life may have taken up residence in your heart without you even realizing what was happening. It can be very flattering to be told you could have a glamorous career, but the truth is more likely that you would only achieve fame by working extremely hard. Gossip on the job may have quite a cruel edge at times and is best ignored. Do not believe even half of what you hear via the grapevine.

29. THURSDAY. Tranquil. You would be unwise to expect too much of yourself this morning. It may help to get up a little earlier than usual so that you can take your time getting ready for the day. If your social life has been a bit sparse recently, you may be wondering where to find a new and more stimulating circle of friends. For a start, you could join a local club or amateur dramatic group. It can be a delight to withdraw into yourself this afternoon, focusing solely on your own tasks. This is an ideal time to write up a report or catch up on letter writing. A romantic evening at the ballet, a concert, or the theater will ensure wonderful dreams tonight.

30. FRIDAY. Happy. Normally you would probably find it extremely embarrassing to receive a declaration of love in front of colleagues. However, when those words come from someone you have been attracted to for a long time, it should be a positive triumph. Financially there is a good opportunity for improving your prospects. It all comes down to picking a job with a future, and there is at least one position that would be ideal. If you are wondering what to buy a friend as a special gift, consider a piece of engraved jewelry or a watch. They are bound to cherish either of these because the gift will always remind them of your friendship, support, and enduring affection.

31. SATURDAY. Enjoyable. A positive electrical energy is in the air, so do not expect to lie around undisturbed. Youngsters are apt to plague you to join in their games until you have to give in. Your nerves have probably been jangled at work recently; now you need a complete change. Think of ways in which you could cut down on the number of tasks you have to do. It can be easier to get a clear perspective when you are away from the working environment. Pets only behave as well as they have been trained to do, and training should start right from the day they came into your home. It is important for you to establish who is in charge before they get a false impression.

APRIL

1. SUNDAY. Uplifting. Quite a lazy mood is apt to overtake you this morning. It is the sort of day to enjoy breakfast in bed and a leisurely look at the newspaper. Later on, you should feel sufficiently energized to think about getting out and about. Romantically this should be quite a surprising day. Someone from your past could resurface, stirring tender emotions that you thought had died out long ago. However, there is no hurry to get involved all over again. A stronger sense of what you want to achieve in life is necessary for your happiness. Find time to look into yourself. Be sure to clarify your career aims, and do not be squeamish about setting a high salary as one of your goals.

2. MONDAY. Expansive. Keep in mind that today is the first day of the rest of your life. Be willing to lift your eyes to far horizons. The usual domestic concerns should not stop you from trying to get broader experience, perhaps by traveling more widely. Cancer people who teach for a living should find students more attentive than usual. This is a good time to practice teaching techniques that might not come off when the class is in a rowdy mood. Although you may balk at organizing a night out with friends, the responsibility will do you good. If everything runs smoothly, you will have the pleasure of having given everyone a lot of happiness.

3. TUESDAY. Helpful. There is money to be made by improving your career prospects. One way to climb higher up the ladder of success would be to lend assistance to a senior staff member. An act of kindness to a close relative might not mean much to you. However, it will be extremely significant to them, as you will discover if and when you are in similar circumstances one day. This is no time for spending lots of money on yourself. Instead you should be concentrating on laying a sound foundation for the future with your mate or partner. Do not hesitate to ask for expert help if you find yourself mixed up about finances; your bank manager or accountant should be able to assist you.

4. WEDNESDAY. Successful. Surprisingly, you might get along better with colleagues once you gain a little power over them. Being put in a position of responsibility can make you realize that there is no need to defer to other people's ideas when you know your way of proceeding is better. Your body will respond well to a simpler diet containing less meat and animal fats. The important first step is to begin by cutting out all junk food. There could be overtime required this evening, allowing you to bank a useful sum of money. Your home would benefit from spending a little on improvements and modernization, particularly in the kitchen and the bathroom.

5. THURSDAY. Enlightening. This quieter day sees you eager to clear up various tasks without being interrupted. Choose fairly menial cleaning and repair jobs that allow your mind to wander freely while you are working. Useful insights into your most important relationships are likely. Quite a mystical outlook on life may begin to attract you more and more, perhaps through meeting someone whose philosophy has impressed you greatly. It would be a good idea to arrange to meet with this person again so that you can ask questions and get some specific guidance. Traveling to a distant conference might not be your idea of fun, but keep an open mind because there is something special for you to learn there.

6. FRIDAY. Tiresome. Having to rewrite a report or correct forms that have been filled in incorrectly could bog down your morning with rather dull, irritating work. But do not hurry or more mistakes are bound to slip through. Even though you may be looking forward to going out with friends tonight, they are unlikely to appear to be as enthusiastic. You could find yourself having to listen to their woes before they relax enough to start having a good time. This is an excellent day to explain in private to youngsters a few adult matters. Unfortunately it is not possible to protect children's innocence forever, since they have to be prepared to cope with a less than perfect world. Be specific in identifying potential dangers without arousing unnecessary fear.

7. SATURDAY. Mixed. If you are hurrying around getting ready to entertain friends, you may be amazed at the cost of doing so in style. However, it would be in your best interests to make a good impression on at least some of your guests, so it is worth splurging on food and drink. This can be quite a dangerous time where romance is concerned. If you feel your emotions being tugged at by an unsuitable person, there is nothing to do but be firm with yourself and say no to their romantic overtures. All domestic matters are favored. This is an ideal day to choose paint and wallpaper to brighten up your living room or any room in your home. Choose soothing, relaxing colors that you can live with for years.

8. SUNDAY. Buoyant. That special someone is not going to know about your feelings unless you come right out and say how you feel. A formal social occasion could provide just the setting for a romantic declaration that might well sweep them off their feet. Even if children are just scribbling with crayons, all of their artistic leanings should be encouraged. The earlier they get a taste of self-expression, the more easily it can be developed. There may be such a contrast between the pace of your home life and of your career that you feel a bit lost on weekends. It is important to try to bring the two sides of your existence into balance by striving for a change of attitude.

9. MONDAY. Strenuous. You need to be constantly on the ball today if handling money for other people. Be sure to write down all transactions, and get both parties to sign if possible. Otherwise mistakes will not only be made, they will be blamed on you. It is inevitable that someone you know nothing about may appear magnetically attractive. That does not mean, however, that you should leap into an intimate relationship. Not all impulses have to be acted on, by any means. If you are taking a driving test, or other official test, be alert for trick questions. Do not allow yourself to relax and let down your guard; quick reactions are wanted.

10. TUESDAY. Suspenseful. Unexpected changes at work may take you completely by surprise. Colleagues could be let go without warning. Despite your concern for their career prospects, there may be promotion in this for you. More vigorous exercise is bound to benefit your health. It would be helpful to join a gym, or to buy an exercise machine to use at home if you feel shy. This is not the best of days to try to mend any electrical equipment. All repairs should be handed over to someone who knows better than you what they are doing. An evening at an avant-garde club could bring you into contact with stimulating new people who soon become good friends.

11. WEDNESDAY. Rewarding. It should be well worthwhile taking notice of financial tips from people who are in the know. Just make sure you are absolutely clear about what is being offered; there is some likelihood of getting the wrong impression. Your dreams are apt to be quite vivid. Even if you do not write them down, at least try to remember them or use a tape recorder to store them in your memory. You should be kept busy with routine matters this afternoon, but there is a lot going on that you do not yet know about. If you do your work well, your dedication will be noticed and marked down in your favor when a future promotion is discussed. Get to bed before that late TV news show tonight.

12. THURSDAY. Pressured. Although you should certainly look after your health, there is no reason to go to extremes. In fact you will simply annoy loved ones if you get too picky about food, or refuse to go out for the evening because you prefer to exercise in private. There may be a lot of pressure being put on from upper management at work to accept voluntary early retirement. If you are caught up in this, it is vital to hold out for as good a deal as possible. You might not always feel comfortable at a formal social occasion, but once in a while it can be fun to get all dressed up and hobnob with the high and mighty or let them associate with you.

13. FRIDAY. Uneven. Get up early if you can bear to do so at the end of this busy workweek. The first part of the day will be easiest and least stressful. Get the major part of your work done then, leaving you free to deal with minor problems that are almost bound to arise. If you are operating heavy machinery, keep your attention firmly focused on what you are doing. Also watch out for other operators, who may not be as alert as you. This is not the most auspicious day to visit the dentist unless you are prepared to have a lot of useful but quite painful work done on your teeth. Cancer singles should keep a new romance under wraps for now.

14. SATURDAY. Good. Children always seem to grow up very fast, so that they get interested in all kinds of touchy subjects. This is a good day to sit down and talk about problem areas such as sickness and death in a very gentle and supportive way. A misdialed number could lead to getting into a very interesting phone conversation with a complete stranger. The way you both feel, you two are unlikely to stay strangers for long. All domestic matters are highlighted. You will be a lot happier after getting heavy cleaning and loads of laundry out of the way. Then allow yourself to relax; all work and no play is bound to make you dull company.

15. SUNDAY. Upbeat. Waking up with a clear head and a sudden knowledge of what you want to achieve over the next few months may not be your style, but this is likely to happen today. You can now make highly useful plans for improving your career options and your general direction in life. This is also a fine day for cooking an exotic and delicious meal, which is a favorite Cancer activity. An impromptu dinner party with a few good friends would be ideal. A close relationship needs to be effective on at least two levels. You should have ideals in common, and also daily habits that harmonize. And both of those areas require constant upkeep.

16. MONDAY. Bumpy. You are apt to wake up on the wrong side of the bed, so that the slightest critical remark really hurts or annoys you. However, since people cannot be expected to walk on tiptoe around you, try to be as brave and calm as possible. Mistakes made in a work presentation could prove quite serious. On no account should you attempt to pass the blame on to other people. Financially this should be quite a positive day. The essential ingredient for success is to be realistic about how much you can afford to put into long-term savings and insurance. Deep emotions could be aroused for someone you never thought of as particularly attractive, but take a second look.

17. TUESDAY. Profitable. Cancer people make sound bankers and financial analysts as well as stockbrokers. Perhaps this is an area that would be worth pursuing. It may be a welcome gesture to buy a pet for a relative who does not get out much. Ask first, of course. Elderly folk can be revitalized by having a living companion to love and care for. Your health may benefit from eating more natural foods. Most large supermarkets have a section for organic produce, which often tastes better than mass-produced fruit and vegetables. Being more versatile at work will get you through the day without the usual grumbles. Just accept whatever tasks you are given and do your best.

18. WEDNESDAY. Variable. There is a risk of an electric shock if you persist in handling old or worn-out electrical equipment. Fiddle with loose wires and you are only asking for trouble. Even if you are usually quite hesitant about learning new technology, a good teacher can make all the difference. It would certainly be a career boost to get up to speed with computer programs, and useful for personal reasons as well. Build muscles by getting regular but small amounts of gentle exercise. This can be built up slowly, but it is vital to pace yourself carefully at first. Do not be too disappointed if friends do not share your enthusiasm for the latest movie or book or television show.

19. THURSDAY. Hectic. The best energy to use is mental. Today you should be thinking quicker than usual, making snap decisions no problem. A financial situation may arise where you have to choose what to do with your own and your partner's funds at short notice. Your first instinct is likely to be the most profitable one. Keep youngsters out of trouble with games that will interest but not overexcite them. They need to have their dexterity and imagination stretched to the limit, and then you will have peace at bedtime. A long journey may be subject to annoying interference from authorities. Make sure your tickets and required proof of identity are all in order. Also keep a close eye on your luggage.

20. FRIDAY. Challenging. It will be difficult to get through the day without having some basic truths brought to your attention. There is no way around this. You will just have to accept criticism and take a long, hard look at your own failings. A romance which you had almost abandoned is about to resurface in your life. The other person probably had unfinished business with a former mate or partner which they had to resolve before getting closer to you. There is extra emphasis on two areas of life, which contrast starkly with each other. On the one hand, an increase in social invitations is likely, but on the other hand you are apt to wish for time alone to sort out your life.

21. SATURDAY. Stimulating. This is not a day to get mired in memories of the past. What is happening with close friends and loved ones should claim all of your attention. It is a great time to expand your social circle by joining a club or organization that will teach you something new. A cooking class or a crafts club would be ideal. If you are currently between relationships but feel ready for a new one, ask friends if they know anyone who would be a match for you. A blind double date could easily be set up, allowing you both to get to know each other but without the pressure of being alone together. Generosity to loved ones will make the evening particularly pleasant.

22. SUNDAY. Productive. On this more serious day you need to turn a critical eye to the appearance of your home environment. It probably could do with a bit of sprucing up, and you have the energy to do a lot of work. At the moment your health is quite good, which should encourage you to keep up with a sensible diet and exercise regime. It also would not hurt to make a few changes. If you have been engaging in competitive sports, a solitary workout would be good and vice versa. This is a great day if you have been promising to entertain some people of importance. Invite them to your home and they are bound to enjoy your hospitality if you relax and act naturally rather than trying to impress them.

23. MONDAY. Invigorating. The workweek should get off to a flying start. In a business meeting you can afford to speak up loud and clear to say what needs to be said. You will get full marks for courage and for your incisive analysis of a work problem. Idealism is vital if you are not to become cynical and sad. At the moment your interest in world affairs is stronger than usual, so it is a good time to join an organization through which you can make a positive contribution to improving the conditions in Third World countries. Younger friends offer a fresh perspective on old problems. There is no reason not to take their advice. Even if you are a little older and more experienced than them, you are not necessarily any wiser.

24. TUESDAY. Cautious. Mistakes with money are easily made. Recently you may have played fast and loose with joint savings, knowing exactly what you were doing. Naturally this was going to come to light. Now that your ill-advised spending has been discovered, no excuses are going to get you off the hook. Some people need to know they can be attractive to others, even if they have no interest in starting a romantic relationship. Do not be fooled into thinking a new acquaintance is bowled over by your Cancer charm: they may just want to prove their power. Check appointments on your calendar or you are almost bound to miss an important social event.

25. WEDNESDAY. Misleading. There is no reason to blindly believe all that a colleague tells you about a secret financial deal. If you question them closely, you will probably find that their story falls to pieces. This should not ruin your day, however. A friend who demands sympathy on a regular basis may not appear to be getting anything positive from your support, which shows that you are wasting your time and energy. If this person prefers to be stuck in their misery, there is nothing you can do about it. Youngsters will probably lead you a merry dance, and their friends will act no better. Do not play hide-and-seek unless you want a very long and worrisome search.

26. THURSDAY. Favorable. Creatively this promises to be an excellent day. However, you will need solitude in order to summon up the best of your imagination, and come up with imagery that speaks to a wide variety of people. This is a good day to consider those who do not have happy lives, and to vow to do something to make their existence less difficult. Regular donations to charity or the occasional hour put in at a local homeless shelter can do a great deal of good. Youngsters and elderly relatives alike are sure to enjoy a few good jokes; after all, laughter is excellent medicine for both body and soul. Treat yourself to a quiet night at home with a favorite novel or video.

27. FRIDAY. Fair. You may be a bit shy today, but that will not hurt since you have private work to do. This is an excellent time to free yourself from old emotional habits. Consider your character traits that others point out to you most often. These are the ones you should work on if you are not altogether comfortable with them. Although it may seem a bit tedious to undo a piece of work and start more or less from scratch, it is surprising how much you can learn from doing so. Former mistakes probably look rather obvious now, which is a sign that you are developing expertise. Trust your judgment in choosing new furniture or window treatments.

28. SATURDAY. Difficult. This is one of those days when whatever you do you will find it impossible to please everyone. Petulance on the part of youngsters should not be tolerated; point out to them how lucky they actually are. When you know both partners in a quarrel, it is never easy to handle confidences from one side or the other. As the onlooker you need to be very tactful in deciding just how much of the situation can be pointed out. Love may escape if you try too hard to catch it. Have faith that what is really yours can never taken away from you. If that person is really destined to be yours, you will not need more than a minimum amount of persuasion.

29. SUNDAY. Low-keyed. No matter that other people might accuse you of being selfish, you deserve to spend a little time doing exactly as you please. A good place to start is with your personal appearance. A little improvement here and there should be enough to enable you to turn heads; it is just a matter of making the effort. Personal plans for self-development can be formulated, although there is little chance at the moment of putting them into practice. However, it would not hurt to start thinking about the importance of money in your life. It is up to you to decide if you are content to do an undemanding job for sufficient pay, or do you aspire to a more luxurious lifestyle and extra work responsibilities.

30. MONDAY. Tricky. The morning should find you deep in serious paperwork. Although you usually are bored by filling out official forms, it has to be done and can be surprisingly absorbing if you get into the right frame of mind. Finding an inner core of stability that cannot be shaken no matter what happens is one of the essential quests of life. Practicing meditation can be an extremely positive way to get in touch with your own core values. Sometimes it seems salespeople see you coming. Your loved ones are bound to be frustrated and annoyed when you spend good money on shoddy merchandise. Wise up; do not buy anything you do not need.

MAY

1. TUESDAY. Rewarding. If it is up to you to persuade customers to buy your product or service, this should be a very rewarding morning. Just be sure you do not overdo the enthusiasm. A long relaxing steam bath would really do you good, steaming away all your troubles and taking the knots out of your muscles. You could also benefit from a session of therapeutic massage or even aromatherapy. There is no point being roped into social occasions that do not really appeal to you. Refuse to allow your friends to make you feel the odd one out; just give them your reasons for not wanting to join in and refuse to be persuaded. Wind down after an active day by talking quietly to loved ones this evening.

2. WEDNESDAY. Tiresome. Traffic this morning is bound to be heavy. It would be wise to allow longer than usual to get to appointments. If a new friendship is not progressing as you want, it may well be due to some reluctance on the other person's part.

A relationship cannot be forced, so do not try to do so. Pin all your hopes on winning a competition and you are almost certainly heading for disappointment. Unfortunately you will probably have to get that dream car or exotic trip by the sweat of your brow and not on a silver platter. Do someone a favor and they will be happy to repay you when you need assistance.

3. THURSDAY. Stressful. Hasty words are almost always regretted. You will probably have to struggle to keep quiet when a friend criticizes you unjustly, but that is exactly what you should do. They will apologize in good time. This is a day when you may be required to make a work decision that you do not really feel qualified to consider. However, there is no way around it, except that you can at least seek advice from your colleagues. Youngsters are apt to be irritable, which may be a symptom of underlying unhappiness. Check that all is well between them and their neighborhood friends. A word with other parents may be in order.

4. FRIDAY. Variable. Thinking and talking too much about what you intend to do with the day can take up valuable time. You may find it is midafternoon before you even begin your tasks. It is not always easy to get along with neighbors; you have every right to complain if you think they are poking into your private life. All the same, there is no excuse for rudeness or for losing your temper. Your parents or another older person may need some cheering up, especially if they show a tendency to live in the past. Invite them for a special meal, and show them how enjoyable the present can be. They will derive great pleasure just from seeing that you are happy and doing well.

5. SATURDAY. Harmonious. The weekend begins with a strong possibility that relatives will make demands on your time. However, you are unlikely to mind this and should lend any assistance they need with a glad heart. As a Cancer you tend to like antiques. This is an excellent day to go looking for a special item to enhance your home. Just do not expect to pick up any bargains. Since loved ones seem to be getting along well, this would be a good day to get out the camera to capture those smiles for the future; they will become precious memories. Youngsters may need to be calmed down before bedtime in order to fall asleep.

6. SUNDAY. Distressing. Sometimes you can be your own worst enemy. Succumbing to negative thoughts about yourself only builds up an unrealistic picture in your mind, holding you back from positive achievements. Try to recognize this tendency when it crops up, and turn to friends and loved ones for positive validation at that time. There is not much hope of getting household tasks completely finished, especially when you are so easily distracted. If your heart is not really in it, do not even attempt chores that at best will be poorly done. The plight of children in underdeveloped countries is likely to stir your compassion. Consider adopting a deserving child by contributing monthly to a reputable charity.

7. MONDAY. Disconcerting. If you expect to slide easily into the workweek's activities, think again. The rhythms of life unfortunately do not take into account your desire for a quiet day, so you will have to cope with whatever is thrown at you. Virtue is said to be its own reward, and that is the best you can expect. However, such lack of appreciation should not put you off helping an elderly or handicapped person, even though they may just take your assistance for granted. The temptation to slip into a daydream should be avoided because it could lead to self-pity. Once you begin to list all the positive aspects of your life, a very different picture begins to emerge.

8. TUESDAY. Difficult. There is no point swimming against the tide where romance is concerned. If a relationship is coming to its natural end, there is little you can do to stop the process. On the other hand, it most certainly is within your power to ensure that the separation is as amicable as possible. Do not go into an interview or a test with too much confidence. A more modest attitude will enable you to see what is within your grasp and what exceeds your abilities. The afternoon is likely to find you struggling to catch up with work that should have been done yesterday or even sooner. Let that be a lesson to you not to procrastinate in the future.

9. WEDNESDAY. Challenging. Being cordial to colleagues can reap unexpected rewards. They might even put in a good word for you if the possibility of a promotion comes up. It is not always smart to get romantically involved with someone you work with, but then again it can be hard to avoid doing so. So if you have been swapping glances during coffee breaks with someone attractive, consider asking for a date. Just try to be discreet in case it does not work out. The last thing you should do is take out your annoyance on pets. All you will do is frighten them and teach them to mistrust you. Instead, try giving them extra care as a therapeutic means of calming yourself down.

10. THURSDAY. Good. This is one of those days when you first must retreat a little in order to make a giant leap forward. This might mean withdrawing from loved ones to fill in a job application to the best of your ability. If you can get asked to go on an interview, you should be ready to drop everything on short notice. Romance can sometimes blossom in the most unfavorable circumstances. You may suddenly notice someone who helps you out every day, perhaps in a local store or on your regular route to work. Cancers who are refurbishing a new home can get a great deal done. Your energy makes even structural work seem like a minor task, but get professionals in for the more technically demanding jobs.

11. FRIDAY. Comforting. In a way it might be quite a relief to have to return to work tasks you thought had been safely passed on to a colleague. There is something quite comforting about slipping back into a familiar routine that you do not have to think much about in order to perform well. The secret life of your heart's emotions can still surprise you. After all, feelings are beyond rational analysis. For this reason you should not be surprised if a former love keeps coming back into your mind; this might be a signal that you should try getting together again. Financially there is a chance for you to improve your position if you are prepared to work a little longer and harder.

12. SATURDAY. Pleasurable. At last you and your mate or partner should be getting on harmoniously. What is most helpful to your relationship is to socialize together with mutual friends. The more pleasurable pursuits you can share, the happier you will be. A formal family gathering could bring you into contact with relatives you have not seen for years. Old memories now seem almost irrelevant, and you can begin a more friendly and positive era of communication. If you hang out with people who do not share your ideals and values, problems are bound to arise. Friends you have known longest are more likely to be there to offer you support and encouragement when you need them most.

13. SUNDAY. Serene. This quiet day allows you to recuperate from the busy week. Current conditions favor taking stock of yourself and doing some emotional weeding out. Get rid of old patterns of behavior that are no longer relevant. In this way you will be making space for a more spontaneous approach to life. There should be time for you and your mate or partner to go over your financial situation together. Two heads are better than one, and as a pair you might come up with a plan that would put your money to better use.

Give some thought to an elderly relative who would welcome a visit, or you might want to invite an uncle or aunt for a meal and a cozy evening of conversation and reminiscing.

14. MONDAY. Cautious. If you feel your energy level is not as high as it should be, you may have been dragged down by recent stress. What you need is a relaxing break or, if that is not possible, a herbal tonic to bring you back to blooming health. Allowing colleagues to take advantage of your helpful Cancer nature is only going to benefit them, and definitely not you. It is vital that you learn to discriminate between those people who genuinely need help and those who are just pretending. Take a good look at children this evening; if their eyes are very bright and their cheeks are flushed, that is probably a sign of a feverish virus coming on.

15. TUESDAY. Demanding. Sometimes you are apt to wish that the phone had never been invented. It can be especially irritating when friends call you at work and expect to chat as if you had all the time in the world. You must tell them that you need to return to work, but tactfully of course. Cancer people who are learning new computer programs should guard against becoming overconfident. Vital information can be lost; perhaps not irretrievably lost, but certainly enough to mess up an already complicated day. Resolve to go for an early evening jog or at least a long walk. Exchange greetings with neighbors along the way; the human touch makes exercise that much more enjoyable.

16. WEDNESDAY. Wearing. If you are traveling a long distance, expect quite a grueling trip. Your fellow passengers may not be very friendly, so unless you take along a good book to pass the time the journey could be dull. Learning should be a pleasure, especially if you have signed up for a course out of choice. There is no reason to worry about it. Try to change your viewpoint and appreciate how much your mental horizons will be widened. A more philosophical outlook on life can give you a better perspective. Setbacks happen to everyone; they are to be coped with rather than moaned about. Do not forget to return a friend's phone call.

17. THURSDAY. Pressured. When your eyes are on a major goal, it can be most annoying to have to deal with the minor details of life. However, if you consider yourself too important to do routine tasks because you are going up in the world, you are riding for a fall. Do at least your fair share of menial, unglamorous jobs. Children should not have to put up with overforceful teachers at school. If you have any reason to suspect that they are not being treated with kindness and respect, make a complaint to the principal in person. Do not ignore your diet, but on the other hand do not invite ridicule by sticking to a rigid program that goes against all reason.

18. FRIDAY. Eventful. Friends from a distance could drop in unexpectedly, which is bound to give you extra work but also a great deal of pleasure. Instead of trying to get everything perfect for them, just do your best with what you have on hand. What is important is your time together. During the middle of the day you should expect a clash between a report that needs to be completed quickly and pressing practical tasks. This is the time to get loved ones or friends to help out. Quietness and retreat are the watchwords to keep in mind this evening. A rowdy night out on the town is not going to be enjoyable when all you want is time to yourself in order to think and plan.

19. SATURDAY. Surprising. Love does not always arrive in the neat package you expect. If you find yourself falling head over heels with a special someone, there is no reason to hold back. Allow yourself to be surprised by the depth of passion the two of you share. An item of jewelry you thought was lost could turn up in a very obvious place, probably in the kitchen or bathroom. Once you again have it in your possession, get that clasp mended without delay. Although money is not often far from your mind, as a Cancer you certainly enjoy splurging when the occasion arises. This is one of those days when you will want to withdraw savings with cheerful recklessness.

20. SUNDAY. Satisfactory. As a Cancer you are often quite sentimental, tending to keep mementos of the past for a very long time. Nor does it do you any harm occasionally to lose yourself in memories while looking over trinkets from past holidays, to say nothing of yellowing love letters. It may surprise you when a friend consults you for advice with confidence that you can provide expert opinion. This is a sign that you may not think highly enough of yourself and your accumulated knowledge. This is a starred day to go somewhere new. Break away from old habits; try an activity that will shake your complacency.

21. MONDAY. Tricky. The most essential item today is your calendar. However, it will only be helpful if you have written down all important appointments, so search your memory to see if there is any date you might have missed. This is not the best day to fiddle with bank and stock accounts, moving sums of money from one to the other. You are unlikely to gain anything at the end of the day by doing this, and you will have wasted a lot of time and energy as well. A friendship you think of as straightforward might actually be costing the other person a lot of effort. Be aware that they could be struggling with a strong romantic attraction to you which they are not in a position to express.

22. TUESDAY. Deceptive. It is absolutely vital to be able to rely on your friends. If you spend time with someone who lets you down, this relationship must be remedied. Make a private resolution to give the person one more chance to honor a commitment. If they fail, let them know exactly how you feel about being treated so casually. Financially you may be sacrificing quite a lot for the sake of what you hope will be future economic security. Life is full of surprises, and it would make more sense to give yourself enough to enjoy the present while still putting away a regular amount. You are not always at your best in a group situation; tonight you may want to avoid crowds of any kind.

23. WEDNESDAY. Delightful. Youngsters are apt to be hatching their own plans which are causing them great pleasure and lots of giggles. As long as you feel nothing negative is going on, you should leave them alone. They may even be planning a lovely surprise for you. An unexpected phone call could start your heart fluttering as soon as you recognize the sound of a special person's voice. It means nothing that you have not heard from them for some time; probably their life has been too hectic to get in touch before now. It is important to give colleagues the benefit of the doubt and allow them to make their own mistakes; they may actually come up with a major breakthrough if left alone.

24. THURSDAY. Fulfilling. This promises to be a busy but fulfilling day for those who are willing to get out of the usual routine. Financially you could receive an offer you cannot refuse, even though other people may have turned it down before you were asked. A romantic affair that has had to be conducted in secrecy can now be shouted from the rooftops. For the first time you will be able to show friends how proud you are of your beloved. Where work is concerned, you are best off staying behind the scenes. Let colleagues make a lot of noise about what they are doing; it should be sufficient for you to know that your contribution is just as valuable.

25. FRIDAY. Burdensome. Mistakes that you make have a way of catching up with you. This is one of those days when you have to eat humble pie and admit to an error. As a result you may have to work late, but that cannot be avoided. A sense of heavy responsibility is not necessarily negative although it can make life somewhat joyless. Other people will get more pleasure out of your company if you are helping them for your own enjoyment rather than just to be dutiful. If parents seem more critical than usual, you may not have fully explained to them the value of what you have been able to achieve in past months. There is no point letting them irritate you to the point that positive conversation becomes impossible.

26. SATURDAY. Uneven. It is not the Cancer style to come on too strong with a romantic partner, so avoid being the heavy in a love relationship. Such forceful behavior smacks of insecurity. If you believe the other person is truly the one for you, have faith that they will feel the same way. Even if you are dissatisfied with your personal appearance, that is no reason to go out and buy outrageous new clothes. Choose some outfits in your usual style, but far-out designs are likely to hang unworn at the back of the closet. When considering your future prospects, do not forget to take loved ones' plans into account as well as your own desires.

27. SUNDAY. Sensitive. Even if you find it hard to make up your mind what you want to do, try to avoid saying one thing then turning around doing another. Your family needs to know where they stand with you. You can afford to be a little unselfish. Nothing will be gained by brooding angrily at friends until you explode. If you feel they have behaved badly, find a tactful and restrained way of telling them. Youngsters may tire you out with their constant questions and demands. There is no way to get your own tasks done unless you can persuade children to lend a helping hand. Just the sense of helping you should cheer them, even if they actually cannot accomplish very much.

28. MONDAY. Fair. Cancer people who are starting a new job are bound to be feeling a little nervous. However, have confidence that you will soon get the hang of it. In fact, the work and routines may seem strangely familiar, and even staff members will probably conform to type. Consolidate the recent improvement in your health by resolving to stick to a diet that has been very effective. If you backslide now, all your good work could be undone in only a few days. Although a romantic affair may be past the exciting stage, there is no reason to feel restless. Learn to appreciate the pleasure of being able to rely on someone for steady, supportive affection at all times.

29. TUESDAY. Helpful. If you are obtaining counseling or therapy, you may feel that progress has been temporarily halted. Such work has a natural ebb and flow, and probably you are now just quietly absorbing all that you have recently learned about yourself. The early part of the day offers the best chance to get practical tasks done. Make the most of the morning to complete shopping and cleaning chores; otherwise they might not get finished this week. Writing a difficult letter could occupy most of the evening. It is important that you take the time to express your feelings clearly and without giving offense. Do not send the letter for a day or two so you can review it.

30. WEDNESDAY. Bumpy. When your attention has to turn to the practical matters of balancing your income and expenses, it is inevitable that inner emotional concerns get ignored. However, that does not mean they do not exist, and today is likely to be the time when powerfully deep feelings of love surge up from the depths of your psyche. This can be quite a difficult time for Cancer people with brothers and sisters who are following a lifestyle perceived as being quite unwise and even risky. Keep in mind, however, that experience is a great teacher. The best you can do is stand by and be ready to offer support when and if it becomes needed.

31. THURSDAY. Profitable. A financial tip could be a real winner, especially one that comes from a stockbroker or financial adviser. However, if it involves complicated efforts on your part, it would be worth finding out if the process can be simplified in any way. There is a fine line between friendship and love, but it is never clear when you have crossed it. Once on the other side there is no going back. Relax and enjoy your newfound happiness. It is important to keep calm if on the road today. You are almost certain to find plenty of reasons to become annoyed, but it will be more satisfying as well as safer to maintain your own high standard of driving while keeping your composure.

JUNE

1. FRIDAY. Excellent. This is an ideal day for finishing off tasks that have been nagging at your conscience. Make those phone calls that you have been putting off; they are bound to be easier than expected. It never hurts to think of other people first. If a friend gives you a hard-luck story, do not just dismiss it but ask how you can be of some help. If you are concerned about the appearance of your home, this is the time to do something about it. Get someone who does not often visit you to look at it with fresh eyes; they should then be able to make some creative suggestions to spruce up every room. Enjoy an evening out by all means, but try not to overdo the food or the drink, and steer clear of smoky places.

2. SATURDAY. Good. Cancer singles who are looking for love are unlikely to get through the day without quite a passionate encounter. The circumstances might be rather unpromising, but there is no doubting the look in that attractive person's eye. Be alert to romantic possibilities while filling up your car at the local gas station or waiting in line at the grocery store. Lost items are almost bound to be fairly easily found within the house. All it takes is thorough looking, and do a bit of tidying up while you are at it. If you are entertaining friends at home this evening, put the emphasis on relaxed conversation. Once you create the right atmosphere, social success is virtually guaranteed.

3. SUNDAY. Misleading. Today's more reckless mood can tempt you into making all kinds of unwise decisions. The last thing you should do is to risk your safety and health by trying a new and possibly dangerous sport. Do not worry about money at the moment; any advice you receive is apt to be be ill-informed. If it becomes possible to concentrate on creative endeavors, you should be able to surprise yourself with unusual images and insights. This takes hard work, however; there is no point expecting to receive inspiration via a dream. Where romance is concerned, take all that is said to you with a grain of salt. Generous promises may never be fulfilled despite the best of intentions.

4. MONDAY. Distressing. The workweek starts in a rather chaotic way. Phone conversations could be cut off and computers go down, so prepare yourself mentally for a day of struggle. Extra care is needed when on the road because other drivers may not have their mind on the road at all. Even if youngsters have been doing well at school recently, their latest grades could be a little disappointing. Rather than berate them for not excelling, try to accept that they cannot maintain the highest grade-point average all the time. Your health will not benefit from a strange diet, no matter how fashionable it might be at the moment. Eat light and right for the best dieting results.

5. TUESDAY. Difficult. There is no reason for you to put up with bullying at work. If someone is trying to impose their will on you without good cause, then make a formal complaint as high up the ladder of authority as you feel is necessary. This is not the best day for trying to cook an elaborate meal. The results may not be anything like you had hoped for, and you might have to wind up going out to eat. Happily there is a chance to make some extra money, even if only for a short time. As long as you are prepared to give up a few evenings, a friend may pay you to help them get a new venture off the ground. Since you really cannot afford to refuse their request, agree willingly.

6. WEDNESDAY. Positive. Today begins a more social period. You will not do yourself any harm dusting off your address book and calling up a few friends who have not been around for a while. Everyone needs ideals to aspire to, and this is a period when you can afford to aim very high. It does not matter so much that you may not live up to your own expectations; the intention is what counts. Unless you change your daily habits, your body is likely to begin to show the strain soon. Do not continue punishing yourself by working too hard; lighten up and allow more time for relaxation in your daily schedule. A job interview can go well if you figure out what the interviewer wants you to say.

7. THURSDAY. Successful. If you are prepared to act quickly, there could be a total revolution in your working life. However, you have to grasp the opportunity and take on a job that no one else wants to do. It is a matter of seeing the potential when other people are oblivious to it. Some extra exercise would be useful. You could benefit from joining a team since you will then have no excuse for not attending training sessions. Talk too much today and you could alienate someone with whom you need to work in close harmony. Without thinking, you might hit a sore spot which they will find hard to forgive. Romantically, this is an ideal moment to ask for a deeper commitment.

8. FRIDAY. Relaxing. At last you can wind down toward the weekend break. This might make you realize how hard you usually work. Take this opportunity to think over your closest relationships. All emotional bonds need conscious thought in order to stay loving and fresh, but that is exactly what usually gets shoved aside by the pressures of everyday life. Cancer people who are entering into a new business partnership should have faith in basic instincts. If you are unhappy about any aspect at all of the business plan, bring it to your partner's attention at the earliest suitable opportunity. An equal partnership is favored to avoid hurt feelings in the future.

9. SATURDAY. Sensitive. Not all friendships are straightforward, especially between men and women. Sometimes there is a lingering feeling of sensual attraction, no matter what other romantic involvements might be ongoing. This needs to be handled carefully, and perhaps even discussed together. Money can be a touchy subject, especially when there is not much of it to spend. If you are asked out to an expensive occasion that you really cannot afford, it is up to you whether to admit that you would rather let it pass. At the moment your future vision is not very clear; the message is that you should be living in the present to the fullest and not worrying about what may be.

10. SUNDAY. Easygoing. Allow the day to begin slowly. An extra half hour in bed will not hurt, for a start. Your energy may not be very plentiful, so it is not a good idea to force yourself to do housework or other practical chores. Instead, get on the phone to a few friends and indulge in some harmless gossip. This is a good time to thoroughly discuss emotional issues with loved ones. Rather than worrying silently, bring your concerns out into the open. Doing so should cause them to simply evaporate. Creatively, today promises to be very fertile. Cancer people who like to get out and paint or write about nature should do just that; go to a favorite beauty spot and capture the inspiring landscape.

11. MONDAY. Fair. If you are handling money in the course of your work, there is no need to take sole responsibility for large sums. Unless you are comfortable with handling a lot of cash, ask a senior staff member to be your partner, taking some of the responsibility off your shoulders. The solution to a personal problem may be almost beyond rational analysis. Since you will not find an answer by thought alone, trust your unconscious to come up with the best approach. Reflect on the problem for a while, then put it to one side. Within a day or two the solution could pop into your mind out of the blue. Candid photos taken today of loved ones will provide many happy memories.

12. TUESDAY. Uneven. Get out of bed early and prepare for a busy day. The daily routine could be complicated by equipment failure, so it may be necessary to fall back on doing work by hand. This will make practical tasks more tiring than usual. A visit to the dentist could reveal that you have quite a lot of work to be done. Instead of wishing you had stayed away, be thankful that you are beginning treatment before your mouth gets any worse. There may be money to be made from unusual investments. Do not turn up your nose at tips which other people consider dubious; just check them out by obtaining a second opinion.

13. WEDNESDAY. Demanding. It is all very well for people to give you health advice, but only you really know what feels right. If a gym instructor or personal trainer lays out an exercise plan that seems too demanding, do not just meekly accept it. Explain that you would rather start gently and work up to the challenging exercises. Sometimes it is your duty to come to the defense of a beleaguered colleague. However, think carefully and make sure you know both sides of the story before putting yourself on the line. Unjustly accusing someone in power is hardly likely to enhance your promotion chances. Unless you make sure all pets are indoors before going to bed, one may go astray.

14. THURSDAY. Hopeful. Sometimes it appears that you have a guardian angel who pulls you out of tricky situations in the nick of time. This is actually probably due to your inner attitude of faith. All the same, you should offer up thanks for having avoided a potentially disastrous financial gamble. Today you can be of great help to relatives whose life experience is not as broad as your own. If they request assistance dealing with authorities or filling out official forms, lend your assistance gladly. Even though you probably would like to have a lot of time to yourself, this is a day for reaching out to other people and making your presence known.

15. FRIDAY. Buoyant. There is something in the air for every Cancer person today. If you are hoping for a romantic encounter, you probably will not be disappointed. Just try not to get too carried away, no matter how attractive the other person is. Someone new on the scene might play on your emotions without getting very involved personally. An unexpected windfall could arrive in the mail as a small but useful sum of money. For once you can spend this on yourself with pure pleasure and a clear conscience. If you want to get ahead in your present job, work harder. A continuing show of competence will make more of an impact on your employer than pleas for a promotion or pay raise.

16. SATURDAY. Changeable. This should be an enjoyable day as long as you can make up your mind what you want to do. There is no point starting and then stopping, or jumping from one activity to another. Make a plan and stick to it, all the while remaining flexible enough to deal with disruptions. Spending more time than usual with children will do both you and them a great deal of good. There is no need to give special treats to youngsters; simply sharing an ordinary day can be quite magical. Check your phone if you do not get any calls by this afternoon. It may be out of order, and you would not want to miss hearing from a special person you recently met.

17. SUNDAY. Variable. The main difficulty to deal with today is a tendency to drift off into a dream world. It would be best not to start any demanding or complicated jobs around the house because it may never get done. Also, your mate or partner will not appreciate the mess you are apt to cause. All social matters are highlighted. Overcome your natural Cancer shyness and boldly introduce yourself to a few new people early in the day. And do not be too bashful to return glances someone on the other side of the room gives you. This evening is a good time to withdraw back into your shell and concentrate on your own thoughts. You may also want to just relax with a favorite video.

18. MONDAY. Rewarding. Although it may not be immediately obvious, as a Cancer you have teaching skills that should be put to use from time to time. Your naturally sympathetic nature makes it easy for you to identify with beginners in any subject. For this reason you can gear material at exactly the right level. Keep this in mind as a possible second source of income; it could be worth taking professional training. The morning hours may mainly be spent on the phone. Even if you find this tiring, you will soon realize that an immense amount of work is getting done through making good contacts. New friends could shock you with their radical ideas, but do not just dismiss them.

19. TUESDAY. Important. Financially there is a real killing to be made. Consult a stock expert and see if you can buy shares that are just about to take off in value. Information technology is an especially appropriate field. Your personal development should be given precedence since you can now progress in leaps and bounds, if you have the courage to face your hidden urges. It might even help to obtain some counseling for a short while. You are likely to feel rather lethargic, which could be Nature telling you to slow down. The way to determine if you need to take it easy is to get some exercise. It will either wake you up or physically drain you, in which case you need to relax more.

20. WEDNESDAY. Cautious. Pets become members of the family very quickly, as everyone in the household forms their own attachment. It is therefore important to be clear from the very beginning whether one person is the owner. This will save children's sensitive feelings. It may be that colleagues are working against you rather than with you. Although you may sense that an open confrontation is inevitable, there should be a less aggressive approach available. You may want to take them aside and explain your perception of their behavior. You could be misunderstanding. Do not allow memories of the past to occupy your mind so much that they block out your present happiness and contentment.

21. THURSDAY. Bright. Conditions today offer you a bright new start with your self-confidence. As a Cancer you are changing all the time, whether you realize it or not. Do not allow yourself to get stuck with an out-of-date image. Buy some stunning new clothes and step out as if you had only just realized how attractive you are. It may be necessary to take a phone call in private, which is not going to make that special person in your life feel to secure. Do not leave them to wonder; explain that unfortunately some of your family business has to be personal. This is a good day for buying electrical items. Spending enough to get top-of-the-line models will be worth the cost in the long run.

22. FRIDAY. Promising. Sometimes you just cannot predict who will be attracted to you. For this reason it can be all the more exciting when you receive an invitation from a friend of a friend who you only met casually. Try to find time to have lunch or an after-work drink with colleagues. This should give you a good chance to talk about something other than work as you get to know each other a little better. Recent savings mean that you should feel quite happy about spending money on yourself. Since you have undoubtedly given lots of consideration to what you want to buy, your purchases are almost bound to be worthwhile. Everyone benefits from a little self-indulgence once in a while.

23. SATURDAY. Peaceful. If you are going away this weekend, get off to an early start, or at least leave on time. It will not matter too much if you do not remember everything; the atmosphere is apt to be so relaxed that nothing can spoil your pleasure. This reasonably undisturbed morning gives you a chance to reflect on your personal plans for the future. It is a good idea to put these down in writing, and keep them somewhere special to be looked at and reassessed in a few months. Shopping can be more of a pleasure than a chore. Stock up as much as possible on essential food and household items, but allow yourself a few treats as well such as out-of-season fruit or vegetables.

24. SUNDAY. Mixed. It may be quite hard to know where you stand today since there is not going to be a smooth flow of energy to carry you through. A feeling of greater security could be shattered by worry about future finances. However, you probably will decide that there is nothing you can do to improve the situation right now so there is not need to let it get you down. This is a good day to work around the house. While you are absorbed in simple chores, the pressures of the outside world should totally disappear. A close friend may be demanding more and more of your time and attention. The sooner you discuss this with them, the better your relationship will be.

25. MONDAY. Productive. A mixture of common sense and inspired imagination could help you come up with the solution to a work problem that has been eluding you. Do not get carried away, however. Work out all the details before putting your new plan into action. Sometimes it can be more of a relief than a sorrow when people connected to your past finally stop being in contact. If you were not particularly close, there is little to be mourned; and you will always have your memories. As a Cancer you are very loving with your family and friends. Whether you are able to rise to the occasion when a slight acquaintance needs your help is a question of how you define your social circle.

26. TUESDAY. Disconcerting. There may be problems with your car, which could mean being without private transportation for at least a day. It is vital to keep phone numbers for appointments with you, in case you get stuck en route. Do not expect too much if you are meeting someone from the classified advertisements section of the local paper. A friendship might spring up, but you would be foolish to expect anything romantic. You might find to your chagrin that older relatives are not always wiser. Turning to them for advice can be flattering for them, but what they tell you needs to be analyzed quite critically. Friends of your own age might be of more practical help.

27. WEDNESDAY. Frustrating. A bright start could arouse unreasonable hopes of success. However, as long as you make the most of your business and social connections, you should get retraining and the time involved in working your way up from the bottom. As a Cancer you like a comfortable life. If you feel that your home is becoming too much of an open house for friends, it is time to put your foot down. Privacy is very important to you, and other people, even family members, must learn to respect this. Remember to eat plenty of fresh fruit and salads while they are in season and plentiful. Buy from a farmers' market if possible.

5. THURSDAY. Stressful. You and your mate or partner may be barely on speaking terms. It is essential that you find time to sit down and calmly talk to each other about recent problems. There is nothing that cannot be solved, if you are prepared to give a little and to take a little less. If you are waiting for the outcome of a legal case, try not to dwell on it too much. Guessing which way it will go is basically a waste of time; the answer will only come when all has been aired and then resolved. Cancer people who recently ended a romantic relationship could benefit from spending some time as a single person before rejoining the world of dating. Rediscover your independence, and enjoy your freedom.

6. FRIDAY. Fulfilling. In one sense this promises to be a straightforward day. You are not in a mood to put up with any beating around the bush, and would much rather know exactly where you stand with friends and colleagues. It can be quite a pleasure to meet up unexpectedly with someone you have not seen for years. There is sure to be a lot of news and gossip to catch up on, and new bonds of friendship to be forged. If you feel like staying at home tonight, do not just lie around idly. Make sure your mind is occupied, either by conversation with loved ones or by getting engrossed in the latest literary sensation. The more open your mind is, the more you will find to enjoy in life.

7. SATURDAY. Low-keyed. You are apt to feel a little fuzzyheaded this morning. Allow yourself some extra time to get going, and do not drive until you are fully awake and alert. Your dreams have a message to convey. It might help to discuss them with someone else, who may be more objective about their imagery than you are able to be. Love does not always begin in an obvious way. If you find yourself reaching for the phone to call a certain person in the middle of the day, that could be a sign that you are beginning to fall for each other. A sense of duty will probably keep you close to home and family members throughout the day. There is much you can do to support your loved ones.

8. SUNDAY. Helpful. On this energetic day there is no need to feel you are the only one interested in getting your home in tiptop condition. Ask for help with chores and you will undoubtedly get the assistance you need. A minor health problem can probably be cleared up by improving your diet. Avoid junk food as much as possible, and soon you are bound to notice the difference. This is a good day for teaching children a greater sense of responsibility. Begin by giving them regular pet-care tasks, such as feeding and grooming. This is likely to be so pleasurable that they come to think of duty as something they actually want to do as a reward in itself.

9. MONDAY. Useful. Expect to be on a bit of a short fuse this morning. There is no point blaming other people for a foolhardy financial decision you made yourself. Do not attempt to pretend you were persuaded into it against your will. It would be good to get acquainted with the latest in office technology rather than relying on the expertise of your colleagues. Also, if you understand how most equipment works, you can make yourself indispensable. The best part of the day is likely to be the time you spend alone. Even half an hour of solitude can be deeply refreshing, to the point that you might want to make it a rule that you take a similar break every day of the work week.

10. TUESDAY. Manageable. If something seems to be holding you back, it is probably more a feeling of reluctance rather than an outside force. It could be that you are caught up in work which you do not enjoy. Examine your reactions closely, and consider making a change if necessary. It can be a nuisance to have to visit relatives at a distance, but sometimes there is no choice. A family gathering that has a certain historical importance is not to be missed no matter what your personal feelings might be. Try to become more aware of a tendency to be as hard on loved ones as you are on yourself. At the very least, show your appreciation for a lovingly cooked meal.

11. WEDNESDAY. Satisfying. The key to making this a reasonably satisfying day is to focus above the daily treadmill of existence. Look for the larger meaning in life, especially for what makes life a profound pleasure for you personally. If you are dealing with people living overseas, it is important to put as much of your own personality into negotiations as possible. The sense of communicating with a real human being rather than someone who is repeating information by rote will have a very positive effect. Later in the day watch that you do not get trapped into supporting someone you actually do not have much faith in. Do not let this person play with your feelings.

12. THURSDAY. Sparkling. The air may glimmer with a special sparkle when you come face-to-face with someone who seems extremely attractive. Although this is not the moment to declare your feelings, it should be memorable just to make contact and let unspoken thoughts pass between you. Today marks the beginning of an encouraging period in which to take a positive yet critical look at yourself. Focus on how well you are fulfilling your ambitions, and whether they are giving you the pleasure you expected. It can help to start a diary for occasional notes about life in general. If you have financial worries, discuss them with an expert; your bank should be able to offer useful advice.

13. FRIDAY. Buoyant. Put superstitious fears out of mind. Today's mood of optimism will attract good fortune. At the moment you appear to have enough confidence to tackle whatever life throws your way. Right now other people find you inspiring, but they are bound to be disappointed if you make promises that are not kept. Beware of a tendency to be full of hot air. You can expect deep satisfaction from scurrying around getting minor chores cleared up before the weekend begins. You can do twice the ordinary amount of work, but make sure other people pull their weight as well. Healthwise, you should be reaping the benefits of a better diet. Vow to stick to your current eating plan despite a certain degree of boredom with it.

14. SATURDAY. Lively. Quite a lively day beckons you. This is a great time to go out with kids. Surprise them with a mystery tour to a place they have never visited before. They are sure to love it. If you enjoy poking around in out-of-the-way shops, indulge yourself this morning but take along plenty of money. You are almost certain to be tempted beyond resistance by unusual and exotic items for yourself and your home. A formal social occasion could prove beneficial as you meet people who could help advance your career. However, it would neither be tactful nor effective to plunge straight into that subject; save such a discussion for a second meeting later on.

15. SUNDAY. Frustrating. It may well be that you are doing yourself no favors in your choice of romantic partners. Secretly you might not believe yourself to be worth a really good match. This is a good time to sit down and consider that you will attract a better sort of person if you can increase your overall sense of self-esteem. Money may be in short supply at the moment, entirely due to your own fault. If you have been spending a lot on pleasure recently, realize that it will not hurt to have a quieter time for a few weeks. Family members will offer more solid emotional support than friends, since they understand you so well. Consider advice even if you do not want to hear it.

16. MONDAY. Exhilarating. Even though you are usually quite shy, it can be exhilarating to have to speak in front of a group. If you have to address a meeting, summon up your courage and let the strength of your convictions carry you through. Hopes and wishes only come true if you work diligently at achieving them. This is a basic truth that has become very obvious in recent weeks. If you want to achieve a personal aim, do not rely on other people. It is primarily through your own efforts that you will eventually be successful. It might be necessary to leave an idealistic organization when their methods begin to diverge from your own sense of what is right and proper.

17. TUESDAY. Sensitive. Romance is lovely as a dream, but the reality of getting involved with someone can be very different. Keep in mind that every relationship has to make the transition from candlelit dinners to sharing the daily chores. This natural progression must be coped with even though you both may regret the heady excitement of the early days. There is no point hoping to get rich doing menial work. No matter how many extra hours you put in, a low wage is never going to amount to much. Reorder your priorities, and reconsider your talents. Find time to lend someone a hand, even if that just involves helping someone across the road.

18. WEDNESDAY. Inspiring. A tactful approach to a friend's emotional problems can work wonders for them. Your understanding of how they think and feel can be just what they need. There is opportunity for you to make a clean break with past memories that have been causing you some unhappiness. All you have to do is learn not to brood on negative feelings, which of course takes a bit of discipline. This is a promising day for all charitable work. You could even be put in charge of a sum of money to be distributed to a worthy cause. This might give you such an appetite for the work that you are eager to do more on a volunteer basis.

19. THURSDAY. Promising. After a long period when it seemed that romance was doomed to fail, new light is dawning on the horizon. The other person probably needed to shake off a lesser attachment before they could truly get emotionally involved with you. Now you have the green light to proceed, so make the most of it. There may be quite an inner conflict going on at the moment because part of you is very happy living a well-organized life. Another part of you, however, is yearning for creative freedom and unusual experiences. The good news is that sustaining such a dual existence without overlooking either side can be immensely positive. Put more of yourself into everything you do.

20. FRIDAY. Pleasant. This is your chance to accomplish a complete makeover on yourself. Decide which aspects of your character you want to bring to the fore, then make a conscious effort to do so. It would not hurt to get some advice on altering your image as well. Where business is concerned, it is important to remember that colleagues and partners must be given their chance to be heard. Even if you are convinced that your plans are better than theirs, they still have a great deal to contribute. Do your utmost to avoid all legal entanglements; try to work out an out-of-court agreement if possible and you will save yourself a great deal of worry as well as expense.

21. SATURDAY. Enjoyable. Even though you may feel like lying around and not doing much, that is not going to happen. Loved ones have different plans, beginning with work being done on your home. Buckle down and finish off minor repair jobs that have been outstanding for so long. Your finances are not in the best of shape. If you have been dipping into savings, that has to be remedied. It might help to work out exactly how your weekly expenditure tallies with your income. Looking through old photo albums can be pleasantly nostalgic, but remember that loved ones might be embarrassed if you share this experience with friends.

22. SUNDAY. Mixed. This is a good day to check your home security. Make sure all window locks work properly, and that doors are not left open. More outdoor lighting can also help. A greater sense of inner confidence can be achieved if you listen to what loved ones say about you. Do not think that they are biased because they are fond of you; actually, this enables them to appreciate your good points to the full. Shyness will get you nowhere in a romantic situation. All the same, it is not necessary to wear your heart on your sleeve. Sooner or later you will have to make the first move. Try to relax this evening without allowing certain events of the day to totally occupy your mind.

23. MONDAY. Successful. Fortunately you have the mental energy that will carry you through this busy day even if you do not feel physically on top of the world. This will count for a lot when you are expected to take on more responsibility than usual. This morning is likely to be a rather frustrating time because you cannot get a project finished due to circumstances beyond your control. The best thing you can do is get on the phone and explain the difficulties; do not try to bluff your way out of it. Take extra care of yourself during the latter part of the day. Guard against missing meals or snacking as you go. You need good food and proper rest to be at your best.

24. TUESDAY. Uneven. The last thing you should do is to start gossiping about neighbors, no matter what the provocation. If you have a problem, face them with it. Going behind their backs is sure to create a bad atmosphere. Cancer parents who are looking for a suitable private school for youngsters to attend this fall should go by instinct. As important as academic excellence is a warm and supportive atmosphere is equally important. Where love is concerned, you have to keep your feelings to yourself for a little while longer. The other person in your life may seem to be unaware of your interest, and it would be foolhardy to come on to them too strong.

25. WEDNESDAY. Hopeful. Moving can be quite traumatic for you, but right now all should go smoothly. If you have found somewhere that is perfect for you, the house itself may seem to be cooperating in your move. Parents or other older relatives could come up with quite promising suggestions for making extra cash, and they might be willing to loan you the amount needed to get a small business off the ground. The ending of a love relationship is bound to leave you feeling a little wistful, but if you are honest there is probably a good deal of relief involved as well. Now you need to take your time before looking around for another romantic partner or even beginning to date.

26. THURSDAY. Happy. Keep an open mind and your heart's desire could appear on the scene. However, this may not occur in quite the form you expect, so it is essential to be receptive to whatever happens and whoever you meet. You might receive a tip-off that would enable you to make some extra money through an astute investment. Any money that is made in this manner should be put away for future use rather than spent now. Since Cancer people are usually happiest when surrounded by family members, a gathering of relatives should bring you deep pleasure.

Of course you do not always have to be the one who organizes such get-togethers; let other loved ones take their turn, too.

27. FRIDAY. Variable. It is difficult to say just how a romantic involvement is going to evolve. One thing is fairly certain, however: your intended is not being totally honest with you. This may be with the best of motives, so it is an issue that needs to be handled with delicacy. Quite a playful mood is apt to strike you as the workweek comes to an end, making you rather disinclined to do any serious work. Indeed, you would be better off inspiring other people rather than forcing yourself. Unfortunately, though, you may have to buckle down for a while. Money does not grow on trees, and this fact must be impressed upon youngsters who expect any and all kinds of luxuries.

28. SATURDAY. Unsettling. A quiet day is the last thing you can expect, so resign yourself to not getting much done without being frequently interrupted. Plans to concentrate on your favorite hobby may have to be abandoned. A close friend in some sort of emotional crisis could require immediate attention. Practical support will be valued, as will a shoulder to cry on. If you have been making serious attempts at photography, you may be finding it a lot harder than you expected to produce a good picture. It could be worth taking a class, which may be more helpful than how-to books. Avoid socializing in a crowded venue this evening; stay home if possible.

29. SUNDAY. Encouraging. Romance is definitely an option if you are so inclined. Curiously, however, at the moment you may feel you better off fully appreciating your circle of friends and avoiding the emotional roller-coaster of a closer romantic relationship. This choice is actually is a very healthy sign. Children's talents may be at an embryonic stage, but that is no reason not to encourage them. Nor should you feel threatened if they show signs of excelling in an artistic or musical field in which you have little ability. A quieter afternoon allows you to get your affairs in order before settling down to a relaxing evening with loved ones.

30. MONDAY. Disruptive. Changes at your workplace appear inevitable. If you attempt to resist them, you will simply be swimming against the tide. No one enjoys profound upheaval, but in this case the consequences should be positive. It is just a matter of hanging in and biding your time. If you have been letting your health take a back seat recently, this is the day to consider your general level of physical fitness. Measure yourself against a friend who exercises regularly, you might be shamed into doing likewise. It should be possible to earn extra money by diversifying your skills. There may even be a leisure pursuit you could practice for spare cash.

31. TUESDAY. Uncertain. When you are given additional responsibility, there is no point pretending that you are not up to it. Many people do not feel grown up, no matter what their age. For this reason it is vital to square your shoulders and accept that you can do what is being asked of you. A sudden whim could lead you to rearrange everything in your kitchen or bathroom but this will have the unfortunate effect that no one can find anything. Consider whether you have made an improvement or created change simply for the sake of it. It is best to keep quiet about your physical attraction to a colleague. If you were to get romantically involved, working together would become very difficult.

AUGUST

1. WEDNESDAY. Disappointing. If you expect a close relationship to fulfill you in every way, you will inevitably be let down. No one person can be everything to you, which is why it is essential to remain in touch with friends even when you have settled in a partnership. High hopes of a business deal will probably have to be brought down to a more realistic level once you realize the full implications. For one thing, there may be more expenses involved than you had calculated. The brightest spots in the day should come from compliments concerning your appearance, which can give your confidence a big boost. Do not be so modest that you turn aside words spoken in all sincerity.

2. THURSDAY. Tricky. Although your emotions should be quite stable, something is apt to make you change your mind from one moment to the next. This is perfectly acceptable until money is involved; then you will simply have to make a decision and stick to it. Children may be having a few worrisome dreams. If you are called out of bed to comfort them several nights in a row, do some close questioning to discover what is at the root of the problem. A small item left to you as a legacy could come as a surprise. It might not be anything you particularly want, but a family heirloom should be cherished rather than sold or given away. Do not stay up late tonight.

3. FRIDAY. Deceptive. Although it is a cliché that love is blind, nonetheless the words are true. When your deeper passions are aroused, good sense tends to go straight out of the window. Try to get a grip on yourself and listen if friends try to warn you to stay away from a certain new acquaintance. Joint savings could melt away if you keep on dipping into them for everyday purchases. It would be better to plan on saving a little less, thus freeing up more money for current expenses. If you feel that your present lifestyle is lacking in some significant way, do something about it. Take up the study of religion or philosophy, and start to work out some lifetime answers for yourself.

4. SATURDAY. Fortunate. On this full day there is plenty of opportunity to get weekend tasks done as thoroughly as you would like. This is a good time to knuckle down to more mundane chores that may have been neglected recently. If you can bear it, it may do you some good to clear out your system with a short fast. But you shouldn't miss more than three meals, and it's essential to drink plenty of fluids and not do heavy physical labor. A real turn-around could take place in your money management, if you have the will to get organized. Perhaps a friend or relative can help you sort out your personal accounts, and get a sense of perspective.

5. SUNDAY. Happy. If you have bottled up feelings for some time, express them without waiting a moment longer. The only danger is that pressure has built up in you to such an extent that you blurt out your views. Rehearse what you are going to say, and try to be moderate. Youngsters can contribute a lot to your sense of well-being just by being their own sweet selves. Consider, however, whether you really pay attention to them rather than encouraging them not to disturb you. You are bound to feel more creative than usual. Do not neglect to jot down your bright ideas so that you can work on them at a later date when you are ready to try something new and daring.

6. MONDAY. Uplifting. A new training course could be exactly what you need, giving you the opportunity for personal growth as well as for learning new work skills. Falling in love with someone who lives far away has the advantage at least of never getting to see so much of each other that you become bored. Greater self-confidence can come from launching yourself into cultural events that at one time might have appeared far beyond you. As long as you go along with a friend who is as high-brow as you, such occasions should be highly educational. Try not to become too involved with every health fad that comes along.

7. TUESDAY. Productive. Be prepared to work hard just as long as there is good money in it. You will probably have to negotiate in order to get a wage that is right and fair. Youngsters need to be taught at an early age to protect themselves when outside. This is the time to warn them against talking to strangers or accepting gifts. Your temper could trip you up with colleagues, creating quite an unpleasant atmosphere. As a Cancer you tend to be rather moody; if you indulge yourself in this way too much, other people will get fed up and may actively try to avoid you. An immediate apology would be a good idea to restore harmony.

8. WEDNESDAY. Frustrating. Sometimes you have to be a little more assertive than usual when you are going after a job you really want. If you interview but are not given assurances about how you have done, ask for clarification. It would be foolish to make promises you have no intention of keeping. You may do so with the best of intentions, but it is far better to tell a friend straight off that you cannot help rather than raising their hopes only to let them down with a bang. As far as money goes, you may well think of your wallet as a bottomless pit. Unless your mate or partner is willing to play the role of tightwad, money will keep on flowing right through your fingers. A detailed budget could help a lot.

9. THURSDAY. Rewarding. Get through the early hours of the day and you will then be rewarded with an easier period. Do not ever try to use charm on a senior staff member. This person will see right through you and is bound to take a dim view of your efforts. Since Cancer people like to look after others, it is important that your kitchen be well designed and fully equipped. Consider splurging on a proper remodeling, which will be an aesthetic as well as a functional delight. Rifts with your parents or other older relatives can be healed if both sides are willing to live and let live. You should be the one to hold out the olive branch in hopes of righting your relationship.

10. FRIDAY. Cautious. The best plan for the day is to keep your nose to the grindstone, much as you would like to rest and relax. Actually, doing daily tasks can be very positive since they have the effect of channeling your energy to positive use. A more restless mood can show up in moments of irritation. However, lashing out at loved ones will do neither you nor them any good. Be patient; realize that your mood is to blame, not the actions of other people. Keeping tabs on youngsters is likely to be a real challenge. Their tendency to get into mischief is likely to be even more pronounced than usual. Try to steer them into lots of different activities, in order to wear them out by nighttime.

11. SATURDAY. Buoyant. Cancer people who are setting off for a summer vacation should be in a buoyant mood. However, do not let that mood relax you so much that you leave behind essential items such as medication you might need while you are away. This is an ideal day to enlarge your circle of friends, perhaps by joining a local club. Consider what kind of group would give you the chance to shine; amateur dramatics perhaps, or an environmental organization. Shopping should be fun, if a little expensive. You are perfectly justified in choosing good quality clothes since they always look better and last longer. Enjoy a friendly restaurant meal with relatives this evening.

12. SUNDAY. Disquieting. This is one of those days when you may simply feel that everyone and everything is stacked against you. The truth, however, is that everyone has times like this; it is just part of the natural rhythm of life. Normally you can rely on your friends to drop everything at a moment's notice in order to go out with you, but they all have their own plans today. For this reason you might have to spend a more solitary afternoon than you expected. This gives you the opportunity to reflect quietly on questions that have been bothering you, so it is really a positive period. Try not to succumb to a sense of dissatisfaction; there is much in your life for which you should give thanks.

13. MONDAY. Exciting. An unexpected alliance could spring up between you and a colleague. This will probably be based on an unspoken understanding more than anything else, but all the same it can make work a very harmonious experience. It is vital today to find some time for yourself. You need to sort out a few of the complications in your life, and now is the time to start. Acts of kindness should not be avoided merely because you might feel embarrassed to be seen performing them. Thinking of the recipient's feelings is likely to inspire you to act. A glamorous night out on the town would bring the day to a romantic and meaningful close in the arms of that special person in your life.

14. TUESDAY. Variable. A number of unfinished tasks demand your attention before you can get on to more interesting matters. It will be a good discipline for you to complete this work to the best of your ability. Self-doubt is only negative; do not let what you perceive as a personal failure bring you down. In actual fact, the true victory lies in behaving well under the most trying of circumstances. You can learn a lot from such experience. At the moment avoid any drastic measures to improve your health. Friends might recommend a distinctly odd diet or therapy, but the best method is to act on your own instincts and avoid anything that is untested and unproven.

15. WEDNESDAY. Sensitive. You and your mate or partner are heading for a falling out over shared finances unless you are more careful. Neither of you may quite have grasped that sharing means equal responsibility. You need to take each other into consideration, not act as if you are still single. Major developments in your personal understanding of life can often be quite unnerving. It is not always comfortable suddenly to see things in a new light, but with time you will get used to the changes. If you can give a neighbors' children a helping hand, they will be grateful. This could be the start of a useful arrangement whereby you each take turns watching kids or pets.

16. THURSDAY. Positive. This should be an especially memorable day if you have to persuade someone to accept your point of view. Your seeming willingness to compromise will appeal to them, so that they fail to realize that underneath you are set on having your own way. Spending a bit more money on yourself can boost your self-confidence. Even though it is only superficial, knowing that you look like a million dollars makes you feel that you are a force to be reckoned with. Love will smile on you, but only if you are open to it. In fact, all you have to do is sit and wait for an attractive person to make the first move to get to know you. After that it is entirely up to you to make the most of it.

17. FRIDAY. Manageable. Normally Cancer people are good with money. Your natural instinct is toward caution, which makes it all the more mysterious that you are not able to keep control at the moment. This could be the time to call in expert help to get you back on course financially. Where romance is concerned, your emotions are apt to be all jumbled. This is to be expected however, when you have just launched a relationship and cannot yet see where it is heading. With time you will begin to find your feet and see your way ahead. Everyone needs dreams in their life. A good way to stretch your imagination is to go to a concert or art gallery and immerse yourself in the beauty of the moment.

18. SATURDAY. Satisfying. Local trips with children can be a real pleasure. It is just important that you organize everything thoroughly so that youngsters have a firm sense of who is in control. Bright ideas for making money should spring up during the course of the day. You might even want to try your hand at writing, perhaps for a specialized hobby magazine. Neighbors can be very helpful if you have a problem with your car. In fact, you will probably be surprised at how many skilled people live close to you. Since you are unlikely to be in the most social of moods, it would be more satisfying to stay indoors and enjoy all the comforts of home.

19. SUNDAY. Helpful. Get the day off to a good start by focusing first on financial paperwork. There are probably old bank statements and even insurance policies that can be thrown out. What looks like a daunting task will soon become more manageable. If you resolve to improve your self-confidence, there is little you will not be able to achieve. The first step is to identify whether material possessions or emotional stability makes you feel most secure. Then you will have a clearer idea of what to aim for. A brother or sister may come in handy as a babysitter, happy to help you out in this way. However, guard against falling into the habit of taking them for granted whenever you want to go out.

20. MONDAY. Fair. You need to be quick on the draw this morning, since all kinds of challenges are apt to be thrown at you. With a flexible attitude, you can work wonders. All written work is highlighted. Even if you just have a few personal letters to dash off, make the most of this chance to get them finished. Focus on the pleasure hearing from you will give the recipients. This afternoon you will probably get some experience saying no to an employer who seems to think of you as superhuman. Everyone has definite limits, and it would be foolish to push yourself beyond what is feasible. Nor would you be able to produce good work that way.

21. TUESDAY. Stressful. On some occasions it becomes necessary to bite the bullet when you are criticized. Naturally this hurts your pride, but it is also a useful lesson in humility. Your nerves are apt to be a little jumpy, so that small things going wrong at work will upset you a lot. It would be best to delegate as much as possible to colleagues, and simplify your day. If youngsters seem a bit stressed out, it is probably because of the heavy demands that will soon be made on them at school. Of course you want them to do well, but the trend toward pushing children hard from an early age and during summer vacation has drawbacks.

Get in touch with teaching supervisors if you are very worried about this pressure to achieve.

22. WEDNESDAY. Profitable. This is an ideal day for buying or selling property. If you have an appointment to show a home, be sure to make it look not only neat and clean but also cozy and welcoming. You may need to consult a senior colleague to help you complete a tricky project. Their age and experience is just what is needed to put on the finishing touches. This can be a very positive day for getting rid of past negativity. Do not be surprised if your dreams conjure up sad scenes from the past; a kind of mental purging is taking place. A surprise sum of money could come your way from someone in the family you know only vaguely. Be thankful and enjoy spending it.

23. THURSDAY. Stimulating. There can be a real improvement in your health and fitness if you are prepared to be a bit tough on yourself. As a Cancer you tend to have a weakness for chocolate; if you can cut down on your intake, you will be making a good start toward looking and feeling better. Change is the watchword on the work scene. You may even find yourself receiving promotion to a level that makes your life much more interesting and challenging. Variety in your job will reawaken your original enthusiasm. Communications of all kinds are highlighted. Do not let friendship slip away through laziness; pick up the phone and make contact if you are unable to write.

24. FRIDAY. Promising. If you have been longing to begin a new romance, dress in your best and go out with optimism in your heart. That special someone is apt to be just around the corner, but it is up to you to ask for a date. This is a promising day to take a test. Belief in yourself gives you an air of authority. If you have prepared thoroughly, the test questions should not be a problem. Although you are not normally interested in taking risks with money, the chance of winning on a small gamble may suddenly seem overwhelmingly attractive. As long as you only wager a modest sum, you should find this a pleasurable and even profitable experience.

25. SATURDAY. Challenging. There are several hurdles to get over today. It will help if you realize they stem from your own attitudes to life and other people. It can be immensely positive to realize that everyone's standards differ, and thus to practice a bit more tolerance. A temporary separation from that special person in your life is bound to be upsetting. In a way, however, it can also be a good experience, since you will both begin to realize more fully how much you love and need each other. All leisure activities are primed to be highly enjoyable. You might feel creative urges that lead you toward artistic expression in paint, cloth, or words.

26. SUNDAY. Mixed. Lose yourself in a dream this morning. Ignore the clock and tell yourself that chores are really not important. Romance is very close to home. A friend of a close relative may begin to visit regularly. Do not be so modest that you imagine this person simply enjoys your hospitality. There is a real danger of having a minor accident when making repairs at home. Be sure all your tools are in good condition, and stay alert no matter how small the job may be. Follow all safety precautions. Thorough kitchen cleaning should not be put off. You may also want to stock your refrigerator.

27. MONDAY. Favorable. You can relax a little where money is concerned. As long as you are able to resist the temptation to spend a lot on beautiful items, there should be a steady flow into your bank account that will cushion you against future expenses. Everyone tends to feel more secure when they are loved, and this is certainly true for you. If friends comment on how wonderful you look, that is the reason even though you were probably not aware of it yourself. Set off for any appointments in good time since traffic is likely to be quite a problem. If there is anything you do not understand, ask to have it explained simply but completely.

28. TUESDAY. Demanding. Cancer people who are looking after children need to be active in order to keep them occupied. Youngsters will demand more than a usual amount of your attention, so you will probably have little time to yourself. It is vital to watch your words, especially at work. A critical remark could be taken in the wrong way simply because you are feeling rather irritated yourself. It would be a good idea to try to arrange a varied day, so that you can move frequently from one task to the next. Your boredom threshold is lower than usual because there is a problem on your mind. Relax this evening by taking your mate or partner out for dinner at a local restaurant.

29. WEDNESDAY. Serene. The middle of the week offers an oasis of peace during a busy period. It would be sensible to use this time to catch up on work that had to be put aside. You will probably be surprised by how much is in your in basket. Relations between you and your mate or partner should be reasonably serene, but this might make you feel restless instead of peaceful. Rather than trying to stir up trouble for the sake of it, arrange a romantic weekend away together. Cancer people who are trying to start up a business are doubtless finding it more complicated than expected. It is bound to be a lengthy process, but persist and you will be successful in the end.

30. THURSDAY. Eventful. If you have legal matters to discuss with a lawyer, do so this morning. Your grasp of technicalities should be quite sound, giving you a clearer idea of just where you stand. Cancer people who drive for a living could have an interesting encounter. A chance meeting when you stop at a red light or pull in for coffee might bring a newcomer into your life. This person is apt to become very important to your happiness. Where money is concerned, you need to be more careful than usual. The power of advertising should not be underestimated; you could find yourself buying goods that you do not really need or want.

31. FRIDAY. Good. Swimming is an excellent form of exercise that uses all major muscles, and the rhythmic movements are likely to appeal. Try to go to the local pool at least once a week. Your natural Cancer sense of compassion means that you rarely refuse to help someone who is in obvious need. Remember, however, that you also need to discriminate since some people who make a claim on your heart are not genuine. This can be a truly romantic day. Prepare for an encounter with someone you already know from work or town. Now new depths of emotion are likely to open up, probably because you soon discover that you hold many ideals in common.

SEPTEMBER

1. SATURDAY. Uneasy. If you are looking forward to going on a romantic date, be aware that it may not turn out quite as you expect. The other person is almost sure to have their own ideas of what they want to do, and these are unlikely to match your own. Shopping can be ruinously expensive if you do not use every ounce of restraint that you possess. Unfortunately the goods you buy may not look so appealing once you get them home, so make sure you keep all receipts. This is a starred day for a children's party. Some supervision will naturally be essential, but on the whole the kids should be able to entertain themselves without getting into too much mischief.

2. SUNDAY. Rewarding. By being generous to a neighbor you will establish a good relationship that should work well for both of you in months and years to come. Even if it is only a matter of helping them out of a tight spot financially, they will be deeply grateful. Try to get out locally today. Explore leisure facilities and recreation spots that you are not yet familiar with. Take along plenty of cash wherever you go. Your focus at the moment should be on developing your natural interests in various assorted subjects. It is worth considering signing up for an evening class, particularly if you want to brush up on a foreign language. Be prepared for long-distance calls that escalate your phone bill.

3. MONDAY. Slow. Discussion of a work problem may seem to be getting nowhere due to the stubborn attitude of a senior staff member. It would help your cause to bombard this person with all the facts you can get your hands on, so that your case is solidly grounded. There is no point nourishing your mind while neglecting your body. Both need exercise if you are to live a balanced life. Long-distance travel may be not only uncomfortable but rather slow. If you get stuck in an airport, use the waiting period to let your imagination mull over the most important areas of your life. Solutions to perplexing dilemmas may well arise while you are in a relaxed state.

4. TUESDAY. Strenuous. Heavy demands could be made by those with whom you live. However, it is not your place to take over responsibility that rightly belongs to them, so do not allow yourself to be made into a kind of universal parent. If you harness your energy and focus it on learning a new skill, there is little you cannot achieve. Indeed, you could immeasurably improve your chances for a promotion by broadening your range of abilities. Cancer people who are trying to get written work published may feel a little disheartened. There are many details to be sorted out in order to get your presentation ready to be submitted, but in the end it is just the quality of your work that will count.

5. WEDNESDAY. Promising. This is one of those times when you either feel that you are being attacked from all directions or that you have an immense number of choices regarding what you can achieve. In reality, it is your own attitude that makes the vital difference, so do not choose to be a victim. Young Cancer couples who are looking for a first home could find an ideal place. It would be smart to make an offer quickly, since desirable property is unlikely to stay on the market long. It can be quite amazing how much your mental and emotional state affects your overall health. Meditating on a regular basis can help you stay calm and centered so that you feel physically better.

6. THURSDAY. Happy. Two main topics are likely on your mind: love and money. Happily, romance appears in the cards at your place of work. Someone who is about to leave is clearly gearing up to ask you out before it is too late, but you will have to give them a bit of encouragement. You can hardly afford to turn down the opportunity to make extra money by taking on some of a colleague's assigned work. Even if you are thrown in at the deep end, you can muddle through somehow. A solution may suddenly seem obvious to an emotional difficulty, thanks to the perceptive comments of a close friend who is concerned about your well-being.

7. FRIDAY. Disappointing. Not everything is going to go your way without a bit of extra effort on your part. You may feel you are beating your head against a brick wall in an attempt to finish off important work. Keep in mind that the world will not come to an end if you leave it until early next week. Plans for an exciting evening out on the town may have to be canceled when a friend lets you down. Calling around to find someone to take their place at the last minute may be futile. If you have the courage to drop in on someone to whom you are romantically attracted, there is no telling how the evening might turn out. Spending a bit of money on yourself is sure to cheer you up.

8. SATURDAY. Tranquil. At the moment you can gain great comfort from spending time alone. You are apt to feel as if you are drawing a magic circle around yourself. Reflect on the support and encouragement your family and friends continue to give you. Try to find time to visit a relative or friend who is not well. They will probably be especially grateful if you can do some shopping for them. If you have been worrying about asking your romantic partner for a commitment, this is the day to broach the subject. Almost certainly it has been on their mind, too. Be sure you get some outdoor exercise since you have a lot of excess energy to burn off.

9. SUNDAY. Difficult. Children must develop a sense of discipline, but you should not be too hard on them or expect too much too soon. Allow them to enjoy the freedom that is such a special aspect of youth. There will be time enough as the years go on to learn the constrictions of adult life. Your phone bill may be astronomically high unless you learn to curb your tongue. If you actually listen to yourself talking, a disturbing amount of what you say may turn out to be negative gossip. This is the right time to nourish romantic feelings but not to act on them. Allow your attraction to develop naturally and at its own pace for at least a few more weeks.

10. MONDAY. Challenging. As a Cancer you are normally fairly happy to accept the authority of those at work who are in senior positions. When they begin to pass down ill-judged decisions, however, you have no choice but to challenge them. It might be a good idea to have a quick look at electrical appliances before turning them on. In this way you just may be able to spot a fault before it develops, although it is more likely that you will have to start using it to find out that something is wrong. Because you naturally have a very strong sense of family history, it can be fascinating to come into possession of an older relative's diaries or other papers. You may even want to consider preparing them for publication.

11. TUESDAY. Helpful. Sometimes it is best to do good in secret. If you can help someone without letting on that you are doing so, they will not feel embarrassed. An old packet of letters could turn up while you are looking through a drawer at home. Memories will immediately flood in, and you will probably forget what you were looking for in the first place. As the day progresses, tension is likely to rise between you and your mate or partner. It would be better to allow them to let off steam rather than keeping the lid on their emotions. Children are in a mood to play quietly, and can be trusted to do so without having to be constantly supervised.

12. WEDNESDAY. Fair. Even though you may be rightly proud of having won a prize, try not to let it go to your head. In the greater scheme of things your achievement is not all that impressive, and boasting about it is not going to endear you to friends or colleagues. On occasion you instinctively deal with a difficult situation by finding the humor in it. As long as this is done with sensitivity, it can be an excellent way of defusing potentially explosive emotions. You are apt to be in the mood for taking it easy, even though there is plenty you could be doing. However, it will not hurt to proceed at a slower pace if that would make life more enjoyable for you today.

13. THURSDAY. Good. Summon up all of your willpower and there is a great deal you can achieve. This is a good day to put into action your latest plans for self-improvement. You should soon be able to see encouraging signs of progress. If you are negotiating a contract, you can afford to hold out for favorable terms. Indeed, it would be foolish to settle for anything that does not suit you. As a Cancer you usually like to keep to yourself. However, there is no harm in getting more closely involved in your local community, which can become a kind of extended family. Everyone benefits from a sense of mutual encouragement and support.

14. FRIDAY. Bumpy. You can expect a bumpy ride where romance is concerned. A sudden attraction could turn your world upside down, but the question remains whether they are really suitable for you. There is simply no way to get rich overnight, so do not kid yourself. Of course it is wise to make astute investments, but you probably do not have the really large sums of money necessary to make an impressive profit. Once you have finished up some routine tasks, you will be free to relax, but do not overdo the wining and dining this evening. You will enjoy the company far more if you moderate all of your actions and avoid any overindulging.

15. SATURDAY. Favorable. This is an excellent day to shop for items for your home. There is no need to be extravagant. Even if you want to buy large items such as furniture it is worth looking for bargains. Greater solidarity with your parents or other older people can arise from a sense of shared family history. Encourage them to tell stories of their own childhood, and of your grandparents' earlier life; you will probably be fascinated. The only problem today is your tendency to lash out in sudden anger. In no case should children be subjected to such treatment. It may not be easy to control your emotions every time, but practice makes perfect.

16. SUNDAY. Active. You and your mate or partner may be quite eager to indulge in something adventurous together. It might be fun to try a new sport, or at least watch other people taking risks. Find time to do some creative writing. You will find that attempts at rhyming can be very therapeutic. If you are not sure about the quality of what you write, you do not need to show your efforts to anyone. This is not the right day to devote to household activities because you will probably only feel frustrated and resentful. Leave the dishes in the sink, the bed unmade, and go out for a walk instead. Plans for a quiet evening at home are likely to fall prey to the insistent ringing of the telephone.

17. MONDAY. Refreshing. For once you should be properly refreshed by the weekend, making you ready to face anything. It might even be a bit of a disappointment to find that there is nothing particularly urgent requiring your attention. Attempting to repay all outstanding debts as soon as possible will get a great weight off your mind. This is a starred day to put your house on the market; there may be a full-price offer almost immediately. On the other hand, if you are looking for a new home you could find the right place without trying very hard. A fresh start in a different location could be just what you need to revitalize your everyday life.

18. TUESDAY. Inspiring. Your mind may be in overdrive, with creative ideas welling up from depths you never knew you possessed. Do not forget to write down these ideas before they evaporate. If youngsters are showing flashes of genius in certain subjects, you may want to discuss with their teacher how best to foster the talent. You should not count on a quiet domestic life. Sparks may fly before the day is done because of some quite small detail such as who drank all the milk and ate all the cookies. An ideal evening out should contain fine wine, soft candlelight, inspiring music, and vigilant service.

19. WEDNESDAY. Pleasant. Cancer people who have a garden are probably eager to be out connecting with the earth. And the longer you can spend digging and cultivating, the better. A surprise gift from parents should be a true delight, showing that they understand your taste better than you imagined and that they care for you a lot. This is a good time to consider redecorating your home. Throw away conventional ideas and consider tile inlays or exotic paint effects. You may want to buy a book on interior design to get an idea of exciting possibilities. Phone a brother or sister this evening, especially if you have not spoken for a while.

20. THURSDAY. Mixed. Although romance may seem to be slipping out of your grasp, that might actually not be a bad thing. You probably cannot see it yet, but the person currently in your life may already be giving out clear signals that they are likely to let you down. Creative business plans can be put into action with confidence. At the moment you are full of energy, which almost guarantees success. Strangely enough, as soon as you give up on the idea of winning a competition you could actually achieve a prize. It may be the very fact of relaxing enough not to care that brings out your creative best.

21. FRIDAY. Opportune. Make the most of a chance to meet new people. Even if you encounter them in a business context, there is potential for real friendship. Where romance is concerned, it would not hurt to put your feelings into words and send a tasteful card or a personally written note. It may not be wise to write poetry at this stage, but a simple declaration of your emotions might be extremely effective. There is no point spending good money on a new leisure interest, only to drop it almost immediately. Try not to be so impulsive; decide first whether you really want to pursue this activity. For once you are allowed to indulge in pure pleasure this evening.

22. SATURDAY. Disquieting. Stay close to home if you want to avoid trouble. Your family will provide pleasant companionship, while friends are apt to brood about imagined insults and just be waiting to argue with you. Household chores can get in the way of a shopping trip on which you planned to indulge yourself. In the end, however, you will find it just as satisfying to work around the house as to get tired trailing through crowded stores. Even though it can be very difficult to get youngsters to clean up after themselves, that is no excuse for being dictatorial. Let them do it in their own time and you will get much better results with much less hassle.

23. SUNDAY. Uneven. This morning you may have great plans for getting ahead with practical matters, but even the best plans will probably come to nothing. Constant interruptions and demands from loved ones will eventually make you see that your time is better dedicated to other people. There may be a few upsets with older relatives who do not share your outlook on life. These can be avoided, however, by keeping controversial opinions to yourself. A considerably more exciting atmosphere this afternoon is apt to give you itchy feet. It could be fun just to jump into the car and take off with loved ones. Remember that such a journey is more important than the ultimate destination.

24. MONDAY. Productive. You certainly will not feel like wasting time this morning. Your capacity to see right through a complicated problem to the best solution will be much in demand. Try to spruce up the appearance of your home by rearranging the furniture and even throwing out older pieces. You will be amazed how refreshing it can be to come into a room and be surprised at its unfamiliar appearance. One way of keeping fit is to exercise at home. For this you do not need expensive equipment. Just walking up and down stairs is good for you; additional weights can be improvised out of bottles of different sizes filled with water. There is no excuse for idleness today.

25. TUESDAY. Sensitive. Emotional problems may come to a head between you and your mate or partner. There is no point trying to sweep them under the carpet any longer. You have reached the point where total honesty is the only possible path to take, but that does not mean you should be hurtful in any way. Cancer people involved in legal matters are probably getting impatient for results. However, losing your temper with your lawyer or with a court official will not hurry the process at all; you are at the mercy of the judge. This is not the best time to try to persuade a business colleague to test out a bright new idea. Wait until they appear less distracted and more open-minded.

26. WEDNESDAY. Deceptive. In one way you can look forward to a simple day. The energy is not running your way, so you can be fairly sure that you will spend some time struggling to keep up with other people. Youngsters may have to be kept at home because they seem to be a little under the weather. It is probably something they will recover from quickly, possibly even a temporary allergy to school. If you are involved in buying or selling property, there is a likelihood of less than honest handling of your affairs by someone involved. At any rate, it would pay to get in touch personally with the owners or potential owners to compare notes.

27. THURSDAY. Easy. Today begins with a feeling that a heavy weight has been lifted from your shoulders. At last all the hard work you have been doing to increase your self-understanding is beginning to pay off. Old problems are starting to be resolved of their own accord so that you can shrug them off. Lost items may turn up within your home. Probably they were hidden during the course of a children's game, so it is up to you to impress on youngsters that some of your belongings must be regarded as off-limits. If you are ready and willing for romance, it is almost certain to find you. Someone who at first does not impress you could suddenly seem to be just your type, and the attraction is sure to be mutual.

28. FRIDAY. Disconcerting. You probably will not know whether you are up or down for most of the day. On the one hand, solitude and peace may seem most desirable. However, as soon as you settle down to your work, a restless mood is apt to make you long for excitement and stimulation. Do not let lack of money stop you from making a small donation to a worthwhile charity. Even a little can do a great deal of good if you are not able to volunteer your time.

Take this chance to widen your knowledge of computer technology. An expert who is on hand can give you a few simple but extremely effective tips. This evening is a good time to let your hair down and go out partying with friends.

29. SATURDAY. Positive. Introducing a new person in your life to your parents is always a bit nerve-racking. However, your family is apt to look kindly upon this love interest and, as long as you both behave quietly, all should go well. This is a great day to pursue hobbies, especially of an artistic type. If you enjoy music but do not play an instrument, you can still learn a lot about the theory of composition and about various composers. Whatever you learn will help you to enjoy the complex nature of your favorite pieces even more. Try to get children to go to bed early tonight. It will do you and your mate or partner a world of good to have some totally private time to yourselves.

30. SUNDAY. Variable. Short trips around the neighborhood should be hassle-free, but a longer journey may be slow going. You might even have to turn back for forgotten items that seem essential to loved ones, though possibly not to you. Take this chance to read up on ways of staying healthy. You can go by instinct to a certain extent, but it is very helpful to be informed about what makes a balanced diet. It would be a shame to become a slave to your home; keep it clean and neat by all means, but do not allow yourself to be taken over by it. Satisfy your need for the exotic with a travel documentary or a wildlife program.

OCTOBER

1. MONDAY. Cautious. Unless you keep a close watch on pets, there is a real danger of one running off and getting lost or in an accident. Don't let dogs off the leash when you are out walking them. Declarations of love are not always welcome, since they can come at inconvenient times and places. But are you in a position to turn away love? It is rare enough to cherish and be cherished, whatever form it takes. At work an irritable atmosphere may arise when fax machines malfunction and calls are interrupted. All forms of communication are likely to experience hitches, so prepare yourself for a trying day.

2. TUESDAY. Rewarding. Do not shy away from getting what you want. Sometimes a romance has to be fought for, which could well be the situation today. This will just make your ultimate success all the more enjoyable. Conditions make today a great opportunity to sell your talents and personal skills in the open market. Look around for a job that would normally be out of your league, and have the courage to apply for it. A more imaginative approach to an emotional entanglement will almost certainly cut through the knot. Allow your mind to roam freely over the problem, then see what solution comes up after you have mulled it over in your sleep.

3. WEDNESDAY. Demanding. There has to be such a thing as give-and-take in a close relationship, which often will go on without you even being aware of it. If you feel that your mate or partner is currently demanding too much from you and not giving enough in return, this must be talked out. It is all too easy to get into arguments over ideals. Keep in mind that you are never going to persuade a diehard opponent of the rightness of your opinions, any more than they are going to win you over; then you will begin to see how futile it is to argue. Maintain a low profile where romance is concerned. Your believability is a little low, so you would be best off waiting for the tide to turn in your favor once again.

4. THURSDAY. Tricky. Watch out for trouble if you are buying or selling property. A deal can fall through right up to the last minute, especially if more than two parties are involved. Just do not become too excited. It does not always follow that you should swallow your boss's words uncritically. Outside their area of specialized knowledge, they may be no better informed than you are. If in doubt, get a second opinion. Going on a blind date is one way of meeting someone new, but it is not ideal. You need to retain a certain amount of emotional reserve rather than spilling out your life story and thus making yourself vulnerable to someone you have only just met.

5. FRIDAY. Opportune. If you are going to a work meeting or conference, maintain an optimistic sense of what will be achieved. Not only will you have the chance to absorb useful information, but you could also make some excellent contacts. You only have to be in a positive mood in the first place. This is a good time to start thinking about ways of expanding your social circle. Your personal interests naturally change over the years, so you may now be eager to meet people who share your latest passion. Celebrate the end of the workweek by arranging for you and your mate or steady date to have a special evening out on the town. Close mutual friends will make ideal companions.

6. SATURDAY. Refreshing. It is lucky that Cancer folk are home-bodies at heart because today is ideal for puttering around in the house and garden. There is plenty of work to do outside as the summer growing season ends and winter looms. Indoors you may want to change light summer curtains for warmer, heavier ones in a rich color. Pets can definitely bring a house alive. Cancers who live alone should consider getting an animal companion. The classified ads in your local paper are the best place to look for a nonpedigreed cat or dog. Where cooking is concerned, you could find your mother's recipes are better than cookbook concoctions.

7. SUNDAY. Manageable. There's no point breaking off a romantic affair just because you are beginning to feel a little bored. Every relationship goes through the doldrums, and it is partly up to you to reinject some excitement into your love life. This is not the best time to stray from the norm when thinking of redecorating. You should avoid anything too loud; remember that you are going to have to live with your choice in all kinds of moods. A quiet day would be ideal, giving you the chance to sort through personal papers and photographs. You might decide that you would like to start collecting specific items rather than acquiring pieces in a haphazard fashion.

8. MONDAY. Successful. Cancer people who have recently begun a new job should be feeling quite at home. Colleagues are beginning to rely on your specialized abilities, almost as if you had always been a valued team member. When the chips are down, you can rely on your parents to lend a helping hand. Whether this involves a loan or practical assistance, their help will be freely and willingly given. Unless you actually enjoy nourishing a hopeless love for someone who is not available, there is little to be gained by indulging such feelings. Carrying on in this manner is certainly not good for you, since it could tempt you to ignore reality in favor of a dream world.

9. TUESDAY. Quiet. You have probably been fretting recently about never having time to perfect your plans for self-development or to reflect on your progress so far. Today offers just that opportunity, so make the most of it. Find time to go through your wardrobe; be ruthless, eliminating clothes that you are unlikely to ever wear again. Even though as a Cancer you like to hang on to all of your belongings, unwanted clothes of reasonable quality should be donated to a charity shop. It is important not to assume that your mate or partner will agree with you on every occasion. Decisions should be made jointly but only after a serious discussion of the pros and cons.

10. WEDNESDAY. Good. Some might call you irresponsible, but when you get an urge for freedom there is nothing that can hold you back. A vacation getaway arranged at short notice could be exactly what you need, even if it means expecting colleagues to cover for you. Be careful not to come on too strong if you are trying to make a romantic impression on someone who is new on the scene. They will far prefer you as you normally are, without any pretense. A new local shop could be a great place to buy a beautiful and unusual gift. You might even splurge on a little something for yourself. Try not to arrive home late this evening without at least calling ahead.

11. THURSDAY. Uncertain. It would be wise to put off making any far-reaching decisions if possible. You are apt to be a bit bewildered by all that is happening, and that is not likely to wear off until late evening. Money may be a problem; it is hard to say where it all goes. Perhaps your mate or partner has a better grasp of your joint financial commitments than you do. Try not to expect a romantic outing to work out to perfection. Your high hopes are almost sure to lead to disappointment, since your date is just as human and imperfect as you are. This is a period when you should be strengthening your immune system for winter by eating right and exercising religiously.

12. FRIDAY. Active. Even though it might seem a small and unimportant matter to some people, getting enough shelves and hooks put up in the kitchen can make a world of difference. All of a sudden you will feel you have twice the space, and you will be able to move around that much more freely. Financially there could be some extra work available, just in time to meet a large bill. Be prepared to work antisocial hours, but only for a short while. No matter how sorry you may feel for yourself, there are always other people who are worse off. You can provide help to those who come within your orbit through visits and small gifts, and of course your cheering presence.

13. SATURDAY. Interesting. Since you and your family are so close, it can come as a shock to find that there is relative you had never heard mentioned. Almost every family has at least one secret story to tell, and you can learn a lot from listening to this one. Today is no time for nostalgia; indeed, you might feel like throwing out a lot of old letters and keepsakes. Use a bit of discrimination, however, because once gone those letters can never be replaced. All the same, getting rid of embarrassing old diaries and other papers can only be a positive move. This is a good time to think about having the wiring in your home checked to prevent a possible fire or other trouble.

14. SUNDAY. Sensitive. Everyone has emotional issues to grapple with. It is certainly not fair if loved ones all choose your shoulder to cry on. At some point you will just have to admit that there is only so much sincere emotional support you are able to give. If you are interrupted by the phone while working, make sure you stop what you are doing before you take the call. Otherwise you are almost bound to lose track of where you are and have trouble regaining momentum. Encourage children to tell you about their daily concerns. This is a good way of getting closer and of showing them that you are there to support them. A private conference with their teacher or principal might be an eye-opener.

15. MONDAY. Harmonious. Striking up a conversation with a neighbor could be the best thing you do this week. A warm friendship is likely to blossom from this apparently chance encounter. There are many ways of making new friends. Consulting a brother or sister is one of the best ways since they are almost sure to know people with whom you would get along well, and they would be willing to introduce you. Allow dreams to guide you toward a more satisfying job. Clues are there, it is just a matter of interpreting them. Moving in with a romantic partner is a big step, but this is an ideal day to take the plunge for an agreed-on trial time.

16. TUESDAY. Hopeful. Even relationships that have been steady for many years sometimes need to have new life breathed into them. If you can arrange a romantic break for you and your mate or partner, you are almost guaranteed to recapture that old excitement. There could be all kinds of interesting items concealed in your attic or cellar, especially if your house is old. Poke around among boxes and pieces left and forgotten by former occupants. There are times when it is vital to stand up for what you believe in, and other times when tact and compromise may be more appropriate. Right now you should trust your good Cancer instinct to keep quiet even if your pride is wounded.

17. WEDNESDAY. Confusing. Unfortunately for Cancer people who are taking tests, thought processes are not as clear as they could be. The best approach is to stay calm and tackle each question bit by bit. If you try to get an overview of the whole exam, you may soon get lost in a fog of speculation. Whatever you do, avoid gambling even a small sum of money unless you are willing to lose it all. Promises of romance may tempt you into a rather intense relationship that requires a lot of understanding in order to sustain it. In the end the struggle will probably be worthwhile because you will gain such a lot of self-knowledge along the way.

18. THURSDAY. Encouraging. You should wake up feeling very clear-headed. Much has probably been worked out in your unconscious mind while you slept. Allow your dreams to evaporate naturally, without making any effort to remember them or to write them down. They have done their work, so further efforts at interpretation should not be necessary. Happily, there is a new relationship on the horizon for Cancer singles who have been alone for a while. Time as a single should have enabled you to be more independent, so that you now will not make unreasonable demands on your new partner. Just do not let friendships fade as your love life gathers intensity.

19. FRIDAY. Tiring. Making all the arrangements for entertaining at home can be very tiring. You naturally want everything to be perfect, which puts an extra strain on you. About an hour before the first guests are due, have a small drink and relax so your guests will feel more relaxed too. Youngsters are apt to be full of energy. Their sole aim in life may appear to be to wear you out. This may partly be your fault because you have allowed them to be too demanding on an everyday basis. Now they must be taught more restrained behavior. Buying a new chair or sofa can make all your other furniture look rather old or even shabby, so get ready for more expense.

20. SATURDAY. Excellent. You can afford to wait for the phone to ring with an offer of a dream date. However, it would perhaps be better if you took the initiative and asked that special person out for dinner or to a concert of romantic classical music. This is a starred day for working on your home. Your touch is faultless, so that you can create beauty even out of unpromising material. There is no point and certainly no pleasure in becoming fanatical about pet care. Animals are resilient, so too much fussing over their food and nutrition is probably a waste of time. Just enjoy their company and let them enjoy being with you.

21. SUNDAY. Satisfying. This is one of those rare days when youngsters really are seen but not heard. As long as you look in and check on them from time to time, you will be safe just settling down to a leisurely Sunday in unusual peace and quiet. There is much to be said for being well organized, since life is bound to be simpler when it is well ordered. There is time today to get matters sorted out in many ways, even if the organization does not last long. The value of being able to listen quietly to someone without making comments and suggestions is inestimable. Often that is all that a troubled person needs, and happily one of your special skills is offering a shoulder to lean on in a time of crisis.

22. MONDAY. Uneasy. This slightly touchy beginning to the workweek demands striving not to get on other people's nerves. It may be impossible to leave the house this morning without a minor disagreement, since loved ones are apt to be extremely sensitive. Your own nerves are also somewhat delicate, which means that all business arrangements must be viewed strictly objectively. If you start allowing yourself to imagine that there are personal complications affecting your colleagues' decisions, you will not be able to judge anything soundly. An act of generosity may backfire as the recipient of your kindness takes it for granted that your duty is to help them.

23. TUESDAY. Demanding. There is good news and bad news in your mail. Among it could be a check for which you have been waiting, but there are also almost inevitably some big bills. Be sure to allow plenty of traveling time, especially when picking up children. Heavy traffic and road detours are likely to slow you down. Self-employed Cancer people will be relieved to have some steady work coming in. However, the deadlines are tight, and you will need to buckle down immediately if you are going to finish in time. Happily, a romantic evening out on the town can make you forget all your troubles in the arms of that special person.

24. WEDNESDAY. Strenuous. Getting a mortgage or other type of loan can be quite a complicated business. It would be unwise to take out a loan which you would have to struggle to repay. Before committing yourself, look around to see if you can get the money on more favorable terms. This certainly is not your cup of tea since you do not enjoy paperwork. However, once it is done all you have to worry about is keeping up with the payments. Youngsters usually are able to get along extremely well with older relatives, who might even be willing to baby-sit from time to time. Actually, you may be doing grandparents a favor by giving them time alone with the children, which can be a very revitalizing experience.

25. THURSDAY. Fair. Do not imagine that just because someone is rather shy they do not like you. In fact, they may well be agonizing over how to approach you to ask for a date. Obviously you can help in that regard by being available. Attention to detail can turn even the most mundane task into a minor work of art. It is not what you do so much as your attitude in doing it that offers real lasting satisfaction. A deeper sense of responsibility usually begins to develop with age. Right now you should be realizing that there are very specific ways in which you can assist friends and family members, and that it would be cruel to hold back unless you have a very good reason.

26. FRIDAY. Fortunate. The workweek is hardly likely to end without a romantic encounter of some sort, most likely where you work. You may already feel so at ease with the other person that they are almost like a relative, just a lot more fascinating. Try to finish off whatever work is outstanding so that you can look forward to the weekend without anything nagging at you. An evening spent at a relative's house could turn out to be a lot more interesting than expected. Not only will you be made to feel very welcome, but you could also hear wonderful stories that throw new light on your family history. Listen more than you talk and you are bound to learn a lot.

27. SATURDAY. Stressful. Problems between you and your mate or partner have probably not been solved so much as just gone underground. That is not any kind of a permanent solution; resentment will just fester away until it breaks out again and probably even worse than ever. Sitting down and talking it through is the only way. There is no point constantly changing your mind about where you want to live. Make a clear decision and then follow it through, which will be a relief for all involved. You may have to turn down an invitation to a get-together that you would have enjoyed, because there is simply too much to do at home. Let that be a lesson not to get behind with your chores!

28. SUNDAY. Misleading. It is not that you intended to mislead a romantic partner, just that at an early stage you failed to clarify a misunderstanding. Now this person may be convinced that your relationship is developing in a direction that you never intended. You must decide how much longer you are going to keep them in the dark. Even though your family is supportive in many ways, there are certain areas of your life which they cannot be expected to understand. Nor should you attempt to draw their attention to matters which truly are private. You will get the most satisfaction this evening from a good novel or TV program rather than going out.

29. MONDAY. Deceptive. Take the advice of someone who suggests you risk your savings, and you are almost certainly asking for trouble. No matter how surefire the financial reward is made out to be, it is quite certain that you will not be the person ending up with the cash. Romance can be delightful in the early stages, when you are still in a golden mist of wonder. However, undoubtedly your intended has some very real failings, which you will see only if you look. Cancer people who believe that all is fair in love and war will not hesitate to take advantage of insider knowledge about a good job opening. Certainly it will not harm your chances to get in an application ahead of the competition.

30. TUESDAY. Profitable. A swift look at your checking or savings account could give you a pleasant surprise. Your recent efforts have reaped definite benefits. Old emotional patterns can be discarded as long as you have sufficient insight into why you no longer need to rely on them. You also need the courage to believe that you can act differently. Where romance is concerned, you should not keep quiet. Unless you at least hint at your feelings, you cannot expect the other person to guess at them. Youngsters can be kept amused with crayons and paper for hours at a time, so relax while they are at play.

31. WEDNESDAY. Challenging. Putting your ambitions and hopes for the future into action is not only hard work but can be very lonely. After all, no one but yourself knows quite how important it is to you to achieve your dreams. Look on the bright side. Do not let obstacles depress you; each one that you conquer will make you stronger and more determined. This is a tricky day for friendships. While differences of opinion are bound to occur, there is a limit to what you can be expected to take from someone who is emotionally close to you. Friendship is not an excuse to be rude in the name of total honesty. It may be best to take a back seat during a work meeting in order to avoid open hostility.

NOVEMBER

1. THURSDAY. Buoyant. Your greater mental agility should make it easier than usual for you to solve problems. It is especially important to be honest in assessing friends' emotional difficulties, although it may not be so easy to persuade them to take your advice. A fresh romance is just what you need. At the moment try to pursue a relationship that is founded on a sense of friendship and mutual freedom, rather than intense emotional bonding. This can be very liberating. A new leisure pursuit may be burning itself out, leaving you looking for new ways to harness your talents. Follow the promptings of your heart despite what your intellect may be telling you.

2. FRIDAY. Uneasy. Even though you have learned a great deal during the past year, it will probably be quite difficult persuading yourself of that fact. You may gain more self-confidence by talking to loved ones in order to get their opinion of how much and how deeply you have changed. There is no excuse for going back on a promise, no matter how insignificant it may seem to you. All vows should be honored, leaving you with a clear conscience. Unless you ease up at work, you could be heading for a stress-related health problem. Naturally you wish to help other people, but you run the risk of getting overloaded with work that is not really your responsibility.

3. SATURDAY. Promising. All family matters appear harmonious, making this a starred day to spend time with loved ones. You may even want to invite relatives to dinner in order to show how much you appreciate your extended family. Procrastination is the thief of time. If you continue to put off finishing essential tasks, the ultimate price could be surprisingly high. Where romance is concerned, do not underestimate the power of persuasion. As long as you intuit that someone is interested in you, there is no reason not to pull out all the stops to get them to go out on a date. They will probably be flattered by your attention and eager to establish a lasting relationship.

4. SUNDAY. Favorable. Your first priority should be mind over matter. It is possible that you could have a real breakthrough in handling a longtime fear or phobia, finally freeing yourself of it for good. This does not mean you should force the issue, however; be gentle with yourself. Children are apt to demand a lot of attention, but that should be a pleasure. There is much you can teach them through the medium of shared games and other activities. As a Cancer you tend to love old furniture and a traditional decorating style for your home. Consider buying a genuine antique to enhance your current decorating scheme.

5. MONDAY. Complicated. Since your instincts are sharp, it should not be difficult for you to intuit that a close friend is holding back important personal information from you. Although they may have sound reasons for doing so, you are apt to be worried about them and want to offer help. Try to get the whole story from them, but tactfully. A romantic affair is unlikely to be straightforward. You must learn to be a little skeptical of someone who sounds too good to be true. If your energy seems to have dropped to a low level, some gentle, rhythmical exercise should help you release more strength from your muscles. Eat light and right tonight, avoid any alcohol.

6. TUESDAY. Happy. This promises to a very cheering day. The chance of beginning a new romance is yours for the taking. Someone you met through a leisure-time pursuit is obviously eager to get to know you better. All personal plans are favored. If you wish to develop your learning skills or just get your life more organized, put your best effort into doing so. Your image could benefit enormously from a fresh style, perhaps a more casual yet elegant look. Promise to buy good quality clothes for yourself from now on, even if that means you can afford fewer of them. You have the potential to learn to dress to impress.

7. WEDNESDAY. Challenging. Life can be an uphill struggle when not everything is going your way. Instead of blaming other people, realize that these are challenges that can and should be tackled in a positive manner. You may currently be suffering an embarrassment of romantic riches. It will not solve your problem to go out with more than one person on a night. Neither will be impressed if you explain you are simply trying to make up your mind between them. Money is probably not exactly filling your pockets at the moment, although it shows a distressing tendency to flow out. Cutting down on luxuries would make a big difference.

8. THURSDAY. Excellent. Given the right circumstances, today could mark the beginning of the most romantic period of your year. You need to be in a receptive frame of mind, however, or Cupid might just strike you with a desire for an unsuitable person. Focus on personal development. Friends who share your interests can point the way forward. All competitive matters are favored, so do not worry if you are going up against a colleague. Do the best you can; you should make an excellent impression on higher-ups. Allow yourself a self-indulgent evening out on the town, with everything you like best.

9. FRIDAY. Pleasant. Right now your focus should be on practical matters concerning finances and your home. It can be very satisfying to work out ways of improving your house so as to increase its value significantly. A greater sense of self-confidence should come from feeling that come what may you have the support of your family. They are very protective of your interests, which is no small thing. This is an ideal day to visit antique shops even if you do not exactly know what you are looking for; something special is bound to catch your eye. Youngsters will appreciate extra cuddles, and perhaps a bedtime story.

10. SATURDAY. Variable. The morning might be a bit dull, although you are bound to be busier than usual. You might well feel that most of the heavy-duty tasks around the house are being heaped on your shoulders, but that is really not the case. There could be a mechanical difficulty with your car. If your vehicle is overdue for servicing, do not put off taking it in. Later in the day you should begin to feel much happier, partly because a surprise present lifts your spirits. It is certainly nice to feel appreciated. A romantic affair could begin in your local library or bookstore. Be sure to get a phone number so that you can arrange a future date.

11. SUNDAY. Tricky. Cancer parents with young children will find them somewhat difficult to deal with and up to all kinds of mischief. Close supervision is essential, unless you want to find bedroom walls adorned with drawings or your best clothes used for dressing up. There is no reason to tell a romantic partner anything other than the truth, no matter what they ask. They will sense if you are only revealing part of the story and, as a consequence, may lose trust in you. That is likely to turn the relationship sour in a very short period of time. Trips are best restricted to your locality unless you are prepared to deal with children getting bored and rambunctious.

12. MONDAY. Fair. All property deals are highlighted, although you must keep in mind that you should not try to pull the wool over a potential buyer's eyes. Defects need to be mentioned so that the buyer knows exactly what would have to be dealt with. This is a great day for getting down to routine daily tasks. If you have allowed laundry to pile up, make a big effort to get it all washed, ironed, folded, and put away. There will be a real satisfaction in having faced up to it. Your health will benefit enormously if you eat at home more. Fast food and snacking while out during the day may be necessary at times, but home-cooked food is much more nutritional.

13. TUESDAY. Surprising. An opportunity to put your creative talents to use and to make some money is extremely exciting. Even if this is a one-time event, it should be not only instructive but excellent for boosting your self-esteem. A romance could be broken off without warning, leaving you wondering just where you went wrong. The truth is probably that the other person panicked, feeling that you were getting too close. Do not try to be too clever if taking an oral test. Attempts to outsmart the examiner are only likely to upset them, so that you will end up getting a lower mark than you rightfully deserve. This is a good time to buy expensive electrical appliances for the kitchen.

14. WEDNESDAY. Mixed. At the moment you may not have a very clear idea of what you want in an ideal romantic partner. This leaves you rather vulnerable to anyone who comes along, since you may be tempted to get into a relationship just for the sake of being paired. It would be more sensible to first do some work clarifying your wishes and expectations. Creatively this promises to be a very fertile day, and great fun as well. You should have time free for self-expression, so make the most of it. Children will love to have you join in their games, and you might get insights into their character that surprise and please you.

15. THURSDAY. Opportune. On one level this is a day when you are expected to put in some hard, tedious work. Events are apt to fling quite a challenge into your lap, forcing you to focus in an entirely new direction. Money is the key; you could end up handling significant amounts of it on behalf of other people. A new romance promises a few thrills as well as spills. Before getting in too deep, ask yourself whether you will really enjoy being on an unending emotional roller-coaster; as a Cancer usually you prefer to know where you stand. Some disciplined exercise would wake you up physically while toning up all your muscles.

16. FRIDAY. Sensitive. While swift decisions may be required, that does not mean you should speak without thinking, especially where close relationships are concerned. If you act too impulsively or in a moment of anger, you will undoubtedly regret it. Pets unfortunately get old and die, which can be very hard for children to accept. If one of your animals is showing signs of age and ill health, at least prepare youngsters for the inevitable by beginning to explain what is happening. Carrying out daily chores provides an opportunity to let your mind roam freely over a problem. An answer may soon seem obvious even though you were not focused on the problem.

17. SATURDAY. Exciting. Just the romance you have been hoping for is finally within your grasp. What is so great about this relationship is that the lines of communication are open, which is the foundation for a good and lasting alliance. You are apt to be feeling highly energized; it would be a pity to let this pep go to waste on ordinary shopping and cleaning. Get some more intensive exercise than usual. Set yourself new limits for fitness; you stand a very good chance of reaching or even exceeding them. Children can be extremely amusing, but there is also an amazing amount of astute knowledge in some of their most casual observations.

18. SUNDAY. Refreshing. Today offers an ideal opportunity to catch up on lost sleep and then to spend a really refreshing day. Be nice to yourself, and also to loved ones. Even though you probably do not feel like exerting, there are tasks around the house that need your personal attention. Take them at a steady pace, and try to enjoy what you are doing. Cancer people who have recently moved in with a new roommate may still be trying to establish a routine that suits. This period of discovery for each of you should be approached with an attitude of tolerance. Start as you mean to go on, with love and mutual consideration.

19. MONDAY. Chancy. Legal matters can be a lottery, or at least that is how it can sometimes seem. At the moment a case you are involved in is going well, so you can afford to be quietly optimistic. Fresh business ideas could turn out to be financially very rewarding. Just bear in mind that there is a world of difference between having a bright idea and putting it into operation. There is no cause to be overbearing with loved ones. Such behavior usually stems from a feeling of insecurity. If this is the case, you need to discuss with your mate or partner why you have such negative concerns. Romantic feelings should be expressed in a letter rather than on the phone.

20. TUESDAY. Lucky. As a Cancer you tend to have strong and deep emotions. It can therefore be quite a relief to get involved with someone who is habitually cheerful and reliable. The contrast between the two of you is apt to be so great that you are amazed there is any attraction at all, but it is a case of opposites attracting. There is a good chance of making a small win in a competition, so have a go at it. You might even be lucky enough to win a vacation in some exotic location. Answers to practical problems involving money could come to you in a dream, thanks to your unconscious mind getting to grips with the matter you have been trying to avoid.

21. WEDNESDAY. Troublesome. Creative ideas might seem wonderful to you, but it would nevertheless be wise to put them aside for now. If they still look good when you review them in a few weeks, you could be on to something, but that is unlikely. Cancer people who are spending the day with children will probably have trouble holding back an angry outburst. Deliberately naughty behavior should not be tolerated. If you want to break off a relationship, do so cleanly and kindly. The last thing you should do is gossip about the other person to your friends first, in the hopes that word will get back to your partner. To do so would be not only cowardly but cruel.

22. THURSDAY. Unpredictable. Your bank account may not be in quite such a good state as you imagine, so getting the monthly statement is likely to be a shock. It is not a mystery, however, why there is less money than you imagined: recent large expenses have taken their toll. Some emotional difficulties can only be worked through slowly, especially when they run very deep. Everyone has weaknesses. Instead of feeling that you must find a solution immediately to each and every problem, just try to be more tolerant and patient with yourself. Romance is apt to be rather unpredictable. Volatile feelings can flare up at any moment, but try to contain them until the time is right.

23. FRIDAY. Worrisome. Although you may be receiving quite tempting financial offers, whether they will produce concrete results is another matter. Caution is advised. You cannot do better than seek expert advice. Long-distance trips are likely to be very tiring, especially if they are related to your work. There will be little time to relax, and you will be expected to keep up an air of authority throughout. Try to schedule time off as soon as you get home, to allow yourself to recover from the stress. While your passions may have been aroused by a special someone, the relationship is not likely to settle down along the conventional lines you are imagining.

24. SATURDAY. Good. As long as you avoid a tendency to get fanatical about minor chores, this should be an enjoyable day. It does not really matter if the bathroom has been left in a mess. That situation is not worth spoiling the day by bawling out a loved one. Feelings of restlessness are probably due to an unacknowledged sense of frustration. You need something fresh to occupy your energy and expand your horizons, such as planning a trip or taking up a new subject of study. You will get great pleasure from an evening out that has a cultural theme. You would probably enjoy a classical dance performance or an inspiring concert by aspiring musicians.

25. SUNDAY. Enjoyable. Enjoy a long day out and about. Find a warm and inviting destination and take a scenic route; a good time is virtually guaranteed. This is a great day for all kinds of writing. Whether you are planning a novel or just jotting down notes for private poems, allow ideas to arise from the depths of your heart and mind. An increased feeling of well-being can stem from getting your life in better order. This gives you a strong foundation from which to face whatever comes along. A dreamy mood can give you time and opportunity to imagine various future achievements. Later on these may become real if you are prepared to work hard to achieve them.

26. MONDAY. Bumpy. Brace yourself for a day in which it will be quite a challenge to get anything done. You are likely to be interrupted constantly by the phone. It might become all too apparent that someone at work is not totally behind you. If you find that your efforts are being undermined, take a firm stand. Itchy feet may lead you to visit a travel agent. It would not hurt to pick up some brochures, even if only for reading in the comfort of your living room. It would be unwise to get too intimate with someone new before you have a clearer idea of their actual character and life experiences.

27. TUESDAY. Fortunate. This is a promising time to concentrate on your career plans. Jot down your current skills and all possible areas in which they could be used. You could meet someone who is able to give you excellent advice concerning savings and investing. If you are prepared to listen to them, your financial future may suddenly become a great deal brighter. The best way to deal with ongoing relationship problems is to bring them out into the open. Once you analyze them, they will almost certainly begin to dwindle away. It is only brooding on them that makes them seem so threatening and potentially overwhelming. Be willing to apologize even if you were not totally to blame.

28. WEDNESDAY. Useful. As a Cancer you have reasonably artistic talents which may be expressed through cookery, fine needlework, or woodworking. However, such crafts are just as valuable as a means of self-expression; you should work to hone these skills to near perfection. There may be an offer of a better job from a slightly obscure source. Perhaps a former colleague with whom you never really got along particularly well will phone to alert you to a promising opportunity. It is apt to be genuine, so do not delay in applying. If you are hoping that a romance can fade into friendship, think again. A clean break would be much easier to manage than a gradual parting.

29. THURSDAY. Sensitive. You are likely to leave your protective armor at home today. The slightest hint of criticism will hurt, just as if you had no self-confidence at all. Before snapping a sharp retort, it would benefit you to ask why you are feeling so sensitive. Love is not easy to handle at the best of times, and right now you and that special person in your life may to be straining in opposite directions. The freedom vs. closeness dilemma is a common one, and the usual solution is a compromise. Do not let friends drag you out to more social events than you really want if you would prefer a few quiet evenings at home. Loved ones and family commitments should be given priority.

30. FRIDAY. Suspenseful. Whispers may be going around at work about possible changes. However, whatever happens is going to be for the good. There may even be a redefinition of your job, with an accompanying higher salary. Although youngsters are normally communicative, at the moment you are probably aware that they are keeping something from you. However, it is more likely to be a surprise than anything for you to worry about, so do not spoil their excitement by prying. Household tasks may have to be left uncompleted due to other demands. Do not let them prey on your mind as you settle down to relax for the evening.

DECEMBER

1. SATURDAY. Slow. Do not berate yourself if you are not up at the break of dawn. Both your body and your emotions need some extra rest. Try to allow yourself a leisurely breakfast in bed, so much the better if someone prepares it for you. Weekend chores can be tedious so you feel you are never going to finish. However, they need to be done. If you are following a strict diet, you may be spending a great deal of time longing for your favorite food. Ideally you will get to the stage where you can enjoy a small amount of rich foods but have enough self-control to know when to stop. Unfortunately you are not yet at that point, so do not tempt yourself.

2. SUNDAY. Pleasant. Ideas to improve your home, especially the bathroom, can come from friends or loved ones. A brighter decor would make bathtime as well as bedtime a more enjoyable experience. Normally Cancer folk are not the tidiest of people, so it may come as a surprise to your family to find you busily putting things away. It might actually be more effective to recruit another member of the family to do this work if they have more of a willingness to get rid of clutter. This quieter time allows difficult emotions that you have repressed to rise to the surface. Talking them over can be enough to help you cease being worried about them.

3. MONDAY. Mixed. Faces from the past are not always welcome if they turn up again. Once you deliberately cut yourself off from some undesirable people, it can be quite a stressful matter letting them know that you do not want to renew the friendship, but it has to be done. Today's more cheerful mood should fill you with an unusual desire to indulge in humor. Your jokes will certainly be enjoyed by family members once they get over their surprise. It is important during winter months to keep close tabs on your health. While it is natural for your energy to diminish a little, it would not hurt to boost your system by taking a daily vitamin supplement.

4. TUESDAY. Positive. Work matters need to be discussed. If there is change in the air, offer your opinion even if it is not a popular one. Your voice ought to be heard. Youngsters may have to spend a day home from school, but they probably are not sick enough to keep out of your hair. Provide some imagination to find activities that will keep them occupied but not overexcited. Consider indulging in a relaxing massage or a day long beauty treatment. Just the experience of being pampered and fussed over can be immensely therapeutic, quite apart from the pleasing results. Your warm feelings for a colleague are apt to be fully reciprocated.

5. WEDNESDAY. Satisfactory. Worrying about money is not going to make the slightest bit of difference to your bank balance. Either forget about it entirely or do something practical such as making more of an effort to save. This is a good day to work in a supportive role, handling the less glamorous tasks that other people might consider beneath them. You will probably prefer being behind the scenes, where you are likely to be left on your own without being disturbed. It would be kind to help out an elderly relative who is short of money. A tactful way of doing so would be to offer household items or foods, which can be given and accepted without much fuss.

6. THURSDAY. Uneven. If so-called friends are making critical remarks clearly designed to erode your self-confidence, consider dropping them. Realize that they are the ones with a problem, not you. Financially you may be up one moment and down the next. It would be a good idea to put money for your regular expenses in a separate account, so that you have a clearer idea of what you are spending monthly. It is never a good idea to listen to gossip at work, and there is no excuse for passing on what you do hear. If you know a rumor is incorrect, do your best to stop it from going any further. If unsure about its truthfulness, check around to find out.

7. FRIDAY. Rewarding. Despite your emotional Cancer nature, you have a great deal of inner strength. When there is a last-minute crisis at work, it is likely to be you who keeps things going and prevents colleagues from panicking. This can be a very significant time for improving your overall health. Either you discover just exactly what suits you best by way of diet, or you recklessly throw all caution to the wind. The choice is yours. Where romance is concerned, avoid sinking into a dream of perfection so that you miss out on everyday fun. Even the most ordinary experiences have a touch of glamour when you are totally enamored with a special someone.

8. SATURDAY. Easy. The early part of the day is ideal for shopping. It would be a good idea to take along as much cash as possible, since you might want to begin loading up with presents for the holiday season. Entertaining the family should not be difficult since everyone is well able to look after themselves, which takes a burden off your shoulders. This is a good time to introduce yourself to new neighbors, perhaps also offering help of some kind. The earlier you establish a good relationship with them, the better. Since you are not likely to be in much of a social mood, it will be more pleasant to spend a quiet evening at home with friends rather than go out partying.

9. SUNDAY. Good. Take the opportunity this morning to relax fully. When waves of tiredness sweep over you, that is a sign of how you have been fighting off restorative sleep while you struggle on. Make a resolution not to push yourself too hard. Parents may be better able than you to deal with a financial crisis. Today is an excellent time to get together with them to discuss how they might help. While love is definitely in the air, you are probably content to let it develop at its own pace. Right now, you and that special person should be getting to know each other better rather than making the social rounds all the time. An experiment with a new recipe this evening should be dramatically successful.

10. MONDAY. Buoyant. Start the workweek with a clean sweep of minor tasks. This will clear the way for more important jobs that are likely to arise later on and will also make you feel more confident and capable. Youngsters will probably enjoy helping around the house while you and they talk, laugh, and sing together. It is not only important but fun to stretch their imagination by making up stories to amuse each other. Cancers with a garden should spend a little time preparing it for the winter months. Also keep in mind that house plants need less water unless they are kept in very warm conditions. Inject a little romance into your life by making this a night full of surprises.

11. TUESDAY. Disconcerting. A romance that seemed to be blossoming with someone at work could fizzle out into nothing more than a lukewarm friendship. Although you are bound to feel a little disheartened, try to realize that this is a blessing in disguise. You might take on extra work with the understanding that it will be well paid, only to discover that you are hardly better off financially. To avoid this happening, make sure you receive written confirmation of the hourly pay involved or of the lump-sum payment before committing yourself to anything. Even home-loving Cancer folk like a bit of excitement, but taking in a good movie would be enough of a charge for you this evening.

12. WEDNESDAY. Disquieting. No matter how bad a disagreement you have with your mate or partner, it can be patched up.

You may walk around seething all day, even planning to break up. However, if your motivation is to inflict hurt, no good can come of that. This is not the time to commit money to any type of speculative venture. Nor should you redistribute your funds on impulse; such matters need to be thought through thoroughly. Children may seem to be asking to be firmly disciplined with their deliberately provoking behavior. Just try to remember that you should not respond to their actions from a position of anger.

13. THURSDAY. Productive. New responsibilities at work could take you into the area of research. This will be a real learning phase for you, although you are bound to feel a little unsure of yourself at first. Entertaining friends from a distance can create a lot of extra work, but it is up to you whether you make a martyr of yourself. Help is available if you want it, so do not hesitate to ask. If you feel that a mongrel dog or cat is not the sort of pet you want, look into buying an exotic breed. Such an animal can be quite an exquisite addition to your life, but you must be prepared to pay the high veterinarian bills that delicate creatures always seem to run up.

14. FRIDAY. Happy. You could be literally swept off your feet in quite a normal situation. Love is not choosy about whom it selects. Today is one of those times when you are apt to feel a magnetic attraction to someone which is almost too strong to resist. Financially there may be rewards for taking on a colleague's work while they are otherwise occupied. Nor should you hesitate because you doubt your own ability. Resolve to get into tiptop physical condition; at the moment you have the willpower to do so. Meeting new people this evening might be almost too much after such a busy day, but they can open your mind to some interesting concepts and possibilities.

15. SATURDAY. Spirited. Children are the focus of attention this morning. It would be fun to let them come with you while you are out doing weekend chores; they will love to be included in grown-up activities. Later on you and your mate or partner can spend some time alone together. Finding some practical work or a hobby that you can share would be ideal. You need to aim for a sense of being able to work together toward a common goal, and enjoy the results. This is a great day for getting on the phone to organize a family event. Just do not fall into the trap of taking on all of the responsibility; let other relatives contribute as much as they can.

16. SUNDAY. Tricky. It can't be denied that as a Cancer you enjoy being the center of attention on occasion. This can lead to some insensitive behavior on your part. Try to listen to loved ones' needs and wishes, rather than imposing your own on them. Humor can be a great way of defusing emotional tension, although it needs to be doled out carefully. Some jokes which you find funny can be highly offensive to the older generation, so let discrimination be your watchword. Those who have been longing to propose marriage might be tempted to do so today. However, unless the atmosphere is too perfect to resist, it may be best to wait until the end of the month.

17. MONDAY. Fair. Legal matters are apt to be in the doldrums at the moment. Even though you feel frustrated with the lack of progress, this at least gives you a break from worry. Although conditions favor concocting business plans, they need to be discussed and perfected before being put into action. Try to be patient. Remember that good things almost always develop slowly. Your main focus as far as relationships are concerned should be inward. This is an ideal chance to ask yourself some tough questions about what you want and expect from love. Some of your own answers might surprise you, forcing you to rethink the direction of a certain love affair.

18. TUESDAY. Low-keyed. It is not likely that you will get much done this morning, at least not if you have practical tasks to complete. Your dreamy, remote mood will fill you with discontent for the kind of life you are leading. Be aware, however, that your fantasies of an ideal existence are totally unrealistic. This afternoon is a more grounded and positive time, offering you the opportunity to rectify some past mistakes. Even if this means redoing a major work project, be grateful that you have caught the situation before the small error grew into a multifaceted blunder. It would be kind to visit or at best call a lonely or elderly relative or neighbor this evening.

19. WEDNESDAY. Excellent. Just when you begin to think that love has passed you by, someone is likely to appear right out of a clear blue sky. The attraction between you may be so immediate that you feel no qualms about moving right into a close relationship. Your health can take a dramatic turn for the better if you hit upon a wholesome diet that suits your system; a bonus will be that you look stunning, too. Do not hesitate if a colleague asks you to go with them to a contemporary art show or play. It may not be your taste, but there will be entertainment just in observing other people who are there and being part of the unusual atmosphere.

20. THURSDAY. Favorable. Because you have everything under control at work, you can now coast toward the holiday with confidence. Part of the secret of your success is knowing how to list your many tasks in order of priority. You and your mate or partner deserve some special time alone. This is a good day to start planning a romantic winter break in a distant location. If you are studying, there is a great deal you can do over the Christmas season. Use this time for reviewing; all the work you put in will consolidate what you have learned so far. This evening you should have the energy to enjoy dancing or talking into the wee hours.

21. FRIDAY. Hectic. Since this will be the last day of work before the holiday break for most Cancer people, there is bound to be a bit of a hectic atmosphere. Happily you are geared up to cope with all that must be done. More intense focus is on personal relationships. In particular, devote some extra time to getting a business partnership running more smoothly. The key is honesty; each of you must be able to trust the other one implicitly. Demands on your time this afternoon may make it difficult to get some tasks finished, but you can do it with a bit of extra concentration. Last-minute shopping for gifts can actually be fun tonight.

22. SATURDAY. Bumpy. If you are going away for the holiday, your journey is apt to get off to a rather stressful start. There are likely to be delays that wear on your nerves, especially if you are traveling with children. Make sure you bring along plenty to keep them occupied. Getting chores done at home can be quite a task; even jobs that you normally enjoy are likely to seem irksome. However, you are not going to help matters by letting your mind wander off into irrelevant speculation. This is a season when close relationships are put under extra strain, so you need to be even more tactful and sensitive than usual. Try very hard to tolerate your loved ones and to forgive their moments of bad temper or inconsideration.

23. SUNDAY. Sensitive. Although you may wake up in a buoyant and energetic frame of mind, be careful to pace yourself or your nerves will be frayed by afternoon. Some difficulties arising between partners are best talked over, while others can be made worse by analysis. Right now you should avoid talking too much about a subject that could be embarrassing; let it alone for a while and allow some silent healing to take place. There is much enjoyment in store if you concoct some imaginative, unusual plans designed to delight youngsters at Christmas. They are bound to guess something is up, but maintaining the secrecy is part of the fun.

24. MONDAY. Exciting. After a lot of work you are finally coming to a sense of yourself as a person who should be taken seriously. Now it is time to be center stage and to make other people dance to your tune. You have the inner confidence to wield authority that they will respect. Try to get some extra exercise today; a long, brisk walk would be ideal. A journey to visit friends should take place in an atmosphere of good cheer that is a delight. If you repay their hospitality with a generous present, so much the better. Quickly tidying up around the house will make you feel you are on top of chores and ready for the big day tomorrow.

25. TUESDAY. Merry Christmas! This is just the sort of day you are bound to enjoy. You have paid enough attention to details to feel that you will be giving everyone a thoroughly good time. With a lot of emphasis on food, it is important to be providing meals that have been cooked with real love. You and your mate or partner should be happy to welcome guests throughout the course of the day, even to the point of hosting an open house. Friends are willing to help with the cleanup, so you do not have to worry about that. Emotions run high. There may be tears before the end of the day, but of happiness rather than sorrow.

26. WEDNESDAY. Auspicious. As you wind down from yesterday, there are many opportunities to tell your mate or partner how much you appreciate them. This can begin a period when the affection between you is expressed much more openly. Cancer singles who are hoping for romance could receive a surprise phone call from someone who has been thinking of asking for a date. It cannot hurt to arrange to meet without delay. This is a good time to get in touch with friends who have dropped out of your everyday life. It might be better to write rather than call so that you can give them all the news. Once you are out of the normal routine of life, your ideals and beliefs should be given some extra attention.

27. THURSDAY. Stressful. It is not always a good idea to bring together friends that you usually see separately. Different sides of your character come out when you are with different people, so in such a group it can be confusing to know how to act. In addition, not all of your friends are guaranteed to get along well. Even though you are full of big ideas for making money, they are not necessarily going to pan out. Remember that you have to test your plans in the real world before you can get a clear idea of if and how they will work. Romance can be highly intoxicating but up in the air. A settled relationship is not in the cards for you just yet.

28. FRIDAY. Challenging. Do not be misled by the peaceful start to this day, which allows you time to dream. You will very quickly have to sharpen your act and cope with the frustrations and duties of everyday life. As a Cancer you tend to depend on loved ones and friends for emotional support, so it is not always easy for you to cope with solitude. Right now other people are apt to be busy with their own lives, forcing you to develop strategies for making the most of time on your own. Travel can be stressful. It is vital to keep your temper if you are driving in order to avoid a minor accident that would nevertheless increase your insurance premium.

29. SATURDAY. Illuminating. Your more introspective mood allows you to recover your dreams from memory this morning. Some of the imagery can be so obvious that you see in flash what the hidden message is. Try to find time to visit a housebound relative, even if you cannot stay very long. It would be a good idea to plan to get together regularly so that they can rely on your visits. This is a great time to go out and try new photographic equipment. Photos taken casually or almost sneakily are likely to turn out better than stiff poses. Honest discussion of a relationship problem may clear it up just as if it never existed.

30. SUNDAY. Difficult. There is no point knocking yourself out with domestic tasks since no one will thank you for doing so. There is much more pleasure in going out for the day with a loved one or a very good friend. After your recent indulgences in food and drink, it is time to be thinking about a new health regime. Just start slowly and gently. Too much exercise too soon can strain your system, making you feel worse rather than better. Close relationships are now turning a corner to a more serene period. However, do not think this transition will be easy; much tolerance and forgiveness is required by both you and your mate or other relative.

31. MONDAY. Pleasant. The end of the year is naturally a time to look back as well as forward. Even though you may feel that you have not made a great deal of progress in your personal development, that is probably far from true. Those people who are closest to you can explain what they see as your most significant changes. Relationships are apt to be at the forefront of your mind; there is certainly work to be done in this sphere of your life. It would not hurt to resolve to try to achieve better balance in the year ahead between your own needs and those of your loved ones. Write down your vows so that you can remind yourself of them from time to time during 2002.

CANCER
NOVEMBER–DECEMBER 2000

November 2000

1. WEDNESDAY. Demanding. What might at first seem like an ideal romance could let you down badly later on. Do not be persuaded by a flow of words; trust your own good Cancer judgment. Youngsters need to be closely watched or they are likely to get into all sorts of mischief behind your back. A favorite leisure activity may be threatened by lack of funds. It is time to consider changing the focus of your attention, or even taking up another pastime. Loved ones are apt to be in a rather playfully romantic mood, which might not chime in with your own feelings. Rather than brush them off, try to enter into the same spirit and you are bound to enjoy yourselves.

2. THURSDAY. Excellent. Friends may be more eager than usual for you to join in with their activities. Even if this does not at first appeal, you will probably have a good time if you say yes. A contract may be signed sooner than expected, and if it suits your purpose you might be able to hurry the process along. As long as you have done the groundwork, there should be no worries about the fine print. Travel conditions are smoother than usual. Take advantage of this to go somewhere special with a loved one. Relations at work are fairly open, giving you a useful opportunity to bring up for discussion a subject that is normally difficult.

3. FRIDAY. Reassuring. You can strengthen the bonds of affection with your mate or partner by involving them in your plans for personal achievement. Confiding hopes and wishes that normally you keep to yourself will increase the rapport between you. A business association that is based upon shared idealism could be extremely profitable. When you are acting on principle, you put that much more energy into it, and this can only have beneficial results. Sometimes it is just not the right moment to tell someone your innermost feelings. Although your emotional nature makes you prone to act on instinct, today it would be better to hold back until a more appropriate time.

4. SATURDAY. Quiet. You may be eager to brighten up your home this weekend. Strike while the iron is hot. Buy paint and tools while the enthusiasm is on you. Time spent alone enables you to mull over the recent ending of a relationship and come to terms with it. There are bound to be both good and not-so-good memories, but now you must again face the future. If you find it difficult to get out of the house very much, ask for help from relatives and neighbors. You will be delighted at how willing people are to lend a hand even with daily chores. A lost item will turn up eventually; keep looking.

5. SUNDAY. Mixed. Political in-fighting could shake your confidence in a cause that has been important to you for some time. Remember that individual failings should not affect your enthusiasm for the ideals that inspire you. A friend may be making underhanded comments that can be quite hurtful. It is likely that their own inadequacies are at the root of the problem, not that you are truly at fault. Try to shrug it off for now. Give youngsters something to occupy their minds. They will learn at a great rate if their interest is aroused, and it is possible that you will pick up new knowledge as well. Do not stay up too late tonight.

6. MONDAY. Disquieting. Unless you can take the long view, this could be a rather upsetting day. There are bound to be obstacles in your path toward self-development, but right now they probably appear larger than they are in reality. A training course may turn out to be not quite what you were looking for. If you suspect that you are not being assessed fairly, it is probably not worth putting a lot of effort into your studying. It is likely to be hard to get colleagues all working together unless you use the full range of your powers of persuasion. In any event, do not go it alone. You need support and encouragement at work and indeed are entitled to it.

7. TUESDAY. Productive. This is an excellent time to brighten the dullness of winter with plans for a first-class vacation. Consider going to a place where you can get plenty of a favorite sport, especially if you have a partner who shares your interest. Romance is about to move to another level. Someone with whom you have good mental rapport is taking a lot more interest in you. A basis of mutual understanding is helpful in any relationship. There is nothing to be gained from quarreling at work over routine arrangements. Everyone has to toe the line to some extent, as well as respecting each other's individuality.

8. WEDNESDAY. Busy. If you have been waiting eagerly for a letter, this could be the day it arrives. Careful inspection may reveal that it has traveled quite a complicated route to reach you. Cancers who rely on clients for work should have a busier day than usual. People who consulted you some time ago are likely to look you up again. This vote of confidence in your work is bound to give you a new boost of energy. Cancer students should think about term papers and exams seriously. A good grade can do wonders for your sense of self-worth and may also be useful in getting a dream job.

9. THURSDAY. Deceptive. More romantic Cancers may be in for a rude awakening. As the truth is revealed about a loved one, you could realize you never really knew each other at all. Money is probably a prime problem area. It is best to play safe. Fight shy of new or unusual investment schemes; they probably will not last long. Creative work that looked good a few days ago may now seem to need extensive redoing. Although this will take time and patience, you are far better off starting again from scratch than trying to patch things up. Workwise, this should be a productive day, but do not push yourself too hard.

10. FRIDAY. Satisfactory. Hidden problems around the house could come to light just in time to be fixed before real damage is done. Thoroughly inspect potential trouble spots, especially down spouts and interior drainage. A mixture of book learning and intuition can solve a long-term problem with a close relative. Both of you need to define your boundaries more clearly, but the first step is better communication. If you are fond of antiques, look for an auction in your area. You have a good eye and should be able to pick out items of value from the ordinary bric-a-brac being offered for sale.

11. SATURDAY. Stressful. You can no longer go on with a romantic affair on a day-by-day basis. Sooner, rather than later, you have to decide just how serious you are, then abide by your decision. Friends may impose themselves on you just when you want to have some time alone to pursue a hobby. Although it can be a difficult situation to handle, make it plain that you will socialize when you are ready and not before. Youngsters may need more company than usual. The role of parent includes being a friend, as you doubtless know. Your kids will get a great kick from feeling you share their interests and curiosity about their world.

12. SUNDAY. Sensitive. There is no point trying to force yourself to join in an activity just because friends and loved ones are enthusiastic about it. You may only end up being a wet blanket, so it is better for everyone in the long run if you insist on doing your own thing. Delving into old family photograph albums and letters can reveal a wealth of knowledge. The memories of a past generation can shed light on the present; you are apt to be fascinated by the similarity of their hopes and problems and your current situation. A stronger sense of compassion is likely to prompt you to try to help a neighbor or friend who has fallen on hard times, but do not get taken in by a hard-luck story meant only to win your sympathy.

13. MONDAY. Reassuring. Relationships should take a turn for the better as both of you make an extra effort to understand the other's point of view. Relaxing rather than arguing every small point can be surprisingly helpful. In the end, being right is not as important as you may think. Legal matters are likely to be costly. Although you will probably come out on the winning side, consider whether it is really worth the hassle. For once, drop your suspicious tendencies and trust that someone in your social circle truly has your best interests at heart. Only if you open yourself to them will you be able to benefit.

14. TUESDAY. Buoyant. A mood of extra buoyancy makes you especially attractive to the opposite sex. This is fine if you are hoping to attract someone. However, if you have other concerns it may be wisest to tone down your behavior. Cancer writers should find self-expression particularly easy. Even if you think you have no talent, keeping a diary can be a fascinating exercise as you record thoughts and feelings rather than cut-and-dried daily events. The value of a long-term relationship lies partly in the way a partner provides a mirror for you to observe yourself. At the moment, however, you may not be able to learn from this and only be seeing the negative.

15. WEDNESDAY. Confusing. Even the best financial experts make mistakes. This is one day when they are apt to be more fallible than usual. Treat all advice with caution; do not act on it until you get a second opinion. A love affair could suffer unecessary complications because one of you is paying too much attention to rumors and gossip. You need to trust each other enough to sort out the truth between you. Competition results are likely to be disappointing. There may have been a mix-up with entries, but do not let this keep you from trying again. Jobs around the house may end in chaos unless you ask for help and get it.

16. THURSDAY. Lucky. If you are house hunting you could have a real stroke of luck that is likely to come out of the blue. You need to be able to recognize it for what it is. Do not pass over any property without having a thorough look. A family gathering could put you back in touch with relatives you lost contact with some time ago. Take this opportunity to pick up the threads again; there is real affection and the offer of support to be gained. A creative approach to problem solving can get your further than tackling issues head-on. In fact, if you think of the problem in a positive way as a challenge, the answer may turn out to be staring you in the face.

17. FRIDAY. Tricky. Extreme caution is advisable if you are sharing finances with your mate or partner. It is vital to be absolutely clear just what you both expect from each other. Otherwise there could be accusations of unfair spending later on. Bringing up youngsters can sometimes make you feel old beyond your years. Taking the leap of imagination to enter their world will give you a fresh outlook on life that makes you feel young again. Your sense of self-worth can be enhanced by doing some volunteer work that satisfies your conscience. Money spent on your home will increase its value in the long run, so regard it as a long-term investment.

18. SATURDAY. Disquieting. You may have to put your own wishes aside as a loved one requires most of your time and attention. The danger is that you will then resent that they have cut into your leisure time, so do your best to be aware of any negative feelings. Romance is unlikely to settle into permanency if you insist on being overly protective of your privacy. Either you trust your loved one enough to let them into your life or you run the risk of losing them. Youngsters may tend to dominate the day unless you are careful. You need to find the right balance between giving them enough attention and attending to your affairs.

19. SUNDAY. Frustrating. If you would rather be alone today, do not hesitate to say so. However, use some tact or you can hurt friends and loved ones. It may seem that you have pushed a favorite leisure activity as far as you can go. In fact, you may envy others who have more skill or ability than you, but with persistence you can learn more and improve your expertise. Trips could be plagued with minor problems. Make sure you have an up-to-date map, or you might get lost and wind up in heated argument. Relationships will be smoother if you open your hearts to each other. Guessing about feelings is no substitute for actually being told what is going on.

20. MONDAY. Pleasant. This is a very good day for making new contacts and, even more importantly, consolidating old ones. You could pick up a lot of useful information by phoning or traveling around. It will pay to check out the political beliefs of business associates in order to get a sense of their basic standards and expectations. A friend can be relied upon to get you to an appointment on time if your own transportation is unavailable; do not be too shy to ask. Get a report written before the day is out. It should be easier than usual to put your ideas across. Professional presentation will help convince people to follow your lead.

21. TUESDAY. Variable. Take this opportunity to consider doing major renovations to your home. This is especially timely if you have been putting off building an addition or making alterations. Quite tiring exercise can be good for your health; a workout at a gym would be ideal. However, if you are not used to this kind of exercise, make sure you have proper supervision. Although arguments within the family are almost inevitable from time to time, a serious clash of personalities may have a deep effect on youngsters if you are not careful. Put a firm stop to rumors at work about your private life. Colleagues should have more important things to talk about.

22. WEDNESDAY. Disconcerting. Loved ones really know how to rub you the wrong way, but on occasion you can do exactly the same to them. Sometimes quarrels can clear the air. It is important not to let them continue without making the effort to patch up a peace. Think about getting additional insurance for valuables. Leaving it to luck is not going to satisfy your Cancer need for security. Family relationships will be improved by giving each other a little more personal space. Everyone needs a measure of privacy, both physically and emotionally. A romantic affair may now be intense, but be aware that it is not as stable as you would like it to be.

23. THURSDAY. Manageable. Try giving up something harmful to your health. You could be amazed at the difference in the way you feel, and you may even want to stay clear of the habit once you have broken it. Clearing out drawers and closets is likely to reveal articles you thought were lost for good. A gentle approach to loved ones should be more effective than trying to browbeat them into doing what you want. However, do not force them to do anything they may later resent. Romance can disappear in a war of words unless you make an effort to stay in touch with how you feel. There is little to be gained from standing on principle if doing so is only going to alienate a loved one.

24. FRIDAY. Deceptive. Impulse buying can get you out of your depth financially before you even realize what has happened unless you are very careful. It might be wise not to buy anything before you consult your mate or partner. They are likely to act as brakes on your enthusiasm. Cancers looking for love are more vulnerable than usual. Your judgment of character is not all it should be, so beware of getting involved with anyone who is outside your usual range of experience. Plans for the upcoming holidays could be thwarted by a dishonest travel agent, so make sure you check the credentials of everyone you deal with and do not fall for anything that is suspiciously cheap.

25. SATURDAY. Demanding. It takes quite a bit of willpower to be consistently patient with youngsters. They may seem bent on being destructive; and if they are quiet, that is not necessarily a good sign. Leisure activities may be interrupted by more serious events. All will be well as long as you keep your head and encourage loved ones to retain a sense of humor. Regard today as an opportunity to get routine chores done rather than as pure leisure time. Social events are likely to be rather formal and quite stressful. However, there are probably useful contacts to be made among the guests you have never met before.

26. SUNDAY. Helpful. Romance is coming to the fore as your doubts about mutual feelings are finally clarified. Enjoy the relationship for what it is, and do not be ashamed to be sentimental. Youngsters can have uncanny insight into a problem that you did not even think they were aware of. It is as if they are plugged into some source of inspiration, so listen closely to them. Overdoing can undermine your health. Schedule some regular time for pure relaxation; even so-called leisure pursuits can be draining. It is important to get to the bottom of a family disagreement that may seem to be about trivia, but deeper issues are at stake.

27. MONDAY. Challenging. Make a fresh start this morning, sweeping away the cobwebs of routine boredom. If you resolve to take a new approach to work, you can find original ways of dealing with the day's tasks. Your health might benefit from more outdoor exercise. Get out at lunchtime, especially if you usually eat in the office. An unusual character may intrigue you with their quirky views. You could probably learn a lot about the deeper meaning of life by listening to them. This is a good time to improve your understanding of modern technology. A short course can be illuminating, and youngsters are apt to be a gold mine of information about the latest developments.

28. TUESDAY. Tricky. You could jeopardize a great measure of security by taking the word of someone who is less than trustworthy. Do not believe promises that sound too good to be true; that is probably exactly what they are. A pet may need a little extra care to get back to full health. At the same time, resist the temptation to spoil them, which will only make the problem worse. There is no point putting your present relationship at risk by hanging onto memories of the past. Comparisons are only going to be upsetting. Your loved one certainly will not appreciate a past acquaintance being held up as some kind of ideal. Money will flow like water unless you budget carefully.

29. WEDNESDAY. Mixed. After a long period of confusion, true affection is becoming the keynote of a close relationship. This should reconcile you to coping with the inevitable drawbacks that are also involved. A lucrative deal may be tempting, but consider how likely it is to come off. No matter what business associates say, it would be wise to check and double-check all the facts before getting optimistic. Couples moving in together for the first time face all kinds of unexpected issues involving compromise and consideration. It is important to agree on the major issues; minor ones are not worth arguing about and will soon sort themselves out.

30. THURSDAY. Misleading. There may be some mystery surrounding a legacy or prize due you. It might be wise to expect some delay before it is paid so that you do not start to worry about it. A romantic partner could be pulling the wool over your eyes on some score. If they are evasive about a particular area of life, that probably means there is something they want to hide. Come right out and demand an explanation. A bright new way of making money could come to you after talking with a colleague. Take time to make some notes so that you can think it over more thoroughly later on. Do not cut yourself off from friends because you are spending a lot of time with your mate or partner.

December 2000

1. FRIDAY. Variable. For no reason that you can think of, friends may be less than enthusiastic about your plans for shared weekend activities. It is probably best not to try to persuade them. Instead, make alternative arrangements on your own. Creative Cancers are likely to be experiencing a block at the moment. The most positive way of dealing with this is to take a break and become more introverted for a while. Eventually ideas will come to you, but they need time. A small lump sum due you for work you may have forgotten about will come in handy. Use it for a leisure project you are trying to get off the ground, but be sure to spend it carefully.

2. SATURDAY. Fair. Spend some time around the house repairing small problems that may have become so familiar you have almost ceased to notice them. Minor faults can easily be fixed, but do not attempt anything you are not entirely confident about doing. The atmosphere will be improved by frank discussion of joint finances. Both you and your mate or partner need to be pulling in the same direction as far as future security goes. There is nothing to be gained by one person saving and the other spending. Quick action now to end a relationship that has begun to go sour should enable you to part as friends. There may still be a degree of attraction, but you need more than that for happiness.

3. SUNDAY. Disquieting. Youngsters may seem more hyperactive than usual. It might be simplest to leave them to their own activities as long as you check on them from time to time. News of a former lover could set your heart fluttering more than you would have expected. There may still be unfinished business between you. When you meet again, this needs to be sorted out so that you can concentrate on present relationships. You may be pulled between confiding an action of which you are not proud to a loved one or keeping silent. Admitting guilt is never easy, but it will be even harder living with your conscience if you say nothing.

4. MONDAY. Sensitive. Everyone may seem to have gotten out of bed on the wrong side this morning. It may even be difficult to leave the house without starting a quarrel about something as petty as who spends longest in the bathroom. A meeting at work needs very careful handling. Some jockeying for power is going on. Although this may seem unimportant, a lot of unnecessary ill will can be caused. As a Cancer you live so much in your emotions that you are easy prey to fears about your health. However, you are probably worrying yourself into symptoms where none actually exist. A thorough checkup will soon put your mind at rest.

5. TUESDAY. Surprising. A relationship with a friend older than you may be developing romantic overtones. Perhaps you are only taken by surprise because you just did not think of the person in those terms. However, you probably have a lot to offer each other. Getting expert help in regard to a legal matter is far safer than taking the law into your own hands. This advice should not be too expensive and will be well worth the cost. If you are looking to take a step up the career ladder, you should be in a position to make use of contacts among your friends and associates. A quiet word in the right place can put you on the path to achieving your ambitions.

6. WEDNESDAY. Fine. Even if you find yourself going through the daily routine in a dream state, do not worry about it. Just get small tasks done and let your mind wander. Your unconscious self is probably busy solving a problem, whose answer will surface in its own good time. This is a good day to take up a relaxing form of exercise rather than anything too strenuous. Rhythmic movement that stretches muscles gently while soothing your nerves can be immensely beneficial. Sooner or later, younger family members have to begin to understand that everyone has to contribute to the family. Touch on this tricky subject now and you will prepare the ground for the future.

7. THURSDAY. Pressured. Most Cancer people are home loving, but it is also necessary to go out and make a living. The tension between these dual needs can cause you more stress than other folk. Maybe it is time to see if you can change your working practices in order to spend more time at home. If you are involved in a property deal, you may find the other party is trying to pressure you into a quick contract. If you do not feel comfortable about this, resist. There will be other opportunities even if this one does not come off. Partnership issues may revolve around a mixture of attraction and resentment. It is true that opposites attract, but envy has no part in a close relationship.

8. FRIDAY. Disconcerting. Just as it seems a special relationship is intimate, the other person may be emotionally unavailable. It could be that something about you is stirring up memories of a past relationship, and they need to sort out past from present before they can give you their full devotion. A dearly held ambition for your future may be more difficult to attain if you have the responsibility of sharing a home. Although the freedom of a single person probably seems more attractive than usual, consider whether you would really want to give up your loved one. Stay at home tonight to wind down from the stress of the workweek.

9. SATURDAY. Promising. Your family can usually be relied upon to offer support when you are in a tight corner, and this time is no exception. A relative is apt to be only too happy to play the role of guardian angel; do not hesitate to accept their offer of assistance. You may have to put more trust than you like in a friend, especially if you must combine funds for a joint project. This is actually good practice in using your powers of judgment, and it is unlikely that you will be let down. Weekend chores should not prevent you from getting out and doing something entirely different and unusual. You need to break the mold from time to time and overcome your self-imposed limits.

10. SUNDAY. Mixed. A romantic daydream may seem about to come true. A new relationship can transport you to a realm of pure pleasure; enjoy it while it lasts. Try to find time to visit a friend or relative who is housebound. Even though it may seem rather tedious, they will get a great deal of pleasure from your company, and you might enjoy it too. It can be harder for Cancers than for others to let go of the past. Your memory is very vivid, but you tend to view past events in a rather idealized way. Do not allow yourself to brood over what is over and done. It would be soothing to spend some time at the movies or concert arena and forget the world.

11. MONDAY. Fair. You should be able to get a great deal of work done today as long as you are not interrupted. Put up a mental do not disturb sign and make others keep their distance. An unusual investment opportunity may tempt you even though there is an element of risk. For once you can afford to take a chance, but do not commit more money than you can comfortably spare. Unless you get a grip on yourself, life can be taken over by dull daily routine and you will lose sight of your objectives. It might help to write down what you want to achieve, just to remind yourself. Spend a quiet evening at home with loved ones. Enjoy talking together rather than watching TV.

12. TUESDAY. Tricky. Fears and worries you thought you shook off long ago could return, though in less force. It is particularly important not to get hung up over matters such as tidiness and cleanliness. Keep objective and you should not have any trouble. A youngster's health may present a few small problems; keep them home from school if you are in any doubt. Romance is in the cards, with the likelihood of a call from someone you had not realized was interested in you personally. Once into this relationship, it may be difficult to end it, so be sure it is something you want to take seriously. Otherwise you face problems later.

13. WEDNESDAY. Challenging. The decision to buy a home is a big step in life, particularly if you are doing it on a shoestring. However, having a home is more important to Cancers than to most, so you probably will not regret taking the plunge. A family gathering could arouse all kinds of emotional cross-currents. As much as you love your relatives, it can be annoying when they attempt to pry into your affairs. Keep in mind that you have every right to tell them only what you want them to know. As a personal project comes to an end, it may leave you with a sense of anticlimax as you ponder what you are going to use your energies on next. The only solution is to find a new quest.

14. THURSDAY. Problematic. You maybe tempted to spend a serious amount of money without considering the consequences. Not only could this put a big dent in your savings, but the actual purchase may turn out to be a disappointment. Unfortunately you cannot rely on romance to bring you happiness right now. Although you may be flinging everything you have into it, the other person may not be so deeply committed. Hopes of improving security in the future may seem rather vague, but that is no reason not to discuss plans with your family. Fulfilling a duty to an older relative will make you feel better about indulging your own whims this evening.

15. FRIDAY. Variable. A sudden brainwave could change the way you and your mate or partner deal with joint funds. Day-to-day living expenses can be handled far more efficiently than you are now doing, which would make a lot of difference to your savings. Frayed nerves can benefit from getting away from the daily round. Plan a weekend away or an afternoon off. What at first seemed to be a good idea for reorganization at work might run into stiff resistance from those who like to do things their own way. You may have to work hard to make more stubborn colleagues think the idea was their own. Guard against making any threats you do not mean.

16. SATURDAY. Cautious. It is safest not to make hard-and-fast plans for a trip. There are bound to be complications as relatives demand or request some of your time. Try to spend some time completing paperwork that should have been done a while ago. Get old receipts and banking information in order so that you have a clearer idea of where you stand financially. You are likely to receive a larger phone bill than expected unless youngsters are kept away from the phone. You could even consider getting a lock to prevent long calls to young friends at a distance. Neighbors can be particularly helpful if you need assistance in a hurry.

17. SUNDAY. Easy. Use this day of rest to relax and unwind. Get in touch with old friends. There is no need to prepare anything elaborate; just being in pleasant company should be enough to ensure enjoyment. This is not the best time to play energetic sports; you will feel far more comfortable getting gentler exercise such as walking. Parents or in-laws may have very useful advice to offer. Although you may at first resent their intrusion, actually there is some wisdom in their words. Throwing away accumulated magazines and newspapers will give you more storage space than you might expect. Take it all to a recycling site if available locally.

18. MONDAY. Helpful. An extra surge of energy can help you clear up tasks that have been preying on your conscience. Recent efforts to live more healthfully are doing you good. Now is the time to resolve to carry on this way, particularly with the temptations of the holidays right around the corner. Paperwork requires detailed attention. Only if you retain sight of the overall plan can you make sense of current options and opportunities. Family members rally around when you need a bit of emotional support. After all, they know you best and care the most.

19. TUESDAY. Favorable. A workplace flirtation promises to brighten up your days. Although neither of you may have made your feelings known, the attraction is apt to be quite strong on both sides. Loved ones could be keeping a secret from you, but this is nothing sinister. You will be let in on it when they deem the time is right. If you are looking for property to buy, consider focusing on older houses. As a Cancer you have a strong sense of history. Although there are undoubtedly problems modernizing fixtures, older properties are often very well built. Relax in a leisurely bath tonight; you need to unwind more often.

20. WEDNESDAY. Busy. Youngsters are bound to be getting excited about now. Their enthusiasm for the festive season is likely to influence even the most harried parents. Let them decorate the tree and they will be happily busy for hours. Arguments may arise when relatives seem to be taking too much interest in your private life. This is something for you to sort out with them personally rather than getting into conflict with other family members. Cancers who work from home should try to get tax forms and the like cleared out of the way. You will then be able to concentrate on your work all the better. A romantic partner cannot be relied upon this evening.

21. THURSDAY. Misleading. The focus is on close relationships. There is more need than usual to understand each other's points of view. Harmony will not come unless and until both of you put in a bit of work on developing a more tolerant attitude. Money may seem to disappear almost without your noticing it. Your normally frugal habits could be breaking down, but without careful planning there will be little to show for the outlay. Cancers involved in romance face the prospect of losing all you have by continuing to be stubborn. When you pause and consider all the other person means to you, it is obviously worth giving in a little in order to keep their affection.

22. FRIDAY. Quiet. A mood of camaraderie reigns on what is probably the last day of work for most Cancers before the holiday break. The traditional parties and celebrations may be a little more quiet in tone than usual. All the same, you could be getting together with people you do not usually see socially. Do not fall into the trap of taking unfinished work home; there is little to be gained, since you probably will not even touch it. A last-minute call could mean the week ends in a rush, although the work is apt to be very valuable. Do not be tempted by friends to go out tonight if you would prefer to stay home. You need to tighten the purse strings a little and keep gift buying to a minimum.

23. SATURDAY. Sensitive. It is almost inevitable you will overeat during the next few days, but it is really important at this time of year to look after your health. Overindulgence just is not worth it, so recognize when enough is enough. Cancers who are looking for love could receive a pleasant surprise as someone plucks up courage to call or even to declare their feelings. In fact, you may be rather taken aback at the suddenness of this development. Give yourself time to mull over a proposal or proposition. Last-minute shopping may turn up some inspired gifts, but they will not be cheap. However, if they give pleasure to loved ones you will be amply rewarded.

24. SUNDAY. Happy. A friend who gets in touch with you out of the blue could whisk you back to a past era when you were both young. If you resist the temptation to get bogged down in memories, this person could bring a new focus of interest to your life because they have been living a very different lifestyle from you. Cancers who are parting from special friends or a lover to return to the family for the holiday are bound to feel a little sad. However, a period of separation should make your reunion all the sweeter. It is all too easy to slip into arguments over final details of arrangements, but remember it is simply impossible to please everybody.

25. MONDAY. Merry Christmas! The accent is firmly on relationships on this special day. There is the possibility of a fresh start due to the season of goodwill; resolve to put the past behind you and renew bonds of affection. If you have organized every last detail of the celebrations, you can now sit back and relax more than usual. Youngsters should be a real joy with their innocent approach to the festivities. Make a point of calling relatives and friends who are too distant to visit. This is a season when you need to feel your loved ones around you. Although this is likely to be a busy and talkative day, the undercurrents are very loving and supportive.

26. TUESDAY. Relaxing. Today's harmonious atmosphere makes it easy to sit back and allow stress to fade away. It is important to spend as much time as possible with loved ones, especially to talk. Past problems can be cleared up with little effort once you look them squarely in the face. Confine exercise to gentle walking. A new pet will take some time to be integrated into the family. It is not too soon to introduce youngsters to a sense of responsibility about caring for pets. This is not a day for putting your own wishes first; real pleasure will come from doing little things to make loved ones happy.

27. WEDNESDAY. Tranquil. Old friends can always be relied on to provide the security and roots that are so necessary to you. Just getting in touch by phone for some gossip may be all you need to feel loved and wanted. This is also a good time to discuss future plans with a loved one. You both have hopes and dreams, and you can help each other achieve them. Parents can become more like friends as time passes and they begin to accept that you have almost as much life experience as they have. However, they will always appreciate it if you show them proper respect. Stay close to home tonight. A quiet evening will restore your energy.

28. THURSDAY. Disquieting. Your dreams are likely to be rather vivid. Even if they contain uncomfortable imagery, they are probably addressing a real-life problem and deserve close attention. Once again romance may have you feeling somewhat lost. The other person may just not seem to know what they want, even if you do. It may be time to decide whether you really want to hang on to this relationship much longer. A quick look at your finances could reveal that savings are less than you expected. Investments may not have fulfilled their promise; you might want to consider alternatives. Do not let a loved one provoke you into losing your temper.

29. FRIDAY. Problematic. It could be more difficult than you expected to recover a loan to a friend. However, at the moment your need is greater than theirs, so do not hesitate to put pressure on them. Cancers who are back at work are likely to find all in good order. There should be time to think of new and improved ways of organizing the daily routine. Loved ones will not thank you for making a financial decision without consulting them. It is immaterial whether or not they understand as much as you; what is important is that you act as a team. A breakthrough in romance is foreseen if you both have the courage to be honest.

30. SATURDAY. Uneasy. The weekend begins with a certain pull between your sense of duty to others and a deep desire to cut yourself off from the world. It would be good to arrange an hour or so of total privacy; then you will feel more in the mood for being with friends and family. A past relationship could be obsessing you to the point where you cannot really enter into a new one. However, you can no longer afford to go on basing your life on a dream; wake up and live in the present! If you are looking for love, you may be happiest with someone who shares all of your ideals and interests. Considering taking a class or joining a club to contact like-minded people.

31. SUNDAY. Harmonious. You have an ideal opportunity to share ideas with your mate or partner. Resolve to improve communications between you in the future. After all, if you do not know what each other is thinking, you can never understand how the relationship is evolving. Now more than ever it is important to bear in mind your process of self-development. Allowing the daily routine to blot out deeper and more enduring concerns will only frustrate your search for life's meaning. You have cleared a lot of deadwood out of your life during the course of the year, making it possible to look forward to new developments and achievements. Keep a sense of perspective and all will be well.

"Famous Talk Show Host"
MOTHER LOVE
♥ Love Psychics ♥

1-800-218-2442 from $2.79/min
1-900-370-5330 $3.99/min

★ CELEBRITY PSYCHIC NETWORK®
Paula Jones
Has your life been turned upside down?
Make your life right again!
1-800-471-4292

BARBARA NORCROSS
THE PALM BEACH PSYCHIC
psychic advisor to police departments, government officials and celebrities for over 25 years.
CALL NOW ★ TOLL FREE
1-888-461-3663

LA TOYA JACKSON'S PSYCHIC NETWORK
AMERICA'S #1 PSYCHIC LINE
1-800-994-1800 from $2.79/min
1-900-737-2442 $3.99/min

CELEBRITY PSYCHIC NETWORK®
Laura Bryan Birn "Soap Opera Star"
3 MINUTES FREE
Don't wait...CALL NOW!
1-800-232-0052

BRIGITTE NIELSEN'S
WITCHES OF SALEM®
Have Faith and Courage • Don't Hesitate • CALL NOW!

1-800-799-5959 from $2.79/min
1-900-370-1586 $3.99/min

US PAT. 5,802,156 • 5,960,069 • THE ZODIAC GROUP, INC. • MUST BE 18 YEARS + • FOR ENTERTAINMENT ONLY

Find Love & Happiness

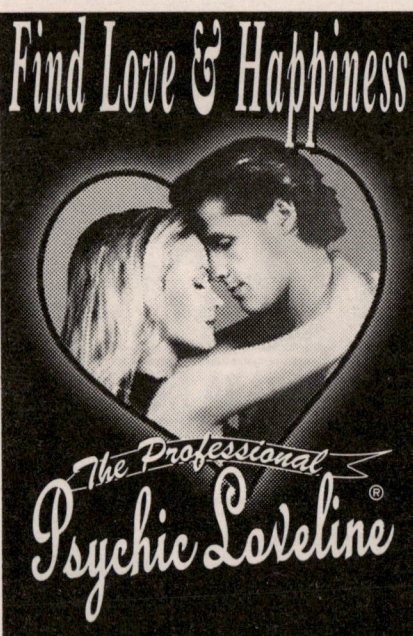

The Professional Psychic Loveline®

Talk live to our genuinely talented Psychics in matters of the heart. They have helped thousands of people just like you find true love, wealth and lasting happiness. Call anytime and get the answers you need from psychic who care.

**NUMEROLOGY · TAROT
ASTROLOGY · CLAIRVOYANT**

FREE 2 MIN!

AS LOW AS $1.93/MIN
1-800-472-9015
CREDIT CARD OR CHECK
1-900-420-6500
FIRST 2 MIN FREE $3.99/MIN. AFTER

24 HOURS. 18+. ENTERTAINMENT PURPOSES ONLY.

AMERICA'S BEST PSYCHIC SOURCE

Astrology · Clairvoyants · Tarot · Numerology

Have the life you always dreamed of with amazing insights from gifted psychics

AS LOW AS $1.93/MIN
1-800-472-4966
CREDIT CARD OR CHECK
1-900-420-0033
FIRST 2 MIN FREE $3.99/MIN. AFTER

24 Hours. 18+. Entertainment purposes only.

The PSYCHIC Romance SPECIALISTS

Try our elite group of gifted Psychics specializing in your personal questions about romance, love and mysteries of your heart. Our Specialists will empower and help guide you to the true happiness you deserve.

FREE 2 MINUTES! $3.99/MIN. AFTER
1-900-740-4466
1-800-784-9758
AS LOW AS $1.93/min.
CREDIT CARD OR CHECK ONLY

24 HOURS. 18+. ENTERTAINMENT PUROPSES ONLY.

WHAT DOES YOUR FUTURE HOLD...?

DISCOVER IT IN *ASTROANALYSIS*—

COMPLETELY REVISED TO THE YEAR 2015, THESE GUIDES INCLUDE COLOR-CODED CHARTS FOR TOTAL ASTROLOGICAL EVALUATION, PLANET TABLES AND CUSP CHARTS, AND STREAMLINED INFORMATION FOR ANYONE WHO HAS EVER LOOKED TO THE STARS AND WONDERED....

__ARIES	0-425-17558-8/$12.95
__TAURUS	0-425-17559-6/$12.95
__GEMINI	0-425-17560-X/$12.95
__CANCER	0-425-17561-8/$12.95
__LEO	0-425-17562-6/$12.95
__VIRGO	0-425-17563-4/$12.95
__LIBRA	0-425-17564-2/$12.95
__SCORPIO	0-425-17565-0/$12.95
__SAGITTARIUS	0-425-17566-9/$12.95
__CAPRICORN	0-425-17567-7/$12.95
__AQUARIUS	0-425-17568-5/$12.95
__PISCES	0-425-17569-3/$12.95

Prices slightly higher in Canada

Payable by Visa, MC or AMEX only ($10.00 min.), No cash, checks or COD. Shipping & handling: US/Can. $2.75 for one book, $1.00 for each add'l book; Int'l $5.00 for one book, $1.00 for each add'l. Call (800) 788-6262 or (201) 933-9292, fax (201) 896-8569 or mail your orders to:

Penguin Putnam Inc.
P.O. Box 12289, Dept. B
Newark, NJ 07101-5289
Please allow 4-6 weeks for delivery.
Foreign and Canadian delivery 6-8 weeks.

Bill my: ❏ Visa ❏ MasterCard ❏ Amex _____ (expires)
Card# _____
Signature _____

Bill to:
Name _____
Address _____ City _____
State/ZIP _____ Daytime Phone # _____

Ship to:
Name _____ Book Total $ _____
Address _____ Applicable Sales Tax $ _____
City _____ Postage & Handling $ _____
State/ZIP _____ Total Amount Due $ _____

This offer subject to change without notice.   Ad # 893 (3/00)

Do you ever need someone to turn to for advice?

Let Our LIVE PSYCHICS be there for YOU!

**24 Hours a day 7 days a week
They'll never let you down!
Call Now!**

1-800-831-TRUE
_{8 3 5 5}

1-473-938-4335

The answers to your problems are only a phone call away!

Billed to your Visa/Mc/Amex or directly to your phone you must be 18+

Supreme Psychic Hotline!

No Callers Refused!

011-592-599-029

Int'l Ld Rates Apply!

AMERICA'S MOST TRUSTED PSYCHIC NETWORKS
Does He Really LOVE Me?
Will I Ever Get MARRIED?
Is He FAITHFUL?
USE YOUR CREDIT CARD & SAVE 50¢ PER MINUTE
1-800-472-8769
$3.49 PER MIN.
1-900-255-7636
$3.99 PER MINUTE
10 MINUTES FREE!
PSYCHIC ANSWERS
Love • Health Money
30 FREE MIN
1-800-781-7836 $3.49 PER MIN.
Use Your Credit Card & Save 50¢ Per Min.
1-900-378-5858 $3.99 PER MIN.
NOSTRADAMUS has FORECAST the FUTURE for more than SIX CENTURIES!
HIS PREDICTIONS CHANGED THE WORLD!
14 FREE MIN
1-800-781-7896 $3.49 PER MIN.
Use Your Credit Card & Save 50¢ Per Min.
1-900-378-6386 $3.99 PER MIN.
your Guardian ANGEL
Knows Protects Guides
10 MINUTES FREE!
CALL NOW TO HEAR WHAT SHE NEEDS TO TELL YOU!
1-800-781-7865 $3.49 per min.
Use Your Credit Card & Save 50¢ Per Min.
1-900-378-6277 $3.99 per min.
Will I Meet My Soulmate Today? Tomorrow?
1-800-372-6062 $3.49 PER MIN.
Use Your Credit Card & Save 50¢ Per Min.
1-900-378-6468 $3.99 PER MIN.
IS LOVE IN YOUR TAROT? IS LOVE IN YOUR STARS?
1-800-431-7529 $3.49 PER MIN.
Make The Most Important Call Of YOUR LIFE!
12 MIN FREE
ISABEL "WEEZY" SANFORD Star of "The Jeffersons"
AS SEEN ON TV
MASTER PSYCHIC READINGS
USE YOUR CREDIT CARD & SAVE 50¢ PER MIN.
1-800-988-6785
$3.49 PER MIN.
1-900-378-6225
$3.99 PER MINUTE
SERVING YOU 24 HOURS A DAY!
10 MIN FREE
Is it... TRUE LOVE?
OR IS YOUR LOVER USING YOU?
Our PSYCHICS have ANSWERS to MARRIAGE, ROMANCE & SEX problems
1-800-277-6661 $3.49 PER MIN.
USE YOUR CREDIT CARD & SAVE 50¢ PER MINUTE
1-900-378-6661 $3.99 PER MIN.
Call NOW!
When Will He Call?
Will He Come Back?
Does He Love Me?
Suzanne Amour
Call Suzanne Today!
1-800-444-5511 $3.49 PER MIN.
Use Your Credit Card & Save 50¢ Per Min.
1-900-255-5385 $3.99 PER MIN.
Discover the HIDDEN SECRETS in Your Life!
AS SEEN ON TV
Gain insight into HEALTH, LOVE and ROMANCE!
20 MIN FREE
1-800-478-6298 $3.49 PER MIN.
Use Your Credit Card & Save 50¢ Per Min.
1-900-378-5959 $3.99 PER MIN.
SUSAN BROWN Known as the respected "Dr. Gail Baldwin", Psychiatrist, Port Charles
10 minutes FREE
"Where the Love is..." FOR YOU!
MY AUTHENTIC Love Psychics
WILL HELP YOU FIND THE Love of Your Life
& MAKE YOUR Dreams Come True
CONNIE FRANCIS
1-800-781-7865 $3.49 PER MIN.
Use Your Credit Card & Save 50¢ Per Min.
1-900-378-6800 $3.99 PER MIN.
6 MINUTES FREE
PAST LIFE READINGS
YOU MUST LEARN ABOUT THE PAST IN ORDER TO SAVE YOUR FUTURE
Use Your Credit Card & Save 50¢ Per Minute
1-800-781-7836 $3.49 PER MIN.
1-900-378-6161 $3.99 PER MIN.
ANCIENT ACCURATE ANSWERS
from Authentic Psychics
LUCK - LOVE
20 MINUTES FREE
TRUE CHANGE
24 HRS LIVE! Incredible Readings
1-800-781-7865 $3.49 PER MIN.
Use Your Credit Card & Save 50¢ Per Min.
1-900-378-6663 $3.99 PER MIN.
PSYCHIC BELIEVERS NETWORK • BOCA RATON, FL • MUST BE 18 YEARS OR OLDER TO CALL • FOR ENTERTAINMENT ONLY.

Are love and money in your future?

WE KNOW

PSYCHIC SOURCE
1-877-468-8588

MC1153 Toll Free Call www.psychicsource.com

The Psychic Zone

The Ultimate LIVE 1 on ! Psychic Center
No Extra Charges - No Credit Cards - Instant Credit

011-683-2896
011-678-739-53

Int'l LD Rates apply

The Live Psychic Hotline
1-800-239-SOUL
7 6 8 5
1-800-813-4625

From $3.99/Min. Credit Cards / Checks by Phone / Direct Bill 18+

FREE Psychic Readings!

BO GRIFFIN

AMERICA'S MOST TRUSTED PSYCHIC NETWORK

AS SEEN ON TV

THE PSYCHIC READERS NETWORK AMERICA'S MOST TRUSTED OFFERS YOU FREE ADVICE

What your Free Psychic Reading reveals may shock you, amaze you and make a huge impact on your future. Find the true answers to love, money, and more from a Real Psychic today.

· CALL NOW ·
1-800-662-8329

For entertainment purposes only. Must be 18+. First 3 min. FREE.

Irene Hughes
AS SEEN ON TV

AMERICA'S MOST ACCURATE PSYCHIC
LOVE • ROMANCE • MONEY

1-800-861-6998 *from $2.79/min*
1-900-903-0229 *$3.99/min*

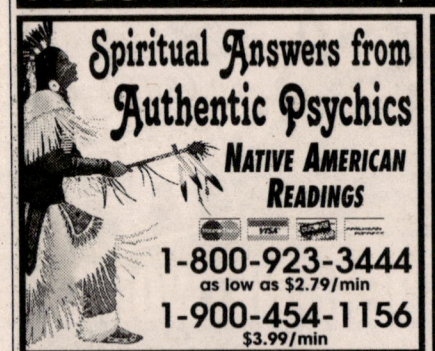

Spiritual Answers from Authentic Psychics
NATIVE AMERICAN READINGS

1-800-923-3444 *as low as $2.79/min*
1-900-454-1156 *$3.99/min*

MASTER PSYCHIC Leah Lusher
AMAZINGLY ACCURATE
2 MINUTES FREE

1-800-232-0160 *as low as $2.79/min*
1-900-786-5775 *$3.99/min thereafter*

JoJo Savard
CANADA'S SUPER PSYCHIC

Is love in your tarot?
Is love in your stars?

1-800-556-8599

FREE Tarot Cards
With every reading

Call Now • Toll FREE
1-888-732-4733

Is your lover being true?
SISTER LOVE has the answers!

1-800-457-9173 *from $2.79/min*
1-900-407-0174 *$3.99/min*
request ext. 1155

US PAT. 5,802,156 • 5,960,069 • THE ZODIAC GROUP, INC. • MUST BE 18 YEARS + • FOR ENTERTAINMENT ONLY

You Don't Have To Be Alone

Talk to a psychic love specialist

1-800-692-LOVE
5683

18+ From $3.99/min.

Live psychics devoted to serving

CANADIANS

seeking love, happiness, wealth & success.

1-900-451-3885
1-644-492-7844

900 $3.99/min. 1-644 Int'l Rates Apply 18+

SH1-2001

GET BACK ON TRACK!

Your road to true freedom can begin now with just one phone call

Gifted psychics available 24hrs/day

1-900-255-0444

18+ $3.99/min.

PSYCHICS 4 LESS
Up to 24 Minutes
Free Psychic Advice

BILLED TO YOU PHONE

1-900-745-0226

ALL MAJOR CREDIT CARDS ACCEPTED

1-800-568-6363

*First two minutes free From $3.99/min. thereafter. Be 18+

You're In Love... But Is He?

Hear from a live clairvoyant

1-800-826-TELL
8355

18+ 800 $3.99/min.

INSTANT ANSWERS FROM MASTERFUL PSYCHICS!

1-900-745-0113
1-644-492-5799

18+ 900 $3.99/min. 1-644 Int'l Rates Apply

LOVE, HAPPINESS, WEALTH, SUCCESS,
Will come to you
Powerful Psychics

1-800-756-4SEE
4733

from $3.99/min. 18+ credit card

BEST LIVE PSYCHICS

"We'll unlock the door to your future."

1-800-596-4897

18+ $3.99/min.

PSYCHIC EXPRESS

Call for your free sample reading

1-900-745-0420

Billed to your phone

1-800-796-LIFE
5433

$3.99/min. 18+ [VISA] [MC] [AMEX] [DISCOVER]

100% LIVE 1-2-1 EXPERT PSYCHICS

011-678-73514

For Guaranteed Access
Dial: 101 0288 011-678-73514

18+ Int'l Rates Apply

Have you ever needed someone to turn to for advice on love, marriage, romance?
Let Our LIVE PSYCHICS be there for YOU!
24 Hours a day 7 days a week
They'll never let you down!
Call Now!

1-800-873-TEAR
8 3 2 7

or

1-900-745-5601

The answers to your problems are only a phone call away!

Just $3.99per min. Billed to you Visa/Mc/Amex or directly to your phone you must be 18+

Direct Connect
Connect Directly with our Amazing Psychics, No Credit Cards, No Hassles!

011-683-9121
011-678-739-53

Win Big $$$
www.PLAYTIMECASINO.com